D0942461

Reflections on Constitutional Law

Other Books by George Anastaplo

The Constitutionalist: Notes on the First Amendment (1971, 2005)

Human Being and Citizen: Essays on Virtue, Freedom, and the Common Good (1975)

The Artist as Thinker: From Shakespeare to Joyce (1983)

The Constitution of 1787: A Commentary (1989)

The American Moralist: On Law, Ethics, and Government (1992)

The Amendments to the Constitution: A Commentary (1995)

The Thinker as Artist: From Homer to Plato & Aristotle (1997)

Campus Hate-Speech Codes, Natural Right, and Twentieth-Century Atrocities (1997, 1999)

Liberty, Equality, and Modern Constitutionalism: A Source Book (1999)

Abraham Lincoln: A Constitutional Biography (1999)

But Not Philosophy: Seven Introductions to Non-Western Thought (2002)

On Trial: From Adam & Eve to O.J. Simpson (2004)

Plato's "Meno," Translation and Commentary (with Laurence Berns) (2004)

Reflections on Freedom of Speech and the First Amendment (forthcoming)

REFLECTIONS ON CONSTITUTIONAL LAW

George Anastaplo

THE UNIVERSITY PRESS OF KENTUCKY

Publication of this volume was made possible in part by a grant
from the National Endowment for the Humanities.

Copyright © 2006 by The University Press of Kentucky

Scholarly publisher for the Commonwealth,
serving Bellarmine University, Berea College, Centre
College of Kentucky, Eastern Kentucky University,
The Filson Historical Society, Georgetown College,
Kentucky Historical Society, Kentucky State University,
Morehead State University, Murray State University,
Northern Kentucky University, Transylvania University,
University of Kentucky, University of Louisville,
and Western Kentucky University.
All rights reserved.

Editorial and Sales Offices: The University Press of Kentucky
663 South Limestone Street, Lexington, Kentucky 40508-4008
www.kentuckypress.com

06 07 08 09 10   5 4 3 2 1

Library of Congress Cataloging-in-Publication Data

Anastaplo, George, 1925-
Reflections on constitutional law / George Anastaplo.
p. cm.
Includes bibliographical references and index.
ISBN-13: 978-0-8131-2396-7 (hardcover : alk. paper)
ISBN-10: 0-8131-2396-8 (hardcover : alk. paper)
ISBN-13: 978-0-8131-9156-0 (pbk. : alk. paper)
ISBN-10: 0-8131-9156-4 (pbk. : alk. paper)
1. Constitutional law—United States. 2. Constitutional history—
United States. 3. Constitutional law—United States—Cases. I. Title.
KF4550.A7297 2006
342.73—dc22
2006012088

This book is printed on acid-free recycled paper meeting
the requirements of the American National Standard
for Permanence in Paper for Printed Library Materials.

Manufactured in the United States of America.

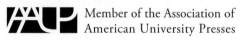 Member of the Association of
American University Presses

To
the Memory
of
My First Constitutional Law Teacher,
William W. Crosskey
(1894–1968)

Contents

APPENDIXES

PREFACE

My mother had to abandon her quest, but managed to extract from the restriction itself a further refinement of thought, as great poets do when the tyranny of rhyme forces them into the discovery of their finest lines.

—Marcel Proust, *Swann's Way* (Overture)

At the foundations of the series of reflections offered in this volume are my *Commentaries* on the Constitution of 1787 and on its Amendments published by the Johns Hopkins University Press in 1989 and 1995.

I observed, at the outset of those *Commentaries,* "I was surprised to discover, upon preparing [them] for publication, that there evidently had not been, since the Ratification Campaign of 1787–1788, any other book-length, section-by-section commentary upon the United States Constitution proceeding primarily from the original text itself. Even during the Ratification Period the longer expositions, as in the *Federalist* and in the State Ratification Conventions, were not systematic but rather were tailored, properly enough, to local interests and concerns. There have been, of course, many instructive systematic accounts of constitutional law in our own time [as well as heretofore], but these have relied far more than I want to do [in my *Commentaries*] upon judicial and other official interpretations and applications of the Constitution and its Amendments."

I believe that those documents were examined in my *Commentaries* with an appropriate rigor, providing a reliable guide for those interested in a coherent account of the 1787 Constitution and its twenty-seven Amendments. My hope was to offer my fellow citizens an account that would exhibit in our Constitution the admirable features that William Blackstone (as his *Commentaries* draw to an end) was able to find in his:

Of a constitution so wisely contrived, so strongly raised, and so highly finished, it is hard to speak with that praise which is justly and severely its due: the thorough and attentive contemplation of it will furnish its best panegyric. It hath been the endeavor of these Commentaries, however the execution may have succeeded, to examine its solid foundations, to mark out its extensive plan, to explain the use and distribution of its parts, and from the harmonious concurrence of those several parts to demonstrate the elegant proportion of the whole.

A learned reader observed about my *Commentaries* that this had been the first time anyone had tried to read the Constitution like a book.

Underpinning the foundations that my *Commentaries* provide can be said to be even deeper foundations, those surveyed in my eight-hundred-page treatise, *The Constitutionalist: Notes on the First Amendment,* published by the Southern Methodist University Press in 1971 and republished in 2005 by Lexington Books, with a 2004 foreword and preface. That treatise not only examines judicial and other readings of the First Amendment but also draws upon the literary, philosophical, and theological materials that can illuminate how we should think about self-government and the common good.

At the outset of each Part of these *Reflections* our constitutional foundations are once again noticed. The Organic Laws of the Anglo-American system and of the United States are recalled in my first five essays. But the bulk of the discussions in this volume of some two dozen sets of constitutional sonnets is about cases decided, for almost two centuries now, by the United States Supreme Court.

I offer, in these discussions, suggestions about how such cases might be read by citizens who approach the text of the Constitution with the seriousness and the care that it invites, requires, and deserves. All but a few of the score of cases investigated are prominent in constitutional law courses. The exceptions are cases that deserve more attention than they usually get.

Of course, there are still other prominent cases that are not examined here. Some of these are considered in *Reflections on Freedom of Speech and the First Amendment* (forthcoming) and still other volumes that are in course of preparation. Even so, the reader familiar with my work should be able to make reliable guesses about how the cases not mentioned would be addressed. Of course, wherever one begins, it should soon be obvious to the reader that I do not attempt to provide exhaustive, or even extensive, accounts of any of the cases considered in this volume. Rather, an attempt is made to suggest aspects of these cases and of the relevant constitutional provisions that are not generally noticed by jurists and scholars. Some repetition among the essays in this volume is inevitable if each case that is discussed is to make sense in this context.

The organization of the discussions of cases in the two parts of this volume can remind the reader of the organization of the typical year-long study of constitutional law, that study for which materials are provided in the typical casebook. But I do much more than does the typical casebook editor with the Organic Laws of the United States. And I encourage the student to work with judicial Opinions in their entirety, something that casebook editors have little room for in their useful comprehensive collections.

The reader is especially encouraged to notice those features of the prominent cases which are apt to be neglected by those constitutional law authorities who do not consider it necessary to read the Constitution rigorously. On the other hand, the intricacies of the Constitution can sometimes be illuminated when the recurring problems posed by challenging cases are probed.

Most of the topics addressed in this volume of reflections will be familiar to the experienced student of constitutional law. But some of these topics are not apt to be given much attention in the typical course. One of them has to do with the pervasive effect of the slavery issue on the development of constitutional law in this Country, as may be seen, for example, in the use and abuse of the Commerce Clause in the first half of the nineteenth century.

Perhaps even more significant is that fundamental change in jurisprudence which culminated in the 1938 case, *Erie Railroad Company* v. *Tompkins.* The *Erie Case,* which is examined at length in Part One, Essay Seven, and in Part Two, Essay Three, of these *Reflections,* has been described in this fashion in *The Guide to American Law* (St. Paul: West Publishing Company, 1984), 10: 371–72:

> Harry J. Tompkins was walking on a footpath alongside railroad tracks on land owned by the Erie Railroad Company when he was struck and injured by a passing train. He claimed that his injuries resulted from the negligence of the railroad in operating the train.
>
> Tompkins wanted to sue the railroad and recover monetary damages for his injuries. He was a citizen of Pennsylvania, and the Erie Railroad Company was a New York corporation. He instituted an action in Federal court which was empowered, by virtue

of its diversity jurisdiction, to hear the case because the plaintiff and the defendant were citizens of different states.

The issue before the Federal trial court was what law to apply in deciding the case. The court would have applied a Federal statute to decide whether Tompkins was entitled to damages, but none existed. The court would have applied a state statute since there was no Federal statute, but Pennsylvania did not have one.

The highest court of Pennsylvania had established a rule to be followed in state courts whenever a case like this occurred. The Pennsylvania [common law] rule was that people who use pathways along railroad right-of-ways, not railroad crossings, are trespassers to whom railroads were not to be held liable unless the trespassers were intentionally injured by the reckless and wanton acts of the railroads.

The trial judge refused to apply the Pennsylvania [common law] rule. He found that *Swift v. Tyson* (1842), which held that there was a body of Federal common law to be applied in such cases, gave Federal judges the right to ignore state rules that were not enacted as statutes by their state legislatures. He held that it was more important for all Federal courts to follow a uniform rule, rather than for each Federal court to apply local state [common law] rules when there was no statute to resolve the case. He allowed a jury to decide whether the railroad company was negligent, and the jury returned a verdict of $30,000 for Tompkins.

The Supreme Court reversed the decision and struck down the rule that allowed Federal judges to ignore state court decisions in diversity cases. Although this rule had been followed since *Swift v. Tyson* was decided in 1842, the Supreme Court ruled that it was inequitable. According to the old rule, Tompkins could obtain monetary damages if he sued in Federal court, but not if he initiated his lawsuit a few blocks away in the Pennsylvania state court. If the plaintiff and defendant were citizens of different states, the plaintiff could take advantage of the right to sue in Federal court. There the plaintiff might win, even if he or she had been trespassing on railroad property. If the plaintiff and defendant were both citizens of Pennsylvania, the plaintiff could not sue in Federal court. Pennsylvania courts would all be bound to follow [their common law] rule that prevented recoveries for those who used paths alongside railroad tracks. The Supreme Court held that it was unjust for the plaintiff's chances of winning to depend on the fact that the railroad was a Pennsylvania corporation.

The new rule of *Erie Railroad Co. v. Tompkins* provided that Federal courts do not have the power to formulate their own rules of law. The Federal courts must apply appropriate Federal statutes in diversity cases. When there is no Federal law to resolve the question in a lawsuit, they must follow the law of the state that is involved. That includes state statutes and controlling decisions made by the highest court of that state.

As a result of this case, the decisions of Federal courts are truly uniform only when a question of Federal law is involved. Otherwise, the states are free to develop their own law and have it applied to state questions that come into Federal court because the parties are from different states.

Quite respectable constitutional law casebooks, these days, can relegate *Erie* to a minor status (if it is mentioned at all). And yet, *Erie* continues to challenge the Framers' understanding of that common law which they considered integral to their system. Perhaps even more serious is the ratification seen in *Erie* of a jurisprudential development which has undermined that respect for natural law/natural right which questions the Nihilistic tendencies of a hedonistic modernity. (See, for references to my discussions elsewhere of these and related matters, John A. Murley's massive bibliography, *Leo Strauss and His Legacy*.)

Appendixes are provided in which useful citations and other materials are collected. Among these materials is the Confederate Constitution of 1861, which exhibits the skill of craftsmen who knew the Constitution of 1787 well enough to be able to identify and "correct" those parts of that document which challenged the institutions and the way of life that they had been unfortunate enough to inherit and that they considered themselves honor-bound to cherish.

Defenders of the Constitution are obliged to know at least as much about it as those "Secessionists" who were unfortunate enough to undertake to replace it.

—George Anastaplo

Hyde Park, Chicago, Illinois
November 7, 2005

PART ONE

1. An Introduction to Constitutionalism

I

Some years ago, not long after I began teaching in the Loyola School of Law, I was invited to a luncheon at the United States Supreme Court. This was during a visit by me to Washington to attend an American Political Science Association annual convention. The invitation was issued on behalf of the Fellows, and of some of the Clerks, at the Supreme Court that year.

It seems that those youngsters had heard something odd about my constitutional law courses which they wanted to look into. They had heard that we actually spend considerable time studying the Constitution of the United States before we begin to look at Supreme Court cases. That preliminary inquiry can run to three or four weeks, a mode of proceeding which is reflected in my two published commentaries on the Constitution.

The typical constitutional law course spends little if any time on the text of the Constitution. Perhaps features of the Constitution will be noticed during the opening class meeting. But soon thereafter, if not even in the opening session of the typical course, the first of the dozens of cases to be surveyed will be examined.

II

Far fewer cases are examined in my constitutional law courses, no more than a score or so during a term. This may seem rather "theoretical" to the typical law students, but it may be the most practical way to lay a sound foundation for them in constitutional law. It is this which I had to explain to my luncheon companions at the Supreme Court—and which I recall here.

Most of the cases studied in the typical constitutional law course when I was in law school a half-century ago are no longer made much of in constitutional law casebooks. Even many of the cases that were in constitutional law casebooks when I began teaching constitutional law a generation later are now ignored. In short, such cases have become obsolete.

This is not surprising, considering how contrived and "topical" many of those cases have always been. I recall, for example, the mysteries of the "original package" criteria to be made sense of by students of the Commerce Clause. Even though cases are constantly being weeded out of the garden of constitutional adjudication, the more popular collections have ever more cases noticed in them, often in no more than snippets from the Opinions of the United States Supreme Court.

III

Despite the constant pruning that is required to keep casebooks both affordable and portable, the typical constitutional law course can easily become a course in constitutional history. Or, depending upon the professor's inclinations, it can become an exercise in political advocacy. Either way, the Constitution itself easily drops out of sight, if it is noticed at all.

The history that judges and lawyers are apt to draw upon tends to be rather skimpy, if not simply unreliable. Something more reliable than such history has to be worked with if sense is to be made of (and with) the historical record that is discussed. Critical to reliability is a grasp of the enduring principles upon which the law naturally tends to draw.

Such principles are not likely to be given sufficient scope in the fragments of judicial opinions which law students are provided, a limitation that is not apt to be corrected by the "research" that is done by the "words and phrases" search engines upon which much legal inquiry evidently depends these days. I have, in recent years, given up altogether on casebooks, asking students to read instead the complete set of Opinions for the one or two cases we discuss each week, along with, for the older cases, the synopses of the arguments of counsel that are often provided in the *United States Reports*. One is more apt to notice there, than in the fragmented Opinions in the typical casebook, the principles, standards, and mode of argument invoked by the contending parties.

IV

It is more important, in a study of constitutional law, to weigh what the United States Supreme Court said and how it was said—what considerations it weighed and how—than it is to know what the Court "decided." Some may wonder, of course, how "practical" this approach is for students of law. I believe it is far more practical than what is usually done in constitutional law courses in this Country today.

If and when one does have, as a lawyer, a controversy apparently involving the Constitution, one must no doubt investigate in some detail what the Supreme Court has recently said about the issues considered relevant. This may be quite different from what was said at the time one's constitutional law casebook was prepared, years before. But what one is not likely to do in practice, when confronted by such a controversy, is to stop to think much about the Constitution itself, especially if one has not been equipped by one's constitutional law courses to do so.

Only if one has a reliable grasp of the Constitution is one likely to be equipped to understand what the Supreme Court has done. A proper reading includes an assessment of what may be intrinsically flawed, or at least quite limited, in what the Court has done and said from time to time. I mention, in passing, that bar examiners, evidently sensing the unreliability of much that passes for constitutional law, do very little with that subject on the typical State bar examination—and that little is adequately prepared for (I gather) by the bar review courses that applicants for admission to the bar usually take.

V

Perhaps unique to the course I prefer—not only as a constitutional law course but perhaps also as a law school course—is that it is very much a course in *how to read.* If one is to learn to read legal documents properly, much is to be said for studying the best-crafted legal document in the annals of this Country, the Constitution itself. Such study depends, in large part, upon habituating oneself to be simpleminded enough to notice what is there.

Essential to noticing what is there is a recognition of a document's vital elements. Central to grasping how something is put together, and hence what is said there, is an awareness of the principle of order implicit in the document one is considering. It helps if one does not underestimate either the seriousness or the competence of the draftsmen whose work one is considering.

The thinking required here is not something to be used only on occasion; rather, it is something that invites one to return again and again to the contemplation of enduring principles. The skills one develops as a reader can be put to good use when one becomes in turn the writer of legal documents, documents for which one must expect both the many typical readers and a few serious readers. As one becomes practiced in these matters, one can develop a reliable "feel" for both the Constitution and Constitutionalism.

VI

Although it is not truly practical to be too practical, it is well to recognize the common sense that a serious study of the Constitution can promote. A proper grasp of the Constitution can put the ever-transitory cases in perspective. Otherwise, one's study of this subject becomes mostly an exercise in memorizing what "the situation" is at any particular moment.

Even so, it can help one see what is momentarily there if one has a reliable sense of how flimsy a particular line of cases might be. One can be helped to anticipate what is likely to be made much of, and not only by judges, especially as one senses the character of our regime. The vulnerability of a line of cases should be evident to anyone who has a feel for that regime.

The classic instance of this kind of recognition in the history of the United States was with respect to the status of slavery "in the long run." This awareness may have contributed, in the first half of the nineteenth century, both to the zeal of abolitionists in the North and to the defensiveness of conservatives in the South. A similar development could be seen in the struggle, in the second half of the twentieth century, with respect to civil rights.

VII

In these and like matters, chance can play a significant part. Chance can affect, for example, where one studies and with whom. The luck of the draw may even be decisive in determining what kind of constitutional law course one is exposed to.

The luck of the draw may also be seen, more significantly, in what finds its way into the *United States Reports*. For example, chance can affect what is-sues are brought before the Supreme Court, in what shape, and by whom. And then there are such factors to be considered as the personnel of the Court of the day—and how the Constitution has come to be talked about.

Chance may have also been critical in the circumstances of the Consti-tutional Convention of 1787, including both the political and economic conditions of the day and those available to serve as delegates. Chance was critical as well in the timing of the Civil War: Union forces would have been markedly inadequate a generation earlier, and Southern forces would have been markedly inadequate a generation later. That is, the timing of the war was such as to make it likely that the struggle would be devastat-ing and hence both soul-searching and revolutionary in its demands and in its consequences.

VIII

History does offer us material to think about—and to think with. Particularly significant, of course, is the Constitution of 1787. Although there was no necessity that it be precisely the way it is, there was much in the circumstances of the day which called for an effort along the lines evident in the Constitution we do have.

The materials offered by history for the constitutionalist to consider include the Confederate Constitution of 1861. That constitution (set forth in Appendix I of this volume) testifies to its drafters' belief that the language of the Constitution of 1787 did very much matter. This is evident in the changes made in 1861—the changes carefully made, it is obvious—to the language (in the Constitution and its first twelve amend-ments) inherited from 1787 and from 1791–1804.

Among the 1861 changes were, of course, those which locked slavery into the new system—that slavery which the Secessionists had come to recognize had been left quite vulnerable by the Constitution of 1787. Reinforcing this effort was the tendency to make the 1861 system more *federal*, less national, than the 1787 system had been. Thus, a study of the Confederate Constitution (to which we return in Part Two of these *Reflections*) can help us to see better than we otherwise might that which preceded it, and which stood as a formidable challenge to it, the Constitu-tion of 1787.

IX

Also instructive, for a proper reading of the 1787 Constitution, are vital documents that preceded it. These include what has long been identified as the other three "Organic Laws of the United States." They are the Declaration of Independence, the Articles of Confederation, and the Northwest Ordinance.

In addition, we shall examine with some care an "Organic Law" of the overarching Anglo-American constitutional system, the Great Charter of 1215. It is odd how little has been said in constitutional pronouncements in recent decades not only about Magna Carta but also about the Declaration of Independence and its immediate progeny. It should not be surprising, therefore, that little is done these days with such documents in constitutional law courses.

We will begin, then, with the study of these documents in their chronological order, culminating in the emergence of the Constitution of 1787. Thereafter we will discuss a series of United States Supreme Court cases and other cases of note, including a couple that are usually ignored in constitutional law courses. I offer indications both of the discussion to be expected in constitutional law classes and of what else might well be said about the subject.

2. Magna Carta (1215)

I

The circumstances of my *Commentary* on the Amendments to the Constitution were critical in the choice of the translation used there for the Magna Carta text. The translation used here as well (in Appendix A of this volume) is one published in 1829, a version which represents the nearest date in time to the Founding Period, available today, for an English translation in the United States. We can thus get a sense of how the provisions of Magna Carta seemed to American citizens during the early decades of the Republic.

This reminder of the importance of circumstances bears upon what any documentary interpretation should take into account. My constitutional law teacher (William W. Crosskey) took as the epigraph for his monumental treatise on the Constitution a sentence from a United States Supreme Court Justice, Oliver Wendell Holmes Jr., who could himself be sometimes rather unreliable in constitutional interpretation: "We ask, not what this man meant, but what those words would mean in the mouth of a normal speaker of English, using them in the circumstances in which they were used." Of course, a reliable grasp of circumstances may sometimes be hard to come by.

It might help, in thinking about Magna Carta, to know more than we do about its drafting: the contribution made by the Archbishop of Canterbury was evidently critical. One has the impression that various Barons had pet grievances which they insisted upon, without much concern about where precisely they should be placed in the document. That is, no draftsmen may have had as much control over the arrangement of the elements of the Great Charter of 1215 as is evident in the arrangement of the elements of the Constitution of 1787.

II

It does seem that the King had some bargaining power, however much he was coerced into accepting this proclamation. We notice, in passing, that coercion can sometimes be used to good effect—and that it does not automatically invalidate what has been "agreed to." Partisans of the King may have contributed such provisions as Chapter 60, obliging the Barons to concede to *their* subjects what they had demanded from the King as *his* subjects, a concession necessary if the Barons were not to surrender the high ground they claimed for themselves.

It is an implicit claim to high-mindedness which has contributed to the enduring reputation of Magna Carta. Indeed, that Charter seems to have become even grander in retrospect than it might have been understood to be from the beginning. This kind of development might be seen as well in this Country for the Declaration of Independence, for the Fourteenth Amendment, and even for the Constitution of 1787, which (despite the passions of the 1787–1788 Ratification Campaign) soon became something of a political icon.

Critical documents can impress us as meaningful, even when we have not had an opportunity to study them. That is, we can get the impression that a document makes sense—and this we can confirm, in the best of cases, when we have disciplined ourselves to examine it. How, then, is Magna Carta, in its original form, arranged?

III

It is by the Grace of God, we are told at the outset, that John is King of England, Lord of Ireland, etc. And we also see at the outset that the King has, or at least is supposed to have, a concern "for the salvation of [his] own soul, and of the souls of all [his] ancestors, and of [his] heirs." However merely formalistic such language may seem, it does draw upon deep-rooted assumptions about both the natural and the divine ordering of things.

Those assumptions are evident in the hierarchy of those who confront the King on this occasion. Mentioned first are "our venerable fathers," with the Archbishop of Canterbury leading this parade of a dozen Churchmen, the Lords Spiritual. One has the impression that there is certainly a recognized organization in the arrangement of these names, and perhaps in the names thereafter of the Lords Temporal.

We should not be surprised, therefore, that the first of the substantive undertakings—those divisions known as chapters (and numbered in the tradition)—should be with respect to "the English Church." That institution (which was then still Roman Catholic, of course) should be free and should have "her whole rights and her liberties inviolable." Once this is understood, "all the underwritten Liberties" of the temporal Barons and others can be recognized as well.

IV

The religious presuppositions of the Magna Carta of 1215 are in marked contrast to those of the Constitution of 1787, with the Declaration of Independence of 1776 and its repeated invocations of the Divine lying between those two documents. The Constitution, it will be remembered, is careful not to express any sectarian bias, even going so far as to provide (in Article VI) that "no religious Test shall ever be required as a Qualification to any Office or public Trust under the United States." The piety expressed in the Preamble of the Confederate Constitution of 1861 can remind us of how different the Constitution of 1787 is in this and in other critical respects.

We come closer to the spirit of the Founding Period in the United States when we notice the Magna Carta provisions subsequent to the confirmation of the rights of the English Church: property rights and transactions are vital from the beginning. This may be seen in Chapter 2 of Magna Carta, just as it may be seen at the outset of the Northwest Ordinance of 1787 (one of the four Organic Laws of the United States). Royal abuses with respect to established property rights, it is evident from Magna Carta, were perhaps dramatically evident when the most critical transitions took place—that is, when a property holder died (especially if his heir was a minor) and when marriages were entered into.

It is evident, again and again, that property should be held with a minimum of interference from the government of the day. This is reflected, further on, in the assurances about merchants and others being able to enter and leave the country with their property, at least in times of peace: we can see accepted here the conditions which permit Jews and others to contribute to the economy of the country (the culmination of this approach may be seen in what we know as globalization). Even so, we can be reminded, by the special restraints placed in critical circumstances of transition upon Jewish creditors, of the fundamentally Christian orientation of the People of Magna Carta.

V

Respect for property includes, in Chapter 12 of Magna Carta, an anticipation of one of the great principles of the American Revolution, "No taxation without representation." This is particularly insisted upon when the King attempts to take more than has been customary for various transitions. Again and again the King, upon having his innovations challenged, is reminded of what has long been done.

We, in turn, can be reminded, upon seeing how these claims are made, that the most successful constitutional pronouncements *tend* to be those cast in the form of reaffirming long-established ways. Such reaffirmations can refine and otherwise improve upon what is believed to have been inherited. Innovations are made respectable, and are more apt to take hold, if their grounding in long-accepted traditions can be thereby displayed.

This means, among other things, that constitution-making for and by various peoples around the world should draw upon the character, language, and experience of those provided for. It is, for example, instructive to see how William Blackstone insisted (in his *Commentaries*) upon beginnings for the English Constitution that were lost in antiquity. Even the legendary Alfred the Great is invoked by him as part of the heritage that eighteenth-century lawyers should respect.

VI

There is evident throughout Magna Carta a reliance upon long-established institutions, among which is what we would call the judicial system, a system traditionally dependent upon the monarch. The innovation here, that critical tribunals should be settled at known places, formally accepts the royal prerogatives in these matters. But it can be expected that judges who are settled and who do not simply follow the royal court will develop practices and perhaps an integrity of their own.

The proper training of judicial personnel is guaranteed. However much of an innovation this may have been in practice, it could be understood to be implicit in the system from the beginning. Here, as elsewhere, the innovation consists in taking seriously and refining what has been said, and somehow or other done, for a very long time.

This may be seen as well in the insistence upon proportionality in exactions. That is, it is said in effect that "property" is to be taken seriously.

One manifestation of this is the requirement of something that we have come to know as "just compensation" upon the exercise by government of its right to "eminent domain."

VII

Another way of putting these observations is to say that Magna Carta is concerned to moderate, if not even to eliminate, the divergences which had chanced to develop over centuries in the kingdom, divergences that the King and his officers had recently exploited to their advantage. An explication of what is implicit (already referred to) may be seen in the insistence upon national standards of weights, measures, and the like. This can be said to be no more than taking seriously the language that everyone already relies upon.

Explication, then, can be seen as reaffirmation and perhaps even as enhancement by way of restoration. It is restoration that is evident in such measures as the removal of obstructions in the Thames and the reduction of the royal forests that had encroached upon the property of others. The Barons, in insisting upon the rollback of royal encroachments, took for granted of course the validity of any titles of theirs which went back to royal grants, grants which might once have meant taking from others what *they* had been accustomed to.

Even so, these reassertions of local authority, as against royal power, seem to have contributed to the centralization of the governance of the country, something that may even be implicit in the insistence upon uniformity in various standards, a uniformity which was grounded in language that was more or less common. That is, the Barons, spiritual and temporal, coming together as they did in opposition to King John, can be understood to have insisted that there were standards and aspirations that all of the country shared. This would eventually lead to the eclipse of the nobility itself, as well as of much of the remaining power of the monarchy.

VIII

The restoration that is anticipated is to be carried further with the return of hostages. The use of mercenaries is to cease. The ways of peace are encouraged—and they too are to be countrywide.

Going further in its reach will be what is to be done to the relations of the English both to the Welsh and to the Scots. It will take several centuries before the entire island can be brought together under one sovereignty, and along with it (at least for awhile) the formidable neighboring island to the west. But already, in the time of King John, the hold of the English monarchs on the Continent is weakening, despite the origins of those monarchs in Normandy.

But all of the restoration sought for and secured by the Barons is not without a price. That may be seen in that provision of Magna Carta (Chapter 60) already referred to: "Also all these customs and liberties aforesaid, which we have granted to be held in our kingdom, for so much of it as belongs to us, all our subjects, as well clergy as laity, shall observe towards their tenants as far as concerns them." This kind of concession on the part of the Barons probably contributed, in the long run, to ever more lawful containment of the monarch as well.

IX

Lawful containment of the monarch may further be seen in the provisions in the closing chapters of Magna Carta. The coalition of Barons, twenty-five in number, is recognized as a continuing institution, able to replenish itself. It is important that it can act by a majority, not only unanimously, if need be.

In addition, there is, in effect, a recognition by the monarch of what we know as the right of revolution, to be exercised whenever he fails to live up to his undertakings. All that had already been done, as well as what may "have" to be done thereafter, has the assurance of a royal pardon. The culmination of all this, after which nothing will ever be the same again, is the execution of Charles I four centuries later.

Magna Carta opened with reliance upon "the Grace of God" and a recognition of the rights and liberties of the English Church, with the freedom (whatever that may mean) of the Church of England reaffirmed in the final chapter, along with the liberties, rights, and concessions recognized for the Barons. The concluding words (before the witnessing provision) speak of a reliance on good faith and of the lack of evil intentions. Thus, the adversaries in this great contest move, at least in speech, from the standoff at Runnymede to the high ground of sincere dealings and the most elevated aspirations.

3. The Declaration of Independence (1776)

I

Each reading of the Declaration of Independence is a challenge and an opportunity. One's circumstances may determine how the Declaration is read on any particular occasion. Such circumstances may include current events, what else one may be working on at the moment, or the questions one is asked by others.

We notice here that "one People" is used at the outset of the Declaration and that the signatures of the delegates appended to this declaration are collected State by State. This juxtaposition anticipates the tension there has always been in this Country between the Union and the States, a tension implicit perhaps in the motto, *E pluribus unum*. As the *unum* becomes ever stronger, it can be wondered what the staying power is of the *pluribus*.

Did those who issued the Declaration of Independence become "one People" in July 1776? Critical differences from their "British Brethren" had been evident for more than a decade: well before then, of course, quite different circumstances had encouraged, perhaps even required, the People of these thirteen Colonies to consider themselves significantly different from the ancestors (across the Atlantic) of most of them. Not the least of the differences was the absence in the Colonies of an entrenched nobility with vast property holdings—in those Colonies where people had been largely governing themselves for decades.

II

The apparent access, for the many, to property in land on this continent must have reinforced the belief that "all Men are created equal." It was evident, of course, that this belief provided a basis for judging what was done to and with various people in various circumstances. Whatever their fundamental equality, grounded in nature or otherwise ordained, it did not mean that differences in capacities and accomplishments could not be taken into account in the ordering of a community.

The status of women tended to be lower than that of men, and children (male as well as female) were subordinated of course to their parents. But not all adult men were on the same plane, with critical distinctions in citizenship, residence, and mental capacity taken into account for various purposes. The last of the grievances recited, with respect to "domestic Insurrections" by some and to uninhibited warfare by others, took for granted the degraded or otherwise troubling condition of all too many human beings.

Implicit throughout the Declaration (set forth in Appendix B of this volume) can be said to be the belief that some forms of association are better than others for developing those still unfit for self-government. Government, it is believed, can very much matter, for good as well as for ill. Circumstances can help determine whether the equality inherent among human beings can find practical expression—but not all governments, or forms of government, are created equal.

III

We have glanced at equality early and late in the Declaration of Independence, but what equality means and how it may be ministered to can further be investigated by considering how the document is organized. When we do that, we can notice anomalies (that is, still another form of inequality) in the Declaration, anomalies that can help us see it better: particularly striking is the shift, in the very center of the document, in the way that nine items in the array of grievances are presented. Theretofore, as well as thereafter, "He" (that is, the King) would be "targeted," but in these nine instances he is identified as having "combined with others to subject us to a Jurisdiction foreign to our Constitution, and unacknowledged by our Laws."

These grievances, we can find upon inquiry, are the oldest of those inventoried in the Declaration. We can also see, when we stop to think about it, that critical to these grievances is what had been done by the British Parliament, not by the King acting alone, or even seeming to act alone. Earlier protests against the doings of the British government had condemned legislative usurpation, protests that recognized the already severely limited power of the British monarch.

It is convenient, perhaps even rhetorically necessary, to attack primarily the King at this stage of the crisis, since the Colonists are about to go to war, with hostilities having already begun. Besides, however much these Colonists intended to repudiate monarchy, they did not intend to abandon parliamentary institutions. In fact, it was a "parliamentary" body which issued this very declaration in an authoritative manner on behalf of the People of what can now be called the United States.

IV

A decade later it will be recognized in the Constitution of 1787 that each State in the Union is to have a "Republican Form of Government"; it is such government, it seems to be believed, that is most likely to respect and to develop the intrinsic equality of human beings. Royalty can be condemned, on occasion, as despotic and tyrannical; it can even be repudiated as the most extreme form of those titles of nobility which are to be forbidden by the Constitution of 1787. In short, the authority of Parliament over the Colonies can be questioned, but not parliamentary government in all circumstances.

A properly constituted parliamentary government is essential (at least in this political tradition) for the legitimation of taxation. We can hear in the Declaration of Independence, with respect to this principle, echoes of Magna Carta, where a proper representation, limited however to the nobility, is provided for. But such representation, because of circumstances, could not be readily devised for the colonists in the British Parliament.

Thus, the Framers of the Declaration of Independence were not proposing to discard in its entirety the system they had inherited. Thus, also, various of the grievances recited depended upon rights long-established in the English constitutional system. Particularly important was the right of trial by jury, which was considered critical as a check on government; it is, in effect, an aspect of self-government, or everyday republicanism.

V

We can recall here the characterization of Magna Carta as "The great Charter of the Liberties of England," something insisted upon in 1628 by a rebellious legislature holding a king to account. The Declaration of Independence, issued by still another rebellious legislature, can be considered the Great Charter of the Liberties of the United States. We can see, again and again, that a People is more apt to be loyal to that which sounds familiar.

The liberties invoked—whether in England or in the United States—include what we do know as the right of revolution, a right that is recognized in effect (as we have seen) in the conclusion of the 1215 Charter and that is made explicit in the 1776 Charter. But this is not done in 1776 without recognizing as well that "Prudence . . . dictate[s] that Governments long established should not be changed for light and transient Causes." Essential to the political principles implicit in the Declaration of Independence is the caution that one should be careful in how one exercises the rights one is undoubtedly entitled to.

Such care depends upon at least an awareness of the standards to be used in determining what makes matters better, and what makes them worse. Whether it is opportune to insist upon one's rights can depend somewhat upon circumstances. It might even be argued that King John proved to be, in 1215, somewhat more prudent than King George's ministers were in 1776, in responding as he did (however insincerely) to the challenge posed by the organized resistance to his innovations by the Barons.

VI

A further comparison between the Declaration of Independence and Magna Carta can usefully be noted. The Barons rebelled against the King's attempt to collect money from those of the nobility who had *not* helped him in his ill-fated campaign in France. The American "Barons" rebelled against the King's attempt to collect money from those of his subjects who had benefitted from the successful (but expensive) British campaign to defend the Colonies during the French and Indian Wars.

In both cases, an attempt was made, in the name of the King of the day, to oblige subjects to contribute what the English government regarded as their fair share to expenditures on behalf of what we would call "national security." Even so, the subjects in each case insisted upon consent as vital to the extracting process. Otherwise, they seemed to believe, a kind of tyranny would threaten them, making all of their property, if not also their lives, vulnerable.

Of course, Magna Carta is understood to have created the precedent of declaring one's grievances. It also created the precedent of insisting upon one's remedies, including a resort to force against long-established authority. Here, as elsewhere, we can see that Ideas Have Consequences.

VII

It is recognized in the Declaration of Independence that government is organized to secure rights. It seems to depend upon circumstances which rights are emphasized from time to time. Thus, some rights may usefully be dramatized, while others are tacitly foregone, at least for the time being, something that is recognized by the Ninth Amendment.

Is the very emphasis upon rights, or upon any particular rights, itself partly due to chance factors as well? We are now accustomed to judging a regime more by whether critical rights are respected than by whether justice is served or the common good is advanced. It is possible to "translate" the former set of terms (the respect for rights) into the others (justice or the common good)—but the emphasis upon rights might still take priority, thereby reinforcing a kind of individualism.

Much is made, at least among us, of "the Pursuit of Happiness." But it can seem a matter of chance what makes someone happy from time to time. Indeed, happiness may even seem to depend, in large part, upon *variety*, upon *change*, and hence upon experimentation.

VIII

We can be reminded by all this of a much older view of political matters, having been told, in Aristotle's *Nicomachean Ethics* (and elsewhere), that happiness is very much dependent upon (even though, sad to say, it is not simply guaranteed by) virtue. This approach to these matters tends to make more of justice and the common good, less of personal liberties and what we now know as individualism. Such individualism does tend to make more of innovation in the service of constantly changing gratification.

The older approach made more of citizen virtue, that virtue upon which an effective common defense depended. In fact, the old-fashioned among us can be startled to see people taken seriously as contenders for high political office who (in their youth) shirked military duty in wars that they approved of, but only if others were conscripted to do the fighting. It can also be startling to notice that such shirkers do not *expect* to be handicapped socially or politically by such selfishness.

Citizen virtue *is* relied upon in the closing lines of the Declaration of Independence. The Declaration concludes, that is, with a dedication to the common cause of the signers' lives, liberty, and honor. It is obvious there that self-interest, even an enlightened self-interest, may not be enough for a healthy political order able both to justify and to defend itself.

IX

It should be noticed that the honor offered up on this occasion is "baptized" as "sacred." This can remind us of how the Divine is recruited for the great patriotic effort called forth by the Declaration of Independence. The culmination of this enlistment of the Divine in this Country's cause may perhaps be heard in "The Battle Hymn of the Republic."

The Declaration opens with the Divine being "naturalized" in more ways than one, beginning with a dependence upon "the Laws of Nature and of Nature's God." Thereafter, a more old-fashioned view of the Divine is drawn upon. The Creation itself, and hence the Divine, is implicit (or so it can seem) in the insistence that "all Men are created equal," an insistence that even nominal atheists can somehow endorse.

The Framers are confident that the Divine cares for the United States—and they seem to hope to be able to justify such caring, even to deserve it, a caring that is very much needed, considering the power of the adversary. The sacredness of honor may suggest as well that political virtue, if not even the Republican Form of Government itself, has been sanctified. With such aspirations the People of the United States were (it turned out) well on their way to regarding themselves as a community with a great destiny.

4. The Articles of Confederation (1776–1789); The Northwest Ordinance (1787)

I

There is evident in the Articles of Confederation something that may be seen again and again in Anglo-American constitutional history, a building on what has already been done. This is particularly obvious when the recognition of various great rights is developed. The institutions and processes provided for in the Articles of Confederation are pretty much those that the Colonies had developed in the course of their decade-long "confrontation" with the British government.

Such continuity with the immediate past meant, among other things, that the Articles of Confederation could be used even before ratification (which was delayed until 1781). That is, Americans in the General Government simply kept doing *from 1776 on* what they had been doing before, much of which had been incorporated in the yet-to-be-ratified Articles of Confederation. An effective political order usually does depend, we have noticed, upon a substantial proportion of familiar things being expected and done.

After all, there was a great war to be fought and new foreign relations to be established, with serious constitution-framing being something that could be postponed to calmer times when the best men were not engaged in desperate activities "in the field." It must have been evident, at least to the more thoughtful Americans, that the Articles of Confederation arrangement was clearly provisional. Even so, the General Government under the Articles of Confederation (set forth in Appendix C of this volume) was remarkably successful, presiding as it did over the attainment of independence, the development of a proper peace treaty, the enactment of the Northwest Ordinance, and the supervision of the process that produced the Constitution of 1787.

II

The permanence of the American Union is repeatedly referred to in the Articles of Confederation, with references at the beginning and at the end to a "perpetual Union." There was a sense of national community, reinforced no doubt by the casualties suffered during the course of the war for independence (perhaps, it is said, with as many as ten percent of the entire population in military service at one time or another). It seems to have been generally evident that there were thirteen Colonies/States to be counted on, with Canada left in an ambiguous relation toward this Union.

The permanent arrangements among the States were still to be worked out. Some of those relations would eventually be developed without explicit adjustments in formal constitutional documents. In the short term, however, a practical equality among the States had to be taken for granted.

The "perpetual Union" insisted upon in the Articles of Confederation was perhaps as much a hope to be realized as a fact to be recognized. A decade of somewhat effective cooperation during very rough times prepared the way for the Constitution of 1787. The "perpetual Union" of the Articles was elevated (in the Preamble to the Constitution) into "a more perfect Union," with the means provided in the new constitution for indeed keeping it so.

III

The continuing importance of the States is both recognized and depended upon in the Articles of Confederation. This may be seen in how the powers of the General Government are defined. This sense of limitations is reinforced by the requirement, for the more important measures, of what we now call a supermajority.

Particularly significant is the use of "expressly delegated" in Article II of the Articles of Confederation. The more such limitations for the General Government are insisted upon in the Articles of Confederation, the easier it is to recognize that the powers of the General Government under the Constitution of 1787 are considerably greater. Indicative of this is the determination of the partisans of the new Constitution in the First Congress to keep the "expressly delegated" language (of Article II of the Articles of Confederation) out of what we now know as the Tenth Amendment.

Thus we can see, again and again, that respect for documents and a reliance upon the proper mode of documentary interpretation can be vital to serious Constitutionalism, at least in the modern world. Such a mode is taken for granted by the drafters of constitutional instruments, a mode that is as much a part of the presuppositions of draftsmanship as the language that is used. Included in that language, we have seen, were the experiences and expectations of the constitutional system that had been inherited.

IV

Limitations upon the General Government are again and again insisted upon in the Articles of Confederation. But, at the same time, the powers that *are* to be exercised by even that government, and only by *that* government, are impressive. They have to do with war and peace, diplomacy, and (eventually) a reliable monetary (if not even a comprehensive commercial) system, dealing thereby with matters that can be all-engrossing.

The thirteen States, on the other hand, are to be left free to deal with the ordinary, everyday activities of the community. These include the education of children, the promotion of morality, the policing of most crime, and the supervision of property arrangements. Auxiliary governments are provided, in effect, by the religious organizations that are both local and countrywide, "governments" that are relied upon to help shape the citizens upon whom effective political governance depends.

The growing importance of the General Government is reflected in the tendency of the most gifted men in the Country to devote themselves to *national* affairs (except perhaps in parts of the South?). In addition, it should again be noticed that the powers identified in the Declaration of Independence as those that "Free and Independent States" may "of Right" exercise are powers assigned even in the Articles of Confederation primarily to the General Government. These are the powers "to levy War, conclude Peace, contract Alliances, and establish Commerce" (with only the last of these seriously questioned since then as to its extent among the powers of the General Government under the Constitution of 1787).

V

The States in the American Union are hedged in at the two extremes of the array of powers recognized in the Articles of Confederation. We have already noticed what is done at one of those extremes, that concerned with relations by the United States with other countries. These are the most national concerns that the People might have, concerns that the States are kept from interfering with.

At the other extreme are the most local activities, those devoted to the allocation, protection, and uses of property. Assurances are given in the Articles of Confederation (echoing here Magna Carta) about the vital right of persons to move from one State to another with their property. A kind of equality seems to be recognized, perhaps promoting thereby what came to be known (after Alexis de Tocqueville?) as individualism.

This Articles of Confederation guarantee, too, can be said to have been anticipated by Magna Carta. This sort of guarantee points up the importance of private property in the Anglo-American constitutional/ political system. A commercial society seems to be not only permitted but perhaps even encouraged thereby.

VI

The form of the General Government provided by the Articles of Confederation was obviously not permanent. After all, *that* form of government had neither a separate Executive nor a permanent Judiciary. There was not even an executive of the kind found in parliamentary governments, an executive that can be quite powerful because of its relation to, if not its control of, the relevant parliamentary body.

The form of government provided by the Articles shows us that the Legislature was regarded as the dominant branch. A legislature, it is assumed, can be depended upon to handle the duties of the other two branches of government, something that would not be expected from either of those other branches. This can be compared to other regimes, such as that of the ancient Persians (as described by Herodotus), for whom the word of the monarch was unquestionable law.

The impermanence of the Articles-form of government is suggested also by its dependence upon a one-house Legislature. We routinely speak of the separation of powers as salutary. But we do not usually notice how much such separation of powers can depend upon the Legislative branch itself being organized into two branches that are substantially independent of each other.

VII

The circumstances very much affected the way that this constitution, the Articles of Confederation, was shaped. It is obvious, as I have noted, that the framers of this constitution believed that they should get on with the war. This evidently meant, among other things, that the smaller States had to be catered to, at least for the time being.

But people generally, in the smaller States as well as in the larger, must have been aware of how much more was required from the larger States than from the smaller for the Country to become viable both at home and in dealings with other powers abroad. Thus, the contributions of both bodies and treasure to military campaigns by the larger States were obviously much greater than what could be expected from the States that chanced, at least for the time being, to be smaller. This recognition did not question the patriotism, but only the resources, of the smaller States.

Of course, the smaller States continue to be catered to somewhat in the Constitution of 1787, as may be seen in how voting power in the Senate and (to a lesser extent) in the Electoral College is allocated. That the smaller States recognized the "deal" offered them by the 1787 Constitution is indicated by the speed and the overwhelming majorities (sometimes the unanimity) with which *their* State conventions ratified the proposed Constitution. This was in marked contrast to how most of the larger States responded.

VIII

The Northwest Ordinance of 1787, enacted by the Articles of Confederation Congress, needs, in this context, to be at least glanced at. This is one of the great Acts of the Congress under the Articles. It was, in critical respect, the same kind of Congress as that which had issued the Declaration of Independence.

We have noticed the significance of the assurances about private property in the Articles of Confederation. Such assurances may be found in the Northwest Ordinance as well, and indeed at its very outset, where guidance is provided for the disposition of property in critical circumstances. The guidance provided there is particularly needed since the people who were expected to settle thereafter in the Northwest Territory were likely to come from States having varying rules of property.

Particularly significant, especially in the light of what we have noticed about the significance of the legislature under the Articles of Confederation, is the provision in the Northwest Ordinance (set forth in Appendix D of this volume) that, pending the election of local legislatures, the Gov-

ernor and judges appointed by Congress would have to make the laws
needed for the Territory. Congress retains a supervisory power with respect to these matters. Also significant is the provision that the laws that
the Governor and judges promulgate on their own authority have to be
taken from the statute books of one or more of the already established
State legislatures, which means that those laws would have originated with
(and hence would have been legitimated by) *some* legislature controlled by
American electorates.

IX

It is significant as well that the new States to be carved out of the
Northwest Territory are to be regarded as all on an equal footing with
the original thirteen. It is anticipated, of course, that there *will* be such
States. Perhaps even more important is the evident understanding that
there should be no permanent colonies made up of citizens of the United
States.

The similarity of the new States to the original thirteen is indicated by
the Bill of Rights addition to the Northwest Ordinance. These new States
are to respect rights which were obviously longstanding and more or less
taken for granted. This was eventually insisted upon as something to be
added to the Constitution of 1787 as well, no matter how vital and long-
established such rights were already understood to be.

We can see once again how much was built upon what was already
understood, anticipating (among other things) what was done with the
Fourteenth Amendment to make sure that the rights that Americans had
"always" had were recognized as applicable to the States as well as to the
General Government. It is taken for granted in the Northwest Ordinance
that a Republican Form of Government would have to be established in
any part of the Northwest Territory seeking admission to the Union. The
way of the future is suggested, moreover, in the provision in the Ordinance of '87 that there would never be any slavery in the Northwest Territory, a provision that must have been considered by many to be in the
spirit of the promise held out in effect by the Declaration of Independence
with respect to an eventual recognition in practice of the created equality
of all human beings.

5. Emergence of the Constitution (1786–1791)

I

A competent grounding in Constitutionalism is evident in how the Constitution of 1787 was developed and implemented. One gets the impression, as steps are taken from 1786 through 1791, that a considerable reservoir of experience and skills is drawn upon. There must have been everywhere in the Country reliable leaders who could not only do what had to be done but who could also explain what was going on, leaders whom the Framers depended upon and had to reckon with.

This is not to assume that there was unanimous agreement as to what should be done with respect to the General Government. But there could not have been much of a mystery about what was happening, whatever reservations some had about the political and other motives of various of the principal participants. Innovations were proposed, but only in the context of much that must have been familiar.

A century later the considerable competence in Constitutionalism, at least among the more enterprising citizens, could find expression in *Robert's Rules of Order*. There was in that compilation eloquent confirmation of what had long been understood, however innovative the post–Civil War compiler of these rules may have been. Guidance was provided, in the formulation of these rules, by parliamentary practices long relied upon in England and the United States.

II

The movements of the 1780s could well have been seen as the next steps in a long process. This was a process that could be felt by some to be several centuries in its making. Precisely what would happen in the United States probably could not have been predicted, but it seems to have been evident that something had to be done to fashion a new constitution, partly because of troubled economic conditions in the Country.

The 1786 Annapolis Conference dramatized the discontents of the day. Political (and eminently practical) men could be seen at work in this preliminary engagement, an early stage in what would be a sustained campaign. The participation of Alexander Hamilton, someone known to be close to General Washington, must have alerted the perceptive to the seriousness as well as to the soundness of this endeavor.

However ineffectual the Annapolis effort may have seemed to some at the time, it can now be recognized as remarkably successful. Its most critical recommendations, with respect to a Convention of the States to be convened in Philadelphia the following spring, found favor in the Articles of Confederation Congress of the day. The way this was done, including when it was done, may have been critical in determining the political complexion that such a Federal Convention would have.

III

Congress, ostensibly conducting itself pursuant to the Articles of Confederation, proved to be remarkably responsive to the proposals of the Annapolis Conference. One can even get the impression that much of what happened between 1786 and 1789 (when the new General Government began to work) was "orchestrated." Much of the turmoil and struggle was hidden from public view.

One could see at work here the men who would pretty much govern the Country for the rest of the eighteenth century, including with respect both to the establishment of the new government in 1789 and to the development of the Bill of Rights of 1791. The more perceptive delegates in the Articles of Confederation Congress could "read" not only the proposals that came out of Annapolis but even more the caliber and interests of the proposers. Such innovators, it must have been suspected, were not likely to be quixotic in their ventures.

The Confederation Congress, in issuing its recommendations to the States, is remarkably laconic. The States, it seems, were relied upon to do whatever might be needed to provide for the Convention anticipated for Philadelphia in May 1787. Here, too, considerable experience and sophistication were put to good use, with all but one of the thirteen States responding favorably (however guardedly, in some instances) to the Congressional recommendation that a Convention be convened.

IV

An emphasis had been placed, in both the Annapolis Conference and the Confederation Congress, upon *revising* the Articles of Confederation. It did seem to be generally understood that something would have to be done, with the inherent limitations of the Articles apparent from the outset. The economic and other conditions of the day reinforced a general sense of the inadequacy of the Articles, at least as originally established.

We can see, in the way that the Philadelphia Convention conducted itself, that the delegates knew from the outset and throughout the summer of 1787 how to use the opportunity provided them. There was considerable social and other contact among the delegates off the floor of the Convention. This must have helped them resolve and refine the issues that were formally dealt with on the Convention floor.

We can get from the Journal of the Convention some idea of how these issues could appear, and be dealt with, from time to time, issues that reflected deep-seated differences among factions in the Country. Of course, the Journal recorded from the beginning the absence of Rhode Island. Far more serious was the absence, after the opening weeks of the Convention, of a quorum of delegates from New York, an absence which anticipated the crucial political struggle in that State which would not be resolved before the following summer.

V

The silence about the New York and other problems must have at times seemed deafening. Among these problems was that of precisely what was happening in the Convention. The talk about "revising" the Articles of Confederation, which had been heard at Annapolis and in the Confederation Congress the year before, was quietly set aside by the Philadelphia Convention.

Thus, there was much that was "irregular" (if not even revolutionary) in what the Convention and thereafter the Confederation Congress and the State Ratification Conventions did. On the other hand, it must have seemed to the more thoughtful citizen that at last the United States might secure a government which would have the powers that the Declaration of Independence assumed that all independent states of right have. That is, it could be said that what was truly irregular was the way that governmental powers in and for the United States had been organized theretofore.

The silence of the day extended to the critical question of what would be the status of the nonratifying States if the proposed Constitution should be ratified by the requisite States. It was evidently believed that that was one of the matters that should *not* be explicitly dealt with, at least for the time being. It was thus that a quiet revolution was accomplished, bypassing the far-too-rigorous amendment provision of the Articles of Confederation.

VI

A series of steps had to be taken, both by Congress and in the States, before the proposed Constitution could take effect. It is striking how much of what happened between 1786 and 1791 depended upon "legislative" bodies. All of the critical "actors" were "legislative" in character—the Annapolis Conference, the Articles of Confederation Congress, the Constitutional Convention, the State legislatures, the State Ratifying Conventions, and the new Congress.

Even so, it must have helped those who guided these developments that it was generally understood that the first President under the new Constitution would be the greatest hero of the Revolution. It also proved vital to the system when that man voluntarily retired from office after two terms. This dramatized the expectation that the People of the United States would have to rule themselves.

Such self-rule takes place primarily through the Legislative branches of the various governments in the Country. And it was evident throughout the Constitution-framing process that the People at large were remarkably competent in the organization and use of their Legislatures. It is those Legislatures that are ultimately dominant in the allocations of powers under the Constitution.

VII

Very little is said about State constitutions and State practices in the materials we are reviewing. State legislatures *were* counted on to do what was needed to provide delegates to the Constitutional Convention, to supervise the State-by-State ratification of the Constitution, and to provide Members for the new Congress thereafter. This reliance upon State legislatures proved to be sound: they did what was needed and expected, and in good time.

Serious men and women all over the Country probably understood what was happening and why. Among the things they must have noticed was the way various State Ratification Conventions voted and when, with the workings of chance, always critical in political matters, quite evident there. That is evident, for example, in what can be called the Pennsylvania anomaly, for that was the one large State to vote early and by a solid majority for the proposed Constitution (sixty-five percent, as compared to Massachusetts's fifty-two percent, Virginia's fifty-one percent, and New York's fifty-two percent [New York being a would-be large State]).

The Conventions of the smaller States tended, we have seen, to vote early and by large majorities (sometimes unanimously) for the proposed Constitution; they knew, we have also seen, they had gotten as good a deal as could be expected, especially with the equality of votes provided for in the Senate. That the smaller States could be catered to as much as they were in 1787 reflected the peculiar circumstances of the framing earlier, under wartime conditions, of the Articles of Confederation, a constitution-making process which had avoided any premature confrontations among the States. As for the Pennsylvania vote in 1787, the Pennsylvania partisans of the Constitution, who had been together in the Convention held in Philadelphia, evidently were able to organize themselves and to get a State convention called and voting before the opposition could organize itself, as it was to do thereafter in Massachusetts, Virginia, and New York.

VIII

That which was seen in the Pennsylvania ratification process could be seen earlier in the way that the Constitutional Convention operated. That is, nationally minded men, who knew what they wanted and how to get it, took charge of matters in Philadelphia. The workings of these eminently political men could also be seen in the First Congress, not least in what they were immediately willing to propose as amendments to the Constitution, amendments which (ever since their ratification in 1791) have tended to be regarded as part of the original Constitution.

The ultimate subordination of the States to a fully empowered General Government was the objective of the leading spirits in the movement from the Annapolis Conference through the First Congress. Thus, they could have George Washington, in his letter of transmittal to Congress as President of the Constitutional Convention, liken the thirteen States to "individuals" entering civil society. This was hardly the language of those who make much of State Sovereignty.

It may well be that the most talented political men in this Country have been those of the Founding generation. It can be startling to notice how confidently *and competently* they moved through one stage after another in defining, establishing, and operating a new system of government. The political discourse of the day both contributed, and testified, to their capacity.

IX

The care with which the Framers and their allies expressed themselves testifies to their political skills. It can be instructive, for example, to trace their creative uses of the term "unanimous" (as in the witnessing provision of the Constitution). Their opponents must, at times, have been exasperated by the skill with which the partisans of the Constitution used the language and the parliamentary practices of the day.

Particularly effective was the appropriation by the partisans of the Constitution of the term "Federalist" (as in the title, *The Federalist*, the eighty-five newspaper articles crafted in New York, in 1787–1788, to urge ratification in that State). Strictly speaking, it *can* be argued, the true Federalists were the *opponents* of the Constitution, who wanted a constitution that retained more of the Federal features (such as the use of "expressly") found in the Articles of Confederation. Nowhere in the Constitution of 1787 is the term *federal* used, however much it was employed by partisans of the Constitution in their efforts both before and after the framing of the document.

One term that George Washington used in his Presidential letter from the Convention to the Congress must have sounded ominous in some quarters. It was "consolidation," a term that opponents of the Constitution made much of, as they prophesied that the new constitutional arrangement would result in the consolidation of the States (that is, the suppression both of vital differences among and of critical powers within the States). The partisans of the Constitution, the so-called Federalists, shied away from the term "consolidation" during the Ratification Campaign, preferring instead to emphasize another sentiment that Washington had used when he invoked "that Country so dear to us."

6. *Marbury* v. *Madison* (1803)

I

Constitutional law courses in this Country traditionally begin with *Marbury* v. *Madison*. One can see there, especially if one is so minded, what it is that our courts aspire to be and to do. But surprisingly little was really done by the United States Supreme Court on *that* occasion, however "big" it talked.

Indeed, one can sense here (whatever *Bush* v. *Gore* [2000] might suggest) the inherent limitations of courts whenever the political stakes are high. The "big" talk of the *Marbury* Court concealed the retreat that it managed in 1803. As far as the immediate controversy was concerned—as to whether duly appointed-and-confirmed justices of the peace in the District of Columbia would be able to take their seats—the Supreme Court did nothing.

Although little, if anything, was evidently "done" on that occasion, what was said by the Court (speaking through Chief Justice John Marshall) proved to be momentous in the long run. We can be reminded thereby of how important opinion and appearance can be in public affairs. This can mean, among other things, that the people involved in such controversies, whether they win or lose, may not know what is going on.

II

To speak of the people involved in this controversy may be to speak loosely. It does not seem that the Jefferson Administration did much to have its position presented to the Court. The "situation," it has been said, was constraining enough to impress upon the Court the limited options that it had.

We notice that it is James Madison, not Thomas Jefferson (his political master), who is named as a party to this controversy. Thus, it is the Secretary of State in what we would call his bureaucratic capacity who is challenged by this suit. It is he who is asked to turn over a document the

33

existence of which (or at least its creation) is not doubted—but which may not truly need to be in the possession of the man serving in the office designated.

After all, we would not expect a judicial or any other officer to vacate his office if his papers should be mislaid, destroyed, stolen, or otherwise go missing. The Chief Justice seems to say virtually this, but he and his colleagues may not have believed it prudent for any claimants (William Marbury et al.) simply to show up in the relevant courtroom, get sworn in by the other judicial personnel, offer to preside over cases, and claim their salaries. However that may have been, it is not mentioned by the Court that, but for the hectic character of John Marshall's last days in the Office of the Secretary of State in the outgoing John Adams Administration (which failed to deliver to Marbury his commission), there would have been no legal controversy at all.

III

In short, this was a trivial matter (with Marbury himself not meriting even a short entry in the twenty-volume *Dictionary of American Biography*). It is because of what is said in the Opinion of the *Marbury* Court, about Judicial Review of Acts of Congress for their constitutionality, that the case became momentous. One must say "became" because the Opinion evidently got little attention at the time, especially since the Administration was not told that it *must* do anything other than what it had been doing.

Thus, the Court did nothing on this occasion but insist that it should be able to declare void for unconstitutionality an improper Act of Congress. This insistence was not backed up by any citations to relevant judicial determinations theretofore in the Anglo-American constitutional tradition. The Court does suggest, however, that a Judiciary entrusted with a written constitution is both authorized and expected to invalidate unconstitutional measures.

But, it could have been pointed out, although the British Constitution has significant parts which *are* written (such as the Habeas Corpus Acts of 1641 and 1679), that has never been taken to authorize any British court to invalidate an Act of Parliament. Furthermore, the constitution known as the Articles of Confederation had also been written—but it was not expected that any court (say, in one of the States) could have properly invalidated acts of the Confederation Congress. And, of course, no serious argument has ever been made that Judicial Review of Acts *of Congress* for constitutionality was ever anticipated or explicitly provided for by the Framers of the Constitution (whatever may seem to be suggested in *Federalist,* Numbers 78 and 81).

IV

The Supremacy Clause in Article VI of the Constitution is sometimes looked to for justification of Judicial Review of Acts of Congress. But it should be clear, upon examination of the Supremacy Clause, that that Clause does not contemplate that the State courts primarily addressed there are expected to pass judgment upon the Acts of Congress, along with the Constitution itself and the treaties there identified, to which they are obliged to defer. A national uniformity, in the application of the Constitution, laws, and treaties of the United States, is thereby provided for and anticipated.

The Judicial Review that *is* anticipated, on the other hand, is with respect to the measures resorted to by State Governments. Such governments are to be supervised by the General Government, somewhat as Colonial governments were supervised by the appropriate arms of the British Government (and somewhat as Territorial governments established pursuant to the Northwest Ordinance could be supervised by Congress). Something of this relation may be seen in the duty that the British courts *now* have to assess Acts of Parliament in the light of Directives issued by the European Union.

It should be recognized, in short, that there is nothing in the Constitution of 1787 which suggests that the Courts of the United States are to pass judgment on Acts of Congress, whatever judges may properly (if not even naturally) try to do to protect themselves from Legislative or Executive encroachments. Nor is there anything comparable to the official assessment of proposed legislation that the President can express through the use of the Veto Power explicitly provided for him. The precise directions set forth with that provision should remind us that no guidance at all is provided for when and how Courts might exercise a power of Judicial Review of Acts of Congress and what the consequence of such an exercise should be.

V

The Presidential Veto Power probably had to be provided in the detail we have it in order to make certain that the traditional absolute veto of the British monarch was not to be continued in the United States. This means, in effect, that the President can express an opinion about the undesirability (including, perhaps, the unconstitutionality) of a just-passed Bill—but his opinion need not be the last word. The care with which the Presidential Veto Power is prescribed points up the uncertainty about what a judicial finding of the unconstitutionality of an Act of Congress should be taken to mean.

For example, as of when is an Act to be considered unconstitutional, especially when there may have already been decades of actions pursuant to it? Then there is this remarkable observation in the *Marbury* Opinion:

> It must be well recollected that in 1792, an act was passed, directing the secretary of war to place on the pension list such disabled officers and soldiers as should be reported to him, by the circuit courts, which act, so far as the duty was imposed on the courts, was deemed unconstitutional; but some of the judges, thinking that the law might be executed by them in the character of commissioners, proceeded to act and to report in that character. This law being deemed unconstitutional at the circuits, was repealed, and a different system was established.

Does not this mean, in effect, that although United States Circuit Court judges (acting to protect themselves?) had found an Act of Congress to be "unconstitutional," it evidently was not (as we would say) automatically considered void, but rather it had to be repealed thereafter by Congress in order for the Country and the judges to get rid of it (and for "a different system [to be] established")?

There is no indication that the situation would have been different if the Supreme Court, rather than a Circuit Court, had issued a finding of the unconstitutionality of that 1792 Act. Thus, it should not be assumed that an Act of Congress is at once to be considered void simply because a Court (even if it should be the United States Supreme Court) has deemed it unconstitutional. A responsible Congress should, of course, take into account such a judicial Opinion when considering what to do about any statute described in this fashion by judges with jurisdiction to hear a case related to that statute.

VI

Thus, the process of Judicial Review can be divided into two phases. First, there is the action of an appropriate court in passing judgment on the constitutionality of an Act of Congress. Then, there is the status of that Act of Congress after an appropriate court has expressed its *Opinion* that it is unconstitutional.

But the puzzles do not end here, for there are the problems that confront us upon our recognizing that relatively few of the measures promulgated by the Congress as well as by the President are ever considered appropriate for review by the United States Supreme Court. Indeed, to make much of Judicial Review can have the unfortunate effect of seeming to absolve the Congress and the President of any duty to assess for their constitutionality the measures that they are responsible for. After all, they *are* the only ones (between them) who have an opportunity, on a day-to-day basis, to make practical assessments of *all* of the measures that are developed and applied by the General Government.

Fortunately, the Congress and the President still do much of this, however tempting it can be to do what they "want" to do, leaving it to the Supreme Court to assess constitutionality "someday." A comprehensive reliance upon the Supreme Court here is both impractical and demoralizing. And it can lead, if the Court does not teach the proper lessons, to a demoralization as well of the People upon whom a respect for constitutionality must ultimately rest.

VII

The happenstance of judicial determinations should again be noted. It can very much depend upon chance what questions get into courts and in what circumstances. This can affect in turn both what is ruled and precisely what is said.

Much has been written about the vulnerability, at the time of *Marbury*, of the Supreme Court Justices and of the bulk of the Federalist judges sitting in the Courts of the United States. It is said that it was simply not known whether the 1801 change in dominant party affiliations in the Presidency and the Congress would lead to a political purge of the Judiciary. This is not a concern that the judges in the Courts of the United States have had once the crises of the early decades of the nineteenth century were weathered.

The safest thing for a self-respecting Court to do, it is further said, is to avoid ordering the Administration to do something that no judge could make it do. This is the course that the *Marbury* Court followed by finding that it really did not have the jurisdiction to deal with the matter that it had examined at length. It could hardly constitute an impeacheable offense, in such circumstances, to abstain from an exercise of power, whatever speculations might have been entertained by the Justices about judicial commissions, writs of mandamus, and findings of unconstitutionality.

VIII

The immediate inconsequentiality of the *Marbury* Opinion is suggested by the fact that the Supreme Court did not presume, for a half-century thereafter, to find any other Act of Congress to be unconstitutional. And when it did so, it was in the remarkably wrongheaded holding of the *Dred Scott Case* of 1857, a holding bearing on the status of slavery in the Territories of the United States, which is sometimes said to have contributed to the coming of the Civil War. Thus, the first recourse to Judicial Review by the Supreme Court was in a trivial quarrel, the second aggravated a cataclysmic crisis.

During the half-century between *Marbury* and *Dred Scott,* the Congress and the President were routinely counted on to make their own assessments of the constitutionality of the measures that they promulgated. It was during this period that serious debates about constitutionality (such as with respect to the use and abuse of tariffs) could be heard in the halls of Congress. The People at large could also be counted upon to contribute to debates in which constitutionality and policy considerations could not help but be mixed.

An informed recognition of the potentially revolutionary act on the part of the *Marbury* Court does not mean that a reliance upon Judicial Review of Acts of Congress should now be immediately abandoned. But it can mean that the limitations of such a power should be appreciated, a power which can be depended upon to "police" far less of what the General Government does than the People have become accustomed to believe that the Court is able to do. Another way of putting all this is to suggest that public-spirited law students should be encouraged to aspire more to political than to judicial careers.

IX

Perhaps the most serious limitation in any substantial reliance upon Judicial Review in the United States today is reflected in the fact that when the Congress and the Court have differed, for two centuries now, as to the constitutionality of *important* measures, the Congress has been right. This has been true, for example, in the *Dred Scott* controversy of 1857, in the Civil Rights Acts controversy of 1883, and in the Commerce Clause controversies of the 1930s. In all such controversies, the Court has eventually come around to the Congress's position, but not without risking serious damage for the Country because of its erroneous rulings.

That we can speak of "error" in these matters does question what may be the principal justification for Judicial Review, the expectation that dispassionate judges are more apt than political men and women to read the Constitution properly. Doubts about the soundness of this expectation can be aroused upon considering *Marbury* itself, where there was a likely misreading of the Article III provision about the immutability of the original jurisdiction of the Supreme Court. One must wonder whether the Chief Justice "knew better," saying in *Marbury* what he did about Article III in order to avoid having to risk issuing an order that would have unpredictable political consequences.

It is not generally recognized that one serious consequence of the *Marbury* reading of the Exceptions Clause in Article III is that the Supreme Court can be effectively stripped of whatever parts of its appellate jurisdiction that the Congress chooses to eliminate. This means, among other things, that the Court can be prevented by Congress from reviewing any statute that the People of the United States permit Congress to keep the Court from considering. Thus, in order to have (on principle) a somewhat reliable system of Judicial Review, the United States Supreme Court would have to reconsider the very provision in Article III of the Constitution that it probably misread when it first ventured (in 1803) to declare an Act of Congress unconstitutional.

7. *Swift* v. *Tyson* (1842);
Erie Railroad Company v. *Tompkins* (1938)

I

We have here two United States Supreme Court cases, a century apart, which are regarded as critical to common law determinations by the Courts of the United States, cases that are difficult, perhaps impossible, to explain to readers not trained in the law. One, *Swift* v. *Tyson,* dealt with negotiable instruments; the other, *Erie Railroad Company* v. *Tompkins,* dealt with tort law. It seems to be widely believed by legal scholars that the ruling in *Erie,* markedly reducing both the authority and the flexibility, in common law and related disputes, of the Courts of the United States (that is, the Federal Courts), was long overdue.

It should be noticed that these and like cases are rarely dealt with in American constitutional law courses these days. It is not generally recognized how much, and in what ways, such cases raise a fundamental question, "What is law?" Nor is it recognized that reasoning about justice and social utility is vital to the common law, as traditionally understood.

It is reported in the *Encyclopedia of the American Constitution,* "Because these federal court decisions [with respect to the common law] did not purport to bind state courts, the result was often the parallel existence of two different rules of law applicable to the same controversy." Why, it must be wondered, were not State Court judges convinced that they should follow the same legal reasoning as the judges in the Courts of the United States? Did their mode of selection and the limits upon their tenure make it likely that State Court judges would prefer to seem primarily local in their allegiances and interests?

II

The stature of Joseph Story, the Justice who wrote the Opinion for the Court in *Swift* v. *Tyson,* is hard to exaggerate. A judge of the highest rank as a scholar, he displays what should be done by any American judges when common law and other such questions are involved in the cases they hear. Such questions are most apt to be raised, in the Courts of the United States, in "diversity of citizenship" cases.

It is a different matter, it is widely recognized, when there is a State statute governing the matter being litigated. Are people more apt to know what a statute provides than what the common law is apt to be with respect to an issue, especially when a local anomaly has to be considered? This is reflected in how Section 34 of the Judiciary Act of 1789 is crafted, binding the Courts of the United States to defer in their rulings to relevant State laws (which "laws" were long taken to refer, for the most part, to statutes).

When the common law rather than a State statute governs the matter under consideration, the 1789 Judiciary Act seems to recognize, judges in the Courts of the United States should continue to do what judges in the Anglo-American tradition have "always" done. How those judges have worked is evident in what Justice Story does in 1842 as he attempts to develop and apply doctrines drawn from the general principles of commercial law. The scope and depth of his inquiry are indicated by the use he makes both of Cicero (by way of Lord Mansfield) and of various cases and treatises of note.

III

The Opinion of the Court in *Erie* (a case described in the Preface for this volume) opens with the announcement, "The question for decision is whether the oft-challenged decision of *Swift* v. *Tyson* [with respect to the relevant authority in common law cases] shall now be disapproved." The *Erie* trial jury, which had found for the injured Harry Tompkins in the amount of $30,000 (equivalent to well over a half million today), evidently did not believe that it should matter precisely where an injured man is, what his legal status is, or what State he is in when a cross-country train hits him in the way it hit Tompkins in this case. And, it seems, this is pretty much the way that judges in the Courts of the United States (known to us as Federal Courts) had, up to that time, thought about this kind of issue, especially with respect to the "trespass" defense advanced by the railroad company.

That the jury's original finding in *Erie* (in favor of the trespassing

Tompkins) "makes sense" is suggested upon considering the guidance provided thereby for "persons" in the position of the railroad company there. Care should be taken, that is, not to have objects protruding from freight cars, no matter where the train happens to be. After all, passersby may be in places where they are entitled to be—and even "trespassers" are not always where they are not supposed to be (as, for example, when the path of the trespass crosses a public highway).

Indeed, it can be said, the railroad company should expect that all kinds of people may be injured by the way it handles its property. In this, it can also be said, it is like the maker of the promissory note in *Swift* v. *Tyson*. Once one has acted, others will be apt to take at face value what one has done, whether it is a promise to pay or the management of a freight car.

IV

Critical to modern complaints that had contributed to the ruling in *Erie* v. *Tompkins* is the phenomenon of "forum shopping." This had come about, it seems, because the rulings of the judges in the Courts of the United States had *not* been regarded as sufficient authority in State courts. This resistance on the part of State courts seems to have been an unexpected development, at least so far as the thinking of the First Congress was concerned.

"States' Rights" dogmas may have contributed to this development. This is particularly odd in that a leader in the movement to restrict, if not to eliminate altogether, the *Swift* v. *Tyson* approach was Oliver Wendell Holmes Jr., a thrice-wounded veteran of the Union Army during the Civil War. It is far from clear that he ever appreciated the irony of his position here, a position that makes much (in effect) of States' Rights.

Be that as it may, the common law rulings of the Courts of the United States should, in a properly explained system, have had considerable influence, if not even authority, in all common law courts (whether State or Federal) in the United States. Also in need of proper explanation is the way that forum shopping continues, even under the *Erie* rule. Only now it is more sophisticated and not readily apparent even to most legal scholars, with the Courts of the United States left even less able than they had been before to compensate for it.

V

Fundamental to complaints such as those about forum shopping are concerns about fairness and the equal protection of the laws. This suggests that there are, or at least should be, determinable standards which must be of general application in a common law system, the kind of system anticipated (for example) in the Northwest Ordinance. To proceed thus is to assume that there *are* standards of good and bad, of right and wrong, which are somewhat independent of authority and power.

To proceed thus is also to question the emphasis, found among "legal realists" such as Justice Holmes and his disciples, upon law as being grounded in authority and hence in power. It is an emphasis that makes much of the *will,* and this at the expense of a deference to the *dictates of justice* grounded in reasoning about the nature of things. The classical source of this will-oriented approach could well be the evidently self-centered Thrasymachus of Plato's *Republic.*

Thomas Aquinas, on the other hand, had insisted that law is, among other things, a dictate of that reason which those in authority should employ. One consequence of the *Erie* doctrine is that the judges in the Courts of the United States are, in effect, forbidden to do what State court judges may routinely do in common law cases: that is, they are forbidden to *think* about the matters they are considering. Rather, they are supposedly limited to determining what the relevant State court has said on any matter at issue—and to be completely bound by *that.*

VI

It should by now be evident to the reader that issues with respect to the ascertainment, modification, and application of the common law can be technical and otherwise complicated. These are matters that judges, with the assistance of lawyers and scholars (including, now, economists), have developed for centuries in the English-speaking world. Critical to this process has been the recognition that legal reasoning, drawing both on precedents and on a reliable sense of what is by nature right, should be deferred to by judges rather than that act of will that it is now so fashionable (in the name of "legal realism," a sophisticated relativism) to depend upon.

However this may be, it is curious that the judges who are generally regarded as the best in the Country, those sitting in the Federal Courts, are the only ones who are supposedly forbidden to think about the common law issues that they must decide. Also curious is the fact that although the United States Supreme Court has assumed powers of Judicial Review of Acts of Congress with which it was obviously *not* entrusted by the Framers, it has managed to surrender a critical power that it was assumed from the beginning that it *would* have as a prominent judicial body in a common law system. Indeed, in the years immediately preceding *Erie* v. *Tompkins,* the United States Supreme Court was quite active in striking down one statute after another that a desperate Congress had developed in its effort to deal with the Great Depression.

Justice Holmes, in developing his legal realism position, insisted that there was no "transcendental body of law outside of any particular State." It is very odd indeed that someone as learned as Oliver Wendell Holmes obviously was in the common law should talk the way he sometimes did, discounting as he evidently did the use of reasons and reasoning by common law judges for centuries. He never seemed to recognize that the United States Supreme Court might have become (indeed, should have become) as influential in State courts for its common law rulings as, say, Lord Mansfield had been for Justice Story.

VII

The timing of the *Erie* case may have affected what the Supreme Court did in disavowing the significant common law influence it had inherited. A generation later, the recognized powers of the Congress of the United States, with respect both to commercial matters and to much of tort law, had been considerably increased—and were steadily growing. There are now, for example, national standards that govern all kinds of railroad traffic and commercial transactions, the activities dealt with both in *Erie* and in *Swift* v. *Tyson.*

In addition, worldwide developments affect local rules, standards, and practices. Justice Louis D. Brandeis insisted, in his Opinion for the Court in *Erie,* that there is no "federal general common law." He was correct in this, but not for the reasons he gave, but rather because there should be only *the* common law.

Perhaps Congress should have, in these matters, provided the Courts of the United States more guidance than it had. Perhaps, that is, it should have addressed whatever abuses there may have been in the way that the dual system of common law adjudications was sometimes manipulated. After all, the common law system always recognized that legislative power was ultimately authoritative, especially whenever the workings of a common law system chanced to lead to difficulties from which the judges could not readily extricate themselves.

VIII

Congressional prerogatives, as well as duties, with respect to these matters should be recognized. Whatever the original intended meaning of the Judiciary Act of 1789, it was somewhat irregular for the United States Supreme Court to attempt in 1938—that is, at so late a date—to correct the long-settled interpretation of the relevant provision in that Act. It is generally recognized that it is up to Congress to make whatever changes may be called for in any judicial interpretation of a statute that is long-standing (and which, it can usually be presumed, the Congress accepts).

It does seem, moreover, that the Supreme Court, with its 1938 reliance upon State *law,* was mistaken in its reading of the 1789 Act. It had long been said, by respectable common law authorities, that the opinions of common law judges are *not* the law, but rather are no more than evidence of what the law is. And so judicial opinions can be constantly reexamined as the judges keep thinking about the best rule in the circumstances in which they find themselves from time to time.

Of course, the Supreme Court sensed that it would be improper for it simply to reinterpret the relevant 1789 statutory provision in *Erie,* rather than leaving it to the Congress to make whatever adjustments might be called for. But, it could properly remind us, mistaken readings of the Constitution are not to be treated the way that mistaken readings of statutes are. The Court suggested, therefore, that the reading theretofore of the relevant 1789 statute, mistaken or not, had not taken into account an unconstitutional assumption of power on the part of the Congress, something which is always open to correction.

IX

The "constitutionality" issue thus recognized permitted, in effect, a reinterpretation of the 1789 statute, however untimely that may otherwise have seemed. But once the purpose was served of somehow permitting a reinterpretation of the statute, the inquiry into constitutionality could be sidetracked. For one thing, the issue of constitutionality had not been raised in the appropriate manner.

That is, the epidemic of judicial invalidations of Acts of Congress had evidently prompted a 1937 Congressional Act providing, among other things, that the Attorney General of the United States should be notified whenever an issue of the constitutionality of an Act of Congress was to be considered. Since this had not been done on this occasion, the Court would have had to hold off its ruling until the Attorney General had had an opportunity to defend the Act of Congress under review. It can be noticed in passing that we can see here one of the bizarre features of Judicial Review of Acts of Congress as it has developed in the United States: a statute can be reviewed for its constitutionality even after it has been used for a century and a half.

So, the "unconstitutionality" issue was raised just enough to permit somehow a remarkably untimely reinterpretation of the Judiciary Act of 1789, but not enough to oblige the Court to invite the Attorney General to participate. But this was not the only questionable use here of the Constitution and relevant Congressional legislation, for there was also the endorsement by the *Erie* Court of a statement, many years before, by Justice Stephen J. Field, in which he uses the term "specifically" in such a way as in effect to read into the Tenth Amendment that "expressly" term which the First Congress had been determined to keep out when it framed that amendment. The spirit of the Articles of Confederation was thereby revived by the Supreme Court, that constitutional arrangement in which the judicial power of the United States was barely recognized, anticipating thereby (it might even be said) that yearning for judicial suicide which later found inglorious expression in *Erie Railroad Company* v. *Tompkins.*

8. *Martin* v. *Hunter's Lessee* (1816); *M'Culloch* v. *Maryland* (1819)

I

There may be seen in these two United States Supreme Court cases, as in several others in the first half of the nineteenth century, reminders of the sectional differences that culminated in the Civil War. The restiveness evident here is on the part of Southerners. Earlier, however, there had been similar restiveness exhibited by New Englanders, in part perhaps because Virginia seemed to monopolize the Presidency.

There may also be seen in such cases the tendency in the United States to translate political differences into legal controversies. It seems to be hoped that legal adjudications can resolve political issues, or at least moderate them. Sometimes, however, the judicial intervention may have made matters worse, as in the *Dred Scott Case* of 1857.

One can be reminded, upon reading the Opinions in *Martin* and in *M'Culloch,* of the man who first encountered Shakespeare's *Hamlet* in a staged production. It was alright, he reported, except that it used a lot of familiar sayings. The pronouncements in these two cases, as well as in cases such as *Marbury* (1803) and *Gibbons* v. *Ogden* (1824), have assumed the status of well-known oracular declarations.

II

We can see in *Martin* v. *Hunter's Lessee* the delicate problem of how the Courts of the United States should deal with the doings of State courts. This may be seen in other cases as well. But the problem is particularly acute in *Martin* because (it seems) of the career, and ambition, of Spencer Roane of the Supreme Court of Virginia.

One aspect of this problem in *Martin* is with respect to the appellate jurisdiction of the United States Supreme Court. The Chief Justice, because of his connection with a party to this litigation, did not participate in the disposition of this case. But Justice Joseph Story, in writing for the Court, does seem to accept the dubious *Marbury* interpretation of the constitutional limitations upon expanding the original jurisdiction of the United States Supreme Court.

It is declared in *Martin* that the powers of the General Government are such that they can affect even property titles in a State. This kind of "interference" with the most local of determinations may also be authorized when there are State statutes (not only the common law) involved. The spirit here is quite different from that which we have encountered in *Erie Railroad Company* v. *Tompkins* (1938).

III

We can see in *Martin* the "reach" of the Supremacy Clause. The question here, however, is *not* of the effect of laws made "in pursuance" of the Constitution, but rather of the effect of treaties "made under the Authority of the United States." An understanding with respect to land titles in Virginia had had to be reached with the British government before arrangements vital to recognition of the very existence of the United States could be agreed to.

This kind of understanding, when developed by way of treaties, may seem to some to be an unwarranted interference with State prerogatives. But the States do have some say with respect to treaties entered into, in that the Senate must ratify all treaties. And, in the Constitution of 1787, the Senate is where the States as States were intended to be represented.

Of course, the treaty provisions critical in *Martin* were never ratified by the Senate, for they were entered into before the Constitution of 1787 went into effect. But the pre-1787 treaties do come within the scope of the Supremacy Clause. And the People of the State of Virginia, when they came to consider ratification of the proposed Constitution, can be understood to have known that such treaties were among those that the Supremacy Clause deliberately placed in a position superior to State laws.

IV

M'Culloch v. *Maryland* is considered by some scholars to be the most important case in the history of the United States Supreme Court. It is evident to anyone studying this case how important the lawyers were who argued it for more than a week. This can remind us of how the common law also worked, something that may not be as apparent today when law clerks do for the Justices much of what counsel once did.

The immediate issue in *M'Culloch* has to do with whether State Governments can so tax the instrumentalities of the General Government as to cripple them. It was evident that what the State of Maryland had done in exercising its tax power was not primarily with a view to raising revenue. Rather, the obvious purpose was to make it difficult, if not impossible, for the National Bank chartered by Congress to do business in Maryland.

All this took place three decades after the establishment of the General Government pursuant to the Constitution of 1787. The longer the life of the General Government, the smaller the proportion of the States in the Union which had ever had an existence somewhat independent of the General Government. Thus, the constitutional arrangement which provided that new States would have the same status as the original thirteen had, as one effect, the subordination of all the States, including the original thirteen, to the General Government, at least with respect to the quite substantial matters assigned to that General Government to take care of.

V

This steady retroactive lowering of the status of the original thirteen States bears upon the critical question repeatedly raised in cases such as *Martin* and *M'Culloch*. That question is as to whether the United States Constitution represents a Compact or a Union. We see more readily in the Confederate Constitution of 1861 (set forth in Appendix I of this volume) what the Compact Theory can mean in practice.

Even so, the Constitution of 1787 (whatever it may mean) is taken to be authoritative. The Supreme Court keeps *saying*, in early nineteenth century reviews of Acts of Congress, that it can assess Acts of Congress for their constitutionality—and that those Acts found to be unconstitutional can be declared void. But it never declares any Act void, between 1803 and 1857, which can remind one of the insistence of Homer's Zeus that he can set aside the decrees of Fate, if he so willed—but he never does, inducing us to wonder whether it was believed (either by Homer or by his audience) that Zeus could ever have done so.

It is asked, from time to time, what the basis may be of the power of the Courts of the United States to declare Acts of Congress to be unconstitutional. But there can be no serious doubt that various acts of State Governments can be reviewed by all branches of the General Government (not just by the Judiciary of that Government) for their constitutionality. Thus, various restrictions on the States, as in Article I, Section 10, and in Article IV, presuppose some supervision of the States by the General Government.

VI

Even so, would it not have been better, even in the *M'Culloch* situation, if Congress had legislated the restraints upon State actions that the United States Supreme Court found to be implicit in the constitutional arrangement? Did the Court, in saying what would be proper taxation and what would not, attempt to do the legislating that Congress is usually better equipped to do? But what the Court did has been so much acquiesced in both by Congress and by the States as to make the judicial initiative here seem less questionable than it might otherwise have been.

It is, in any event, instructive to see how the Constitution can be read in *M'Culloch*. The term "necessary" in "necessary and proper" is, we are told, illuminated by the use (further on in the Constitution) of that term in "absolutely necessary." An invaluable reminder is provided here of the cautions of which every legal draftsman should be aware.

We must, further on in this inquiry, consider challenges in constitutional interpretation that are not addressed by the Court in *M'Culloch*. For example, it is argued, on behalf of Maryland, that the specification of some restraints upon the States implies that other restraints were not intended. But I will attempt, later on, to develop a counterargument illustrated by the chart of the powers enumerated in Article I, Section 8 (found in Appendix F of this volume).

VII

The remarkable career of Chief Justice John Marshall is illustrated by what he was able to do in *M'Culloch* v. *Maryland*. Even though there were, by that time, only two Federalist appointees left on his Court, there had been maintained a decidedly nationalist tone in what was said and done by that Court. This is testimony to, among other things, the part that chance factors—in this case, the remarkable Marshall "personality"—can play in the conduct of public affairs.

Chance may be seen as well in the availability of the "We the People" language that is made so much of by those who stress "Union" rather than "Compact" in their understanding of our constitutional arrangement. It can be wondered, however, whether the "We the People" formulation would have been used in the 1787 Preamble if it had been known precisely which States would be ratifying the proposed Constitution. But however that language came to be settled upon, it has had a profound effect upon constitutional sensibilities ever since, something which is perversely testified to by the adjustments made to the language of the Preamble in the Confederate Constitution of 1861.

The importance of "personality" is further testified to by the way that the *Federalist* can be cited in counsel's arguments in *M'Culloch*—that is, as *Letters of Publius*. Is it not recognized thereby that that which was said by the authors of those papers in a particular historical situation might differ in critical ways from what they might properly have said in other circumstances? We are reminded, in *Martin,* of the importance of circumstances, as Justice Story provides a litany of "historical facts" that can help us understand how the Constitution was understood by its Framers.

VIII

Critical to the decision in *M'Culloch* v. *Maryland* is one of the great principles of Anglo-American constitutionalism. That there should be no taxation without adequate representation can be said to go back at least to Magna Carta. It is invoked in the Declaration of Independence, and in a way which suggests that no explicit constitutional provision is any longer needed to justify such an invocation.

An application of that principle may be seen in what the *M'Culloch* Court says, as it prepares to close its Opinion, about the taxes that Maryland may still levy against instrumentalities of the United States. Still, it might be wondered whether Congress could not immunize those instrumentalities from even such State taxation. But the taxes thus permitted by the Court at least have the safeguard of also being paid by the People of Maryland at large, which makes it likely that such taxes will be sensible, unlike the taxation that had been developed in order to cripple the operations of the National Bank in Maryland.

The "No taxation without representation" safeguard is implicit in the way that the Revenue Power is provided for in Article I of the Constitution, with the House of Representatives given the lead in revenue matters. It may also be implicit in our general understanding of "property." It may be implicit as well in our understanding both of the rule of law and of that Republican Form of Government required for States by Article IV of the Constitution.

IX

We can be reminded of the underlying issues neglected by proponents today of the *Erie* doctrine when we probe further into these matters by considering what the natural right/natural law basis may be of our Constitutionalism. Are there always, or almost always, limitations upon government that do not depend upon explicit constitutional documents? Are such limitations even implicit in the very language we use?

It may well be that a healthy natural right/natural law tradition depends as much on perennial questions as it does on authoritative answers. Among the questions that can be usefully considered are how and why various other peoples around the world can put up, decade after decade (if not century after century), with the kind of governments that *they* have. It can be particularly instructive to remember, for example, what is reported by Herodotus about the way that the Persian kings conducted themselves, and with the expectation that their sometimes insane commands would be immediately obeyed.

Such commands can make the governmental abuses we have seen in this Country from time to time seem to be child's play by comparison. This is not to suggest, however, that deeply-rooted misconceptions among us may not have serious consequences, as may be seen in how our early nineteenth-century political and constitutional debates culminated in the Civil War. It can be wondered whether those vital pre–Civil War struggles continue, in a much tamer form, in the intermittent States' Rights struggles of our own time.

9. *Gibbons* v. *Ogden* (1824)

I

The scope of any Congressional power is recognized in this case, of 180 years ago, to be, for practical purposes, virtually unlimited—and this despite the arguments made on behalf of States' Rights. This is obvious enough when the power considered is that of, say, the power to "establish Post Offices and post Roads." Congress, if it should wish, could open a post office in every block on every street in every town and city in this Country.

Why did it not do so, even in the days when it could create thereby a multitude of patronage jobs? There is nothing in the Constitution which prevents this. But there is much in our constitutional system (including the recourse the People have to elections) that makes such action on the part of Congress virtually unthinkable.

But what about the power of Congress to "regulate Commerce with foreign Nations, and among the several States"? How much local commercial activity may Congress deal with, especially in light of the fact that the States also try to deal with such activity? Suggestive of the scope of Congressional power with respect to the management of traffic on navigable waters within a State is the fact that Congress did, in 1793, take charge of this matter, obviously assuming, from early on in its history, that regulation of commerce includes the power to regulate navigation.

II

It was as obvious two centuries ago as it is today that Congress effectively shares still another power with the States, its great power to levy and collect taxes. Without such a power, government may not be impossible—as could be seen in the government provided for by the Articles of Confederation—but it is likely, without an independent source of revenue, to be quite limited in its scope and effectiveness. It is obvious that State Governments were expected to continue to do much of what local governments had always done, especially with respect to the care of the health and the morals of their inhabitants.

Even so, although the Congressional taxation power is not exclusive, it *has* come to be recognized as preeminent. This may even be seen in how we routinely prepare our income tax returns in many States, calculating first our Internal Revenue Service obligations and thereafter (almost as an afterthought) our State tax. And, it is known, the United States gets to take its cut first out of the assets of any taxpayer's estate.

Of course, governments do not exist in order to tax, whatever harassed citizens might suspect at times, but rather they tax in order to exist—in order, that is, to do or to encourage the doing of things expected of them. Intimately related, then, to the taxation power is the power to spend money, and it is with this money that Congress can (when it wishes) exert considerable control over both the Executive and the Judicial branches of the General Government. These facts of our Constitutional life are critical to an appreciation of the grave threat posed to our system of government, two decades ago, by the Iran arms/Contra aid subterfuge.

III

The principal domestic power of Congress *is* the Commerce Power, which has come to be recognized as a comprehensive power to minister to the economy of the Country. This has been reinforced politically by an observation for which there is considerable support, that the business of America is business. Whatever reservations we should have about the scope of this observation, there is certainly much to be said for it.

The Commerce Power is to be exercised with a view to the prosperity and hence the happiness of the People of this Country. When such terms as "the general Welfare" (found twice in the Constitution of 1787) are recalled, it can be understood that the business of America may also be to make citizens better—as well as "better off"—human beings than they might otherwise be. Indeed, as we have been obliged to notice from time to time, sustained economic activity (and hence a thriving business life) presupposes competent and reliable people both high and low, something that may be difficult to maintain without curbing some economic activity (whether it is traffic in drugs, in guns, in human beings, in tobacco, or in financial manipulations).

State Governments are also concerned to promote the happiness of their peoples and the general welfare. They are most apt to devote themselves to the supervision of those activities over which they can hope to exercise some effective control, such as the management of property relations, of pre-collegiate education, of health, and of morals. But it is virtually impossible for the General Government *not* to take such matters into account also, and even to shape them somewhat, in legislating on the grand matters that it is obviously entrusted with (however misleading such judicial experiments as *United States* v. *Lopez* [1995] may be from time to time).

IV

The comprehensiveness of the Commerce Power of the General Government is no longer seriously doubted. In fact, Chief Justice Marshall's Opinion for the Court in *Gibbons* v. *Ogden* should have settled that issue. The only serious question remaining thereafter, aside from the not-altogether-serious question of what "Commerce" encompasses, is whether the States, in their regulations of commerce within their borders, may be restrained by implications drawn from Congressional regulation.

Sometimes the relevant implication is obvious enough, and hence not in need of being spelled out. In other instances, Congress may have to specify what the States can continue to do with respect to any matter addressed by Congressional legislation. Related to these responses is the "burdens upon interstate commerce" litigation that we will be considering further on in these *Reflections.*

Of course, Congress could enact legislation that simply says that whenever State laws conflict in their operations with the laws of the United States, then the laws of the United States take precedence. But, it can be said, this is already provided for, in effect, by the Supremacy Clause in Article VI of the Constitution. This seems to have been the understanding of constitutional scholars since *M'Culloch* v. *Maryland* (1819).

V

What *is* the scope of the Commerce Power of Congress? We may now appreciate, more than formerly, how much the cumulative effects of minor activities can have national, if not international, consequences. We can even be reminded here of that wing-flapping by a solitary butterfly which may get the weather system moving that culminates in a tornado halfway around the globe.

We can also appreciate now, more than formerly, how ineffectual an individual State is apt to be in coping with economic disturbances within its own borders. This recognition may even have been implicit in a much-quoted passage from *Gibbons* v. *Ogden* as to the scope of the Commerce Power, that passage in which it is observed that the Congress may, if it chooses, concern itself with any commercial activity that affects more States than one. We have come to see—or perhaps it has simply come to be—that our States cannot reasonably hope to cope with any significant economic activity, that nationwide (if not even worldwide) influences are so pervasive that no State can have, with respect to such matters, an effective "oneness."

All this means, in effect, that Congress is empowered to attempt to regulate any activity bearing on the economic life of the Country that it is aware of and interested in. The effective restraint here is "political," not "constitutional," just as it is with respect to most other powers belonging to Congress. In fact, we are now likely to hear States insisting that Congress do more, not less, to regulate activities (such as "outsourcing") which are said to threaten the well-being of States that are powerless to do much, if anything, on their own to protect themselves economically.

VI

The scope of the Congressional Commerce Power is further indicated by the opening provision of Section 9 of Article I, which includes this restraint with respect to the slave trade: "The Migration or Importation of such Persons as any of the States now existing shall think proper to admit, should not be prohibited by the Congress prior to the Year one thousand eight hundred and eight." The implications of this restraint upon Congress is commented on in *Gibbons* v. *Ogden*. It is not generally noticed, by the way, that this provision (which does reflect a widespread abhorrence, in the South as well as in the North, of the international slave trade) did not keep Congress from regulating at once possible importations of slaves into any States created after the original States in the Union.

Congress did prohibit the international slave trade as of January 1, 1808. What authorized Congress to act at that time? Was such a power implicit in the Commerce Clause (in Section 8 of Article I)—or was the authorization provided, in effect, by the restraint that had been placed in Section 9 upon Congress until 1808, a restraint that had originally been insisted upon as protection for particular slavery interests in two or three States?

Defenders of Southern slavery interests eventually became apprehensive lest the General Government, relying in such matters upon the Commerce Clause, consider itself empowered to suppress not only the international slave trade (as it had properly done since 1808) but also that critical slave trade which moved among the States. Their concern is reflected in the question put to Abraham Lincoln by Stephen A. Douglas during their 1858 Illinois Senatorial election debates as to whether Lincoln supported Congressional regulation of the domestic slave trade. It is such regulation which (when extended to the products of a dubious work force) has been seen in the legislation that attempted to discourage child labor in this Country, an effective attempt that was temporarily thwarted by the Supreme Court in *Hammer* v. *Dagenhart* (1918).

VII

We can once again be reminded here of chance developments that can affect constitutional developments, something which can bear upon what lawyers do in their careers as drafters of legal and other documents. A concern was expressed during the 1787–1788 Ratification Campaign about the unintended consequences of a proposed Bill of Rights. Such a Bill, it was argued by some, would, by purporting to negate various powers in the General Government, support the recognition by implication of broad powers that the General Government might not otherwise have been considered to have.

This is aside from the concern, addressed in the Ninth Amendment, about the danger of undermining (if not even surrendering) those rights that did not happen to be listed in the Bill of Rights. Consider, for example, the implications suggested by the insistence in the First Amendment that Congress should not abridge "the freedom of speech, or of the press." Is Congress, then, implicitly empowered to regulate all those kinds of speaking which are *not* protected by "freedom of speech, or of the press" as traditionally understood?

The significance of this question is apt to be concealed by the tendency in recent decades to transform "freedom of speech" into "freedom

of expression," which would thereby seem to leave little for Congress to
regulate here. Or is this sort of reasoning likely to lead to the conclusion that since much expression (such as deceptive commercial advertis-
ing) "obviously" has to be regulated, then that which had once seemed to
have an absolute protection (freedom of political discourse) must also be
subject to regulation? On the other hand, it can be wondered, does the
restraint placed upon Congress's power to abridge the freedom of speech
tacitly empower Congress to protect and even to enhance the freedom of
speech?

VIII

We can return now to a mystery touched upon in our discussion heretofore of these matters. We have noticed that all State officers, including all State legislators, are obliged (by Article VI of the Constitution) to
pledge "to support this Constitution." What is the Constitution that such
officers are obliged to "support"?

It is hardly to be expected of all officers in every State in this Country
that they understand the Constitution. Is the "support" required of them
like the support that the typical Christian testifies to when the Nicene
Creed is routinely recited (as it has been for more than a millennium)?
Concepts such as "Commerce . . . among the several States" can sometimes *seem* as difficult to comprehend as concepts such as "filioque" and
"consubstantial with the Father."

Are such pledges then primarily significant rituals, which do testify
to one's intentions and good will? There is indeed something mysterious
in such transactions, whether political or spiritual. Somehow or other, an
effective understanding (an expression of good will?) is shared upon which
effective communal endeavors depend.

IX

The support and continued effectiveness of our constitutional endeavors depend as well upon factors that are rarely noticed, however pervasive,
important, and effective they may be. There is, for example, the Anglo-
American tradition, which includes both constitutionalism and the common law (which are intertwined). It includes as well the effects of the En-

glish language itself, and that which comes with it, such as the remarkably influential King James translation of the Bible and the sovereign works of William Shakespeare.

Shakespeare continues to shape us, including even those who never read or see his plays. Compare, for example, the diverse rankings of Brutus and Cassius in various parts of the Western World: their reputation is far higher, with profound political implications, in the English-speaking world (evidently, partly because of Shakespeare's portrayal of them in his *Julius Caesar*) than it can be elsewhere, as may be seen when one notices what is done to these conspirators in, say, Dante's *Inferno*. Of course, influences can be misapplied, as may be seen in how John Wilkes Booth patterned himself, most grievously, upon Shakespeare's Brutus.

We can return, however briefly, to the Commerce Power, which is apt to be virtually comprehensive if it is understood as the Chief Justice did in *Gibbons* v. *Ogden*. We need only examine the clothing we wear, the food we eat, and the automobiles we use to recognize that entirely local economic activity is rare these days. This still leaves the eminently prudential question of what it may be useful to try to regulate, in what way, and for how long, something that no constitution or principles of constitutional law can effectively prescribe in detail for any people.

10. Burdens on Interstate Commerce (1905–1981)

I

Some State Governmental interferences with, or burdens on, regulations by the General Government can be said to have been properly curtailed by the United States Supreme Court. One such set of burdens was addressed, we have seen, in *M'Culloch* v. *Maryland* (1819), when an effort was made to put the National Bank out of business in one State. And there was, in *Gibbons* v. *Ogden* (1824), we have also seen, the invalidation of the exercise of a State licensing power which threatened to impede steamboat operations that had been authorized by an Act of Congress which went back to 1793.

The primary concern in these and like cases is not with any particular economic or social policy supposedly incorporated in the Commerce Clause or in any other constitutional provision. Rather, the Supreme Court attempted in such cases to recognize what the Congress had already done in exercising its constitutional powers. It is left open in these and in like cases what the "policy" implicit in the Commerce Clause should be taken to be, in the absence of Congressional legislation.

Policy implications are drawn upon in various "burdens on interstate commerce" cases. Illustrative of these are the cases in which State regulations of transportation companies, such as railroads and trucking firms, are challenged (*Southern Pacific Company* v. *Arizona* [1945], *Kassel* v. *Consolidated Freightways Corporation* [1981]). Also illustrative are the cases assessing State regulations of the marketing of products from out of State (*H. P. Hood & Sons* v. *Du Mond* [1949], *Dean Milk Company* v. *City of Madison* [1951]).

II

Is there a Commerce Clause "policy"? That is, are there practices and objectives of State commercial regulations which are in themselves unconstitutional? It seems to be conceded, by the way, that any such suspect

60

State regulations, if explicitly authorized by Congress, would usually be considered constitutionally acceptable.

But it is assumed by the Supreme Court from time to time that if Congress does *not* provide guidance in such matters, the inherent or implicit policy of the Commerce Clause should govern. That policy, it is further assumed, is in favor of free trade or of a market economy. It does not seem to matter to the Justices involved in these efforts that Congress itself does not consistently take a market economy or any other approach (including price-fixing or the use of subsidies) in exercising its Commerce Clause powers.

If Congress does not act, what does follow by implication from the Commerce Clause? The Supreme Court seems to have said, in the *Southern Pacific* and *Kassel Cases,* that railroad companies and trucking firms, in competition among themselves, are in effect to determine the lengths of the trains and the trucks that move across this Country. We seem to have here, in the depreciation of State power, a resurrection of a variation of the doctrine of *Lochner* v. *New York* (1905), which had long been thought to have been discredited.

III

It is sometimes said, in justification of the Supreme Court's "burdens" doctrine, such as it is, that the Articles of Confederation had been woefully deficient because Congress did not have a proper Commerce Power. This, it is further said, led to ruinous commercial rivalries among the States, hurting thereby the economy of the United States. Indeed, it can be added, the 1786 Annapolis Conference was held, in large part, because of a recognized deficiency of Congress with respect to the regulation of commerce—and this led, soon after, to the Constitutional Convention of 1787.

It does seem to have been agreed, in 1787–1789, that a broad Commerce Power should be available to Congress. But such an agreement does not prescribe how such a power should be used by Congress. How it should be used has to depend, in large part, upon circumstances, leaving Congress free to develop, for example, both anti-trust legislation and subsidies.

Furthermore, that such a Commerce Power is available for Congress does not automatically prescribe what the States may or may not try to do about that part of the commercial life of the Country to which they have access. The States are explicitly restricted with respect to some matters over which the Congress *is* given jurisdiction, such as coinage and custom duties. There would have been no need to place these restrictions upon the States if the related grants of powers to Congress (whether or not exercised by Congress) had automatically immobilized the States with respect to these and like matters, or at least with respect to "burdening" activities that Congress is authorized to deal with.

IV

Thus, it should be evident, a power given is not a policy mandated. Consider, for example, how Alexander Hamilton, as the first Secretary of the Treasury, wanted the Commerce Power used. It could be used, in conjunction with the Revenue Power, to encourage domestic manufactures.

That is, Hamilton did not assume that only a free market policy was consistent with the Commerce and other Powers of the General Government. He knew, of course, the arguments for a free market and against subsidies of one or another branch of commerce. After all, Adam Smith had published his great treatise on that and related subjects more than a decade before, arguing as he did about what contributed to the enduring prosperity of a country.

Much more of a policy about how the Commerce Power should, and should not, be used may be seen in the Confederate Constitution of 1861. Severe restraints are placed there upon some of the things that Hamilton and his successors had tried to do. In fact, the States in the Confederacy were left with far more power, beyond the supervisory power of the new Federal government, than is evidently provided for in the Constitution of 1787, reflecting in this (as in other ways) the Confederate desire for the indefinite perpetuation of slavery.

V

Critical problems present themselves when the Supreme Court undertakes to discover and implement the policy of the Commerce Clause, especially when it does so by discerning and invalidating "burdens on interstate commerce." Certainly, the Courts of the United States find it difficult to develop or implement the policies that may be called for in a variety of circumstances. The most the Supreme Court can usually do is to say "No" to particular programs developed in one State after another, programs which it is asked to consider from time to time.

A key question here is, What standards *do* Courts properly have to draw upon? Anglo-American courts are adept—and centuries of experience testify to this—in applying the common law, drawing on (among other things) principles of justice, principles that are not simply those of a market economy. Properly trained courts are also adept at interpreting and applying rules provided by Congress, or by others, drawing in the process upon the accepted rules of interpretation.

These observations help explain why the Judicial Article in the Constitution of 1787, Article III, is by far the shortest of the articles establishing the three departments (or branches) of the General Government. That is, courts were expected to continue to do pretty much what courts had long done in the Anglo-American constitutional system. Even so, it was also expected that if what the courts said about either the common law or about any statute should be questionable, then an appropriate legislature would correct them to the extent or in the way necessary.

VI

We can now return to a further consideration of the Commerce Clause itself, having suggested what the Supreme Court is properly equipped to do. What, on the other hand, it is likely to be ill-equipped to do is to discern and assess the political concerns implicit in any exercise of the Commerce Power. Such an exercise is bound, in some instances, to require arbitrary judgments, sometimes as the result of negotiations among political agents.

A recognition of these constitutional facts of life is implicit in the dissents of Justice Hugo L. Black in three of the cases we are considering here. We can see in his dissents, a half-century ago, that the presumptuousness of the Supreme Court in such matters could be criticized as the doings of a "super-legislature." Today, critics are more apt to put such objections in the form of attacks upon "activist judges."

It is hard to see what guidance the Supreme Court draws upon when it ventures into these matters, especially when it second-guesses the political and economic judgments of State legislatures. It is also hard to see what guidance the Supreme Court provides others, including lower courts and

State Governments, when it does venture to pronounce on the so-called negative implications of the Commerce Clause. Indeed, it can sometimes be hard to see what guidance the Justices hope to provide even their own successors on the Court in such matters.

VII

All this is complicated by the accidental character of the "burdens" litigation. Also subject to chance can be what is said about such litigation. Accidental as well is the kind and amount of information made available to the Supreme Court in the cases it does happen to take.

The information available to the Court is pretty much determined by who the parties are who happen to be involved in the litigation. This is always a factor in any litigation, of course, but it is a particularly acute problem when attempts are made to use litigation to determine economic and social policies. Even when amicus briefs are permitted and relied upon by the Court, there is not likely to be the kind of thoroughgoing inquiry that is available when there is an announced legislative consideration of the policies to be established.

Chance may also determine the cases taken by the Supreme Court from time to time. These are cases often, if not usually, developed by commercial organizations which try to get from the Supreme Court the establishment of policies which neither Congress nor the State legislatures are likely to endorse. Unpredictable as well is the scope of whatever rulings the Court may be persuaded to issue, rulings which may be difficult to apply in most of the circumstances that a comprehensive legislative policy would have tried to deal with.

VIII

Where, then, are things left in the "burdens" cases? They are pretty much left where one would expect them to be left when circumstances govern as much as they do the piecemeal pronouncements on economic and social policies that are issued by the Supreme Court. It can be hard to predict, therefore, what is likely to happen from time to time—and to whom.

The problems to be noticed here are similar to those encountered when attempts are made by the Supreme Court to exercise Judicial Review of Acts of Congress. The uncertainty there includes the arbitrariness of when any particular Act of Congress is called into question, by whom, and in what circumstances. Is there also seen in the "burdens" cases the "lulling" effect that the availability of Judicial Review can have on a legislature, seeming to spare it from having to make the judgments that it should be making about both unconstitutional legislation and about undesirable burdens on commerce?

Of course, Congress could adopt one of the "burdens" policies that some Members of the Supreme Court have espoused at one time or another. Congress might thereby try both to limit what States do and to authorize others to implement whatever Congressional policy there may be developed. But there is one virtually insuperable obstacle for the Congress, if it should undertake to adopt one of the judicial policies with respect to burdens on interstate commerce—and that is, as Justice William H. Rehnquist observed in his Dissenting Opinion in *Kassel,* that "the jurisprudence of the 'negative side' of the Commerce Clause remains hopelessly confused."

IX

Is there in this corner of the law, as there is generally in Commerce Clause litigation, a tendency these days toward that standardization promoted by the economic globalization that we are witnessing? Is this what the Supreme Court, somehow or other, has tried to encourage? But the Court simply does not have either the information or the perspective that Congress *can* have when dealing with such matters.

The complexity of the problems that the Court now and then, here and there, ventures to "settle" is suggested by what has been happening with the implementation of the NAFTA provisions. What, for example, should various States be able to do about regulating the condition and use on their highways of the trucks that are coming up from Mexico? Is it not obvious that it is only Congress, if anyone at all in this Country, who can effectively deal with such questions in the years ahead?

How, then, should the "policy" implicit in the Commerce Clause be regarded by all of us, not only by the Courts? The relevant policy here, as of most other provisions in the Constitution, may be suggested by its Preamble—and particularly with respect to the use of the Commerce Clause in the promotion of the General Welfare. How the General Welfare is indeed to be promoted, in the regulation of the economic life of the Country, is a question apt to be addressed properly, let alone answered definitively, not by judges and the litigants who happen to engage them, but rather by the duly elected Congress of the United States.

11. *Missouri* v. *Holland* (1920); *Wickard* v. *Filburn* (1942)

I

The absurdity of the situation in *State of Missouri* v. *Holland* is never noticed by the United States Supreme Court. It is remarkable, if not even bizarre, that the Government of the United States had to resort to a treaty arrangement with Great Britain in order to be able to legislate effectively about any hunting of birds conducted solely within the United States. An earlier attempt to handle all this only "among us," by Congressional legislation, had been "held bad" by a District Court of the United States.

It is recognized by the Supreme Court, in the concluding paragraph of its *Holland* Opinion, that the Government of the United States had been obliged to try to deal effectively with serious threats to the migratory bird population in this Country. That concluding paragraph reads,

> Here a national interest of very nearly the first magnitude is involved. It can be protected only by national action in concert with that of another power. The subject matter is only temporarily within [any] State and has no permanent habitat therein. But for the treaty and the statute there soon might be no birds for any powers to deal with. We see nothing in the Constitution that compels the Government [of the United States] to sit by while a food supply is cut off and the protectors of our forests and our crops are destroyed. It is not sufficient to rely upon the States. The reliance is vain, and [even] were it otherwise, the question is whether the United States is forbidden to act. We are of opinion that the treaty and statute must be upheld. (*Carey* v. *South Dakota*, 250 U.S. 118 [1919].)

Far more extensive regulations of everyday activities are routinely promulgated in this Country today by the Government of the United States, in furtherance of "environmental" and other concerns, without recourse to any treaties.

The limitations of the recognized constitutional law scholarship in this Country during the past century are suggested by the general failure to notice the absurdity all too evident in the *Holland Case.* The limitations here are those of both academic scholars and Supreme Court Justices. Officers in the British Government must have wondered why representatives of the Government of the United States had to recruit *them* in 1919 to contrive a treaty that would permit Congress to do on its own what any other national legislature in the world could routinely do on *its* own.

II

Of course, the British must have felt that this was only one of the aberrations of their former "Colonials" that they could not understand. Prohibition must have been another, for which a constitutional amendment had been conjured up. It might even have seemed to the British that the wrong amendment had been ratified in 1919.

Such responses by outsiders ask, one way or another, the question that should have been asked in this Country on this as on other occasions: "How in the world did we get ourselves into this kind of situation?" Critical to consideration of this question is an awareness of what had happened with judicial interpretations of the Commerce Clause in the Constitution of the United States. A related question here is with respect to the significance of States' Rights doctrines in this Country.

Both of these matters—Commerce Clause interpretations and States' Rights doctrines—came to depend upon distortions of the language of the Constitution. These distortions were reflected in the shift in the way we came to talk about these matters—the shift from the "Commerce . . . among the several States" language of Article I, Section 8, to the "interstate commerce" formulation that has long been fashionable. It has not been generally noticed, however, that there *has* been any shift here, beginning with the forgetting of the scope of the meaning of the word "among."

III

How *did* the Congressional Commerce Power come to be limited as much as it was by the 1920s? "History"—that is to say, unpredictable (if not even incomprehensible) events—had much to do with this development. Perhaps most important here was the slavery controversy that began to heat up in the early decades of the nineteenth century.

Southerners—perhaps only a minority of them, but evidently the most influential of them—considered themselves obliged to keep within their immediate control the management of the institutions of slavery. One way of maintaining such control, that complete control they considered vital both to their physical safety and to their economic well-being, was to limit the power of the Government of the United States to interfere with slavery by the use of economic regulations grounded in the Commerce Clause. We have noticed that Stephen A. Douglas, a Northern Democrat whose Presidential ambitions depended upon Southern support, could (during the Lincoln-Douglas debates of 1858) suggest that his opponent, if elected to the United States Senate, would be inclined to legislate against the movement of slaves from one State to another.

The election of a Free-Soil Republican to the Presidency in 1860 was considered by apprehensive Southerners to be a threat to their long-term well-being, leading them to wonder what Congress and the President might do to their vulnerable slavery interests once Republicans assumed substantial control of the General Government. Not only might interstate traffic in slaves be imperilled, but also the traffic in the products of slaves "among the several States." These were not fanciful fears, as may be seen in how effectively child labor has been regulated in the United States by the severe restrictions placed (by taxation and otherwise) upon the movement of the products of child labor in what is known as "interstate commerce."

IV

Justice Holmes, in his Opinion for the Court in the *Holland Case,* speaks thus about the United States Constitution:

> [W]hen we are dealing with words that also are a constituent act, like the Constitution of the United States, we must realize that they have called into life a being the development of which could not have been foreseen completely by the most gifted of its begetters.

But insofar as a national government *was* being set up by the "begetters," would it have been beyond their gifts to provide that that government would be able, when necessary, to exercise the salutary powers that other well-ordered national governments of their day could exercise? Indeed, opponents of the proposed Constitution, in 1787–1788—opponents who did not want any effective national government with broad powers— protested that the new government *would* have comprehensive legislative powers.

Justice Holmes, in the passage just quoted from his *Holland* Opinion, continues in this fashion: "It was enough for [the begetters of the Constitution] to realize or to hope that they had created an organism; it has taken a century and has cost their successors much sweat and blood to prove they have created a nation." This *is* odd talk from a thrice-wounded veteran of the Civil War. It is in marked contrast to the Lincolnian insistence, as in the Gettysburg Address, that "a new nation" had been "brought forth" in 1776.

It should not be forgotten that the Declaration of Independence had proclaimed that these Colonies, as "Free and Independent States," would have "full Power to levy War, conclude Peace, contract Alliances, establish Commerce, and to do all other Acts and Things which Independent States may of right do." It is instructive to remind ourselves that even under the pre-Constitution Articles of Confederation the thirteen States of the American Union were explicitly precluded from exercising the first three of these four powers (the powers "to levy War, conclude Peace, contract Alliances"). Does not this suggest, if only by implication, how broad the fourth of these powers (to "establish Commerce") might be for the General Government established by the Constitution of 1787?

V

The remarkable state of affairs evident in the *Holland Case* is in large part due to what had been by then almost a century of judicial misreadings of the Commerce Clause. These misreadings continued for almost another two decades. It took the pressures of the Great Depression to move the Supreme Court to recognize what everyone else could see, that a nation does need a genuine national government.

It cannot be repeated too often that when the Congress and the Supreme Court have differed in their readings of vital constitutional powers of the Congress, the Congress has turned out (even in the Supreme Court's eventual estimation) to have been the sounder of the two institutions. This recognition is reflected in the observation that the Supreme Court follows the election returns, an observation which testifies perhaps to the long-term good sense of the People of this Country. This is not to deny, of course, that at times the People and their Congress and Courts have all been dismally wrong together, especially when severely shaken by unexpected events that they did not yet understand.

However this may be, it should be asked, again and again, How are judges to be corrected when *they* go wrong? Congress and the President can be corrected by the People, but the Justices (in theory) only by constitutional amendments (of which there have been only two dozen or so). But even here, the People may have some control—not only by means of their election returns but also by means of their responses to the arguments of those who explain what the Constitution does and does not say.

VI

Two decades separate *Missouri* v. *Holland* and *Wickard* v. *Filburn*, two decades during which momentous events and persistent arguments obliged the Supreme Court to make radical revisions in its Commerce Clause readings. The chronic irresponsibility of the Court during the early New Deal years pointed up the limitations of the accepted doctrine of Judicial Review of Acts of Congress. The Court might have reformed itself earlier if it had truly listened to what it itself had been saying.

Even in *Holland,* well before the New Deal, Justice Holmes could make a use of the "in pursuance" language of Article VI, which should have made him wonder about how the Court read the Supremacy Clause. Consider, with a view to the conventional basis of Judicial Review, this passage in his Opinion for the *Holland* Court:

> Acts of Congress are the supreme law of the land only when made in pursuance of the Constitution, while treaties are declared to be so when made under the authority of the United States. It is open to question whether the authority of the United States means more than the formal acts prescribed to make the convention.

Shortly before this passage Justice Holmes made a use in his Opinion of "in pursuance of" that virtually equated it to "under the authority of," having spoken there of an Act of Congress that had not been made "in pursuance of" a treaty.

But, it turned out, the Court had to learn from the Country at large rather than from the implications of what it had been saying. The *Filburn Case* ratified in 1942 developments which recognized that the Commerce Power is, for practical purposes, as broad as Congress chooses to treat it. Only the kid with his sidewalk lemonade stand seems to be clearly beyond the reach of a Congress determined to regulate "Commerce . . . among the several States."

VII

This is not to deny that Congress too can at times be woefully mistaken in the exercise of the powers it obviously has. This may be seen, for example, in its experimentations with the tax code from time to time. But "misjudgment" cannot be equated with "unconstitutionality."

One can even wonder whether it made sense for the Government to regulate wheat production as much as it was shown to do in the *Filburn Case*. One chance consequence of this may have been to make the smaller family farms even more vulnerable than they already were. This probably was not intended, no more than the typical adverse effects on the poor of well-intended price controls.

That is, there is much to be said for allowing a market economy considerable scope. But even the most devoted partisans of a free market must depend upon considerable governmental activity if such an economy is to endure. Private property itself—upon which such an economy very much depends—is not something which comes into being and endures worldwide without substantial guidance from and support by governments.

VIII

There have been, in recent years, occasional indications by Members of the current Supreme Court (as in *United States* v. *Lopez* [1995]) that the Commerce Power of Congress should be reined in by the Judiciary. But, it seems to me, enduring judicial interventions in this realm are likely to be ineffectual in the years ahead. The truly troubling question will be not whether Congress has too much control over the economy, but whether it can have as much effective control as we might like it to have in the face of a globalization of the economies of all nations.

I have recalled the efforts of the slavery interests to minimize the Commerce Power of the Congress. After the Civil War, such efforts were continued by businessmen who often preferred local regulation to national regulation. That is, they often preferred to have no effective regulation of their ambitious activities.

But does not Big Business in this Country today tend to be in favor of more, not less, *national* supervision of the economy? For one thing, their wide-ranging activities can be better conducted if there is national uniformity in standards with respect to product quality, financial routines, and merchandising practices. The globalization of economies is likely to reinforce the desire for a reliable uniformity by which Big Business can take its bearings.

IX

Even so, if Congress tries to regulate too much, it runs the risk of repudiation by the People. Such a repudiation may even hoist the banner of States' Rights, however irrelevant that approach may usually be in our time. But experienced politicians can hear what is really being said when they have misjudged what is needed and what will be put up with by the public at large.

It is sensible in these matters to recognize the importance of prudence. Certainly, if a constitutional doctrine (like the Ptolemaic recourse to planetary epicycles) tends in its complications toward the absurd, a thorough reconsideration is called for. Among the consequences of a reliance upon prudence is the recognition of what fairness calls for in particular situations.

Thus, Courts should be encouraged to rely upon what they are naturally inclined toward: the sensible and the fair. After all, judicial tribunals are routinely spoken of as "courts of justice." This is the kind of talk that judges should be encouraged to notice, something which is made more likely if they are helped to *see* what they do happen to say from time to time.

12. The Presidency and the Constitution

I

An awareness of the timing of events related to *Youngstown Sheet &* *Tube Company* v. *Sawyer,* the *Steel Seizure Case* of April–June 1952, is critical to an understanding of how this constitutional controversy is to be understood. One event, of course, is the Korean War, which had begun in June 1950 and of which much was made in this case by the President and his supporters. Another event was anticipated in some quarters, the 1952 election, but that was not as critical as it would have been if it had been anticipated that the incumbent President would be running for re-election.

Far more critical, at least for our purposes as students of the Constitution, is the fact that the labor relations crisis in the steel industry began to develop toward the end of 1951. This was several months before the President considered himself obliged to take possession of the steel mills in order to avert an interruption of their production while a war was going on. This meant, among other things, that the Congress had had more than enough time to provide, if it had wished to do so, for the kind of measures resorted to by the President in April 1952.

It seems that no serious effort was made by the President to get Congress to provide explicit legislative authorization for what he wanted to do. He evidently recognized that no such authorization would be provided, even if requested by him. A then-recent Congress, when asked thus to authorize the President in the Taft-Hartley Act, had already refused to do so, preferring to allow the contending parties to "fight it out" (subject to eventual Legislative intervention if that should prove necessary).

II

That there was more than enough time for Congress to act is also indicated by the fact that there was time for the President to prepare the regulations that he issued. Those regulations, which (as is recognized in the Opinion of the Court) look like legislation, could have been offered to Congress to enact. But Congressional reluctance to do what a President very much wants done does not in and of itself add to Presidential powers.

There are, after all, many occasions that find Congress and the President differing as to what is essential to "save the country." They may differ, for example, as to the tax policy needed, or as to the expenditures needed for defense, or as to the Executive agencies that need to be established and funded. Congressional reluctance cannot be translated into Executive empowerment, whatever the perpetrators of the 1986–1989 Iran arms/ Contra aid covert action may have believed.

Justice Black's Opinion for the Court in the *Steel Seizure Case* is often regarded by constitutional scholars as less rigorous, and hence as less serious, than the Concurring Opinions in that case. But the Black Opinion does have the merit of recognizing constitutional fundamentals in this matter, fundamentals that have been lost sight of as attempts are made to rationalize repeated unilateral Executive assumptions of power since the Civil War. It should also be noticed that the divisions among the Justices in the *Steel Seizure Case* were divisions among Justices who had all been appointed by Democratic Presidents.

III

One striking feature of the *Steel Seizure Case* is often unnoticed, and that is the recognition by everyone involved that Congress clearly had the power to legislate comprehensively with respect to the matters under consideration. This indicates how broad the Commerce Power of Congress had come to be understood by 1952. Thus, there seems to have been little doubt by this time that Congress has broad powers to deal with the economy of the Country.

Indeed, the solidity of the Commerce Power has become such that it has been relied upon to justify various Congressional actions even with respect to race relations, actions which could have been grounded more appropriately in, say, the Fourteenth Amendment. This kind of Commerce Clause reliance, which is believed to be "safe," does tend to undermine clearheadedness about the constitutional principles of the regime. It is partly because the Supreme Court has at times been unpredictable in its constitutional expositions that Congress has resorted to the use of "safe" formulations in controversial situations.

Be that as it may, Congress does provide for emergency situations, empowering the Executive to act on its own in a variety of circumstances. And, in an unanticipated emergency, the President *can* do what Abraham Lincoln did in 1861, when he presumed to act on his own authority, expecting to get Legislative ratification after Congress returned to Washington. Of course, in a truly overwhelming emergency, the Constitution itself might be temporarily overridden, if need be, for the sake of what could be considered a supra-Constitutionalism (which is itself grounded in prudence).

IV

Chief Justice Fred M. Vinson's dissent in the *Steel Seizure Case* is, in effect, a brief for the Government, reminding us of how the Executive had come to regard its powers. It can be odd to see someone who keeps referring euphemistically to the Civil War as "the War Between the States" nevertheless make so much of the measures resorted to by President Lincoln in his desperate effort to maintain the unity of the Country. One can see again and again, as in this Dissenting Opinion, that this Chief Justice was *not* the man who would be up to the challenge posed two years later by *Brown* v. *Board of Education* (1954).

The Chief Justice concedes that "the Executive cannot exercise [the law-making] function to any degree." But he still makes much of the powers of the President as commander-in-chief, not recognizing that the President he offers looks uncomfortably like Charles I, a monarch who lost his head partly because he usurped one Legislative power after another. We can hear, these days, in the rhetorical exercises in support of a wide-ranging and never-ending "War on Terrorism," a return in effect to the Chief Justice's Dissenting Opinion in the *Steel Seizure Case*.

It seems at times that the Chief Justice does not, perhaps simply cannot, hear what he is saying, especially when he makes as much as he does of the President's duty to make sure that the laws are faithfully executed. He can even invoke Alexander Hamilton on the importance of the President's being able to preserve the status quo in order that the Congress might in turn be able to act—and yet it was evident in this 1952 instance that the Congress had had more than enough time to act, and had deliberately chosen not to do so. The more the dissenting Chief Justice said about an international policy to which the Congress had contributed mightily, the more striking was the absence of Congressional action in support of the President's unilateral initiative on this occasion.

V

It is again and again evident in the Constitution that the Congress is intended to be the dominant branch (*not* the most spectacular branch) of the General Government. This was consistent with the constitutional principles that the Framers of 1787 had inherited from the British. The President is to execute the laws (made by Congress); he is to be commander-in-chief of the armed forces (provided for by Congress); and he is to lead the Country in war (declared by Congress).

The secondary role of the President, however much he may naturally be exalted on the national stage, is repeatedly recognized in the Constitution, sometimes explicitly, as in its impeachment provisions. It is recognized implicitly in the provisions for constitutional amendments and for the admission of new States to the Union, fundamental provisions which have no place for the President. It is further recognized, of course, by the power assigned to the Congress to override Presidential vetoes, an arrangement related, indirectly, to the lack of Presidential participation in amending the Constitution and in admitting new States to the Union.

It would have been sounder if Congress, rather than the Supreme Court, had provided the check upon the Executive seen in the *Steel Seizure Case*. It would usually be enough, in response to this and most other Executive usurpations, for the Congress to cut off access to the funds that permit the President to do what he does (such as going to war) without the proper Congressional authorization. But then, if Congress were properly sensitive about its prerogatives, it would have taken issue as well with the remarkable judicial usurpation evident in *Bush* v. *Gore* (2000).

VI

An insistence upon Congressional prerogatives has as one advantage the elevation in the public esteem of that branch of the General Government over which the People can reasonably believe that they have some control. Congressional resurgence, properly guided and explained, could help to refine and to solidify the constitutional principles of our regime. A good beginning here is to encourage everyone to read carefully not only the Constitution but also the other major constitutional instruments that the Constitution takes for granted.

It is odd, if not even ominous, that there has been little if any Congressional protest *not* about the final decision of the Supreme Court in *Bush* v. *Gore,* but rather about the fact that the Court presumed to involve itself at all in that controversy. I myself believed, and publicly said so at the time (in several published letters to editors of November 10, 2000), that a drawing of lots would have been a healthier way for the Country to proceed once a deadlock seemed highly likely. It was inevitable, in the circumstances, that the decision that would be made by the Court, if it presumed to settle the controversy, would be more "political" than "judicial" both in appearance and in tone, something that can be troubling for those who believe that justice and a sound regime depend upon each part of a government doing its proper job, that which it is best equipped to do.

The *Bush* v. *Gore* controversy and how its resolution was regarded were very much affected by the fact that many Democrats, in Florida and elsewhere, were convinced that more qualified voters went to the polls in Florida intending to vote for Al Gore rather than for George W. Bush. It is this conviction that recounts were sought for to test. And it is this kind of issue, as raised here, that seems to some to be better suited for a political rather than for a judicial resolution—or rather, it might be said, however such an issue was resolved, it would very likely *seem* to have been a political rather than a judicial resolution.

VII

We see in *Bush* v. *Gore* still another instance of an assumption of power for the sake of dealing with a supposed emergency. The emergency there was seen to result from the uncertainty of the outcome of the Presidential election. But, it should be remembered, this was merely an extension for a few more weeks of the uncertainty that there had been for some months.

Perhaps the most heartening feature of this particular crisis was that the incumbent President was not able to settle the matter in the way *he* might have personally preferred. For him to have intervened would have properly been decried as usurpation on his part, setting thereby a dangerous precedent. Less serious perhaps is what the Supreme Court did, but that too should be troubling, depending as much as it did on the chance composition of the Court.

And what the Court did was troubling enough to leave doubts about the legitimacy of the Bush Presidency. It can be wondered whether a more secure Administration would have conducted itself differently both in its opening months and after the September Eleventh disasters. Critics of the Administration can even go so far as to suspect that unnecessary measures (and especially the "preemptive war" against Iraq) have been resorted to partly in order to secure the political legitimacy that the Supreme Court had failed to confer by what it presumed to do in December 2000.

VIII

What, then, would have happened if the Supreme Court had not intervened as it did in the 2000 Presidential contest? Recounts would have been conducted in Florida, perhaps according to varying standards and under various auspices in different parts of that State. Results would then have been certified to Congress by one or more State officials, depending in part upon how persuasively the results of the recounts could have been presented.

The new Congress, meeting the first week of January 2001, would have had to decide among any contending claims that had come out of Florida. Or Congress could have asked for more information, perhaps even establishing a commission to supervise the inquiry it wanted made. It is likely and not improper, considering the political allegiances of the Members of the House of Representatives, that any serious uncertainty in the results would have been resolved in favor of Mr. Bush.

That is, it is *not likely* that the Republican-controlled House of Representatives would have found in favor of Mr. Gore unless public opinion had been convinced by the recounts that Mr. Gore had been clearly preferred by the Florida electorate. One way or another, therefore, there probably would have been someone available to be inaugurated, on January 20, as President or (in effect) as Acting President. That result could have been properly explained as the result of a recognized political process, something that people are accustomed to being reconciled to even when it very much goes against what they might have preferred.

IX

Thus, it should not cause either surprise or alarm if Congress should act politically in such a controversy. After all, the People had acted politically when they voted as they did in November 2000. It is political action that Congress is both empowered and expected to take; but political action is something which can be disturbing (as well as unseemly) for a Court to take, or to seem to take, however much it invokes the Constitution.

We return with these observations to what can be noticed about the insistence by the Supreme Court that it has that power of Judicial Review of Acts of Congress which was not explicitly provided for in the Constitution (in marked contrast, we have seen, to the power of the Legislative veto explicitly provided for the President). It is difficult, and often virtually impossible, to keep political judgments out of constitutional law adjudications. It is such a likely, if not even such an inevitable, combination that is to be expected when Congress acts.

A recognition of Congressional duties here should be accompanied by our encouragement of Congress to keep the Constitution in view whenever it acts, something that it is often discouraged from doing when it can tell itself that the Supreme Court will make the constitutional judgments that Congress would rather not be bothered with making (sometimes because of the political liabilities involved). Furthermore, it should be remembered, the Supreme Court is never able to pass constitutional muster on most of what Congress and the President do and do not do. This is particularly troubling when we observe one Congress after another permitting the President to usurp the Congressional power to declare war, an Executive usurpation that the Supreme Court has (prudently enough) never ventured to challenge, whatever it might otherwise say from time to time about its supposed general power of Judicial Review of Acts of Congress.

13. A Government of Enumerated Powers?

I

Much is made of the Constitution of 1787 as a charter enumerating all the powers of the General Government. This could be said, of course, of any constitution providing for any national government. But the enumerated powers of the Constitution of 1787 usually referred to are particular powers, such as those listed in Section 8 of Article I.

Excluded from this kind of identification are the powers implied by the references, as in the Preamble to the Constitution, to the great ends of the People in establishing the Constitution. Two of those great ends—the Common Defense and the General Welfare—are repeated at the outset of the Article I, Section 8, enumeration. The potency of such terms is testified to by the determination of the framers of the Confederate Constitution of 1861 to omit both of them from the Preamble of their constitution and thereafter also to omit one of them (the General Welfare) from *their* Article I, Section 8.

Little is done by the United States Supreme Court or by most recognized interpreters of the Constitution with the Preamble to the Constitution of 1787. But another general provision, the Necessary and Proper Clause (once known also as the Sweeping Clause) *is* made much of. So much has had to be made of the Necessary and Proper Clause (in order to have a plausible General Government) that it can make one suspect that the conventional opinions about the significance of the enumeration of powers cannot be practical.

II

An examination of the Article I, Section 8, enumeration can be helpful here. Vital to the examination of this, as of any other document that is to be taken seriously, is (as we have already noticed in these *Reflections*) an inquiry as to its principle of order. That there is such an order must be apparent to any reader of the text who lingers over it, especially if the work of William W. Crosskey is taken as seriously as it should be.

Section 8 begins by providing the means (that is, the taxes and other funds) that the General Government would need in order to be able to do whatever it is usually expected to do. This government, unlike that provided for in the Articles of Confederation, does not depend upon the States for its finances. Thereafter the economic life of the Country is provided for, including arrangements for money, for weights and measures, for a postal system, and for copyrights and patents.

Provision is then made in Section 8 for the Judiciary, anticipating what is said in Article III, perhaps leaving us to wonder why this is done here and not there. The foreign relations of the Country are then addressed, including what military forces are to be available and on what terms. Thereupon, before the Necessary and Proper Clause finishes off Section 8, provision is made for the governance of such places (including what we now know as the District of Columbia) acquired by the United States from the States.

III

Students of the Constitution are likely to agree that some such scheme as that which I have just sketched (and which is illustrated in Appendix F of this volume) helps account for the ordering of the Section 8 provisions, however they might adjust my analysis here and there. It is obvious to anyone who looks into the matter that the order evident here is not the order in which the various powers of the General Government had been agreed to in the Constitutional Convention. This is evident throughout the Constitution as well, with its systematic provision first for the Legislative branch, then for the Executive branch, and thereafter for the Judicial branch, before the relations among the States, and between the States and the Union, could be further provided for.

There seems to be taken for granted throughout the Constitution an awareness of the understanding of that English constitutionalism which the republican-minded People of the United States had inherited. Revisions had to be made, of course, in that inheritance, such as with respect to the status of such institutions as titles of nobility and other monarchical forms. There was an awareness as well of what had (and had not) been done in the second constitution for the new nation, the Articles of Confederation.

The first constitution for the United States, it can now be said, is that which is implicit in the Declaration of Independence. A system of government, incorporating elements of such instruments as Magna Carta, is taken for granted by the Declaration. There is also taken for granted in that document an inherited understanding both of what government must deal with and of how that might properly be done and undone.

IV

One may be obliged to consider further the significance of the enumeration in Section 8 of Article I when one notices that there is explicit provision made for some enforcement powers and not for others. Thus, Congress may "provide for the Punishment of counterfeiting." Why is this said, but nothing about punishing those who interfere with, say, the postal system that is authorized?

I do not know of any serious attempt to deny the General Government the power to protect its postal system from criminal interference. For example, the States are not relied upon to provide the primary protection for the United States postal system. The Necessary and Proper Clause obviously empowers Congress to deal adequately with this matter.

We can suspect, therefore, that something about the history of the power to deal with coinage can help explain why the power to punish counterfeiting is mentioned in Section 8 of Article I, but not the power to punish crimes against the post. The uses of history may be critical here, we also suspect, as it is with the difference between the provision for armies and the provision for a navy. Does not the army-navy difference with respect to the duration of appropriations suggest where threats to the liberties of Englishmen had come from, with any leader posing far more of a threat because of long-term control of land forces than because of such control of sea forces?

V

A further use of history may be seen in our effort to explain why the Legislative power to deal with counterfeiting is explicitly provided for in Article I, Section 8. We can, by proceeding in this way, begin to see how intricate the construction of the Constitution may be. Such anomalies are particularly to be noticed and thereafter to be thought about.

Another anomaly can suggest how our counterfeiting puzzle might be dealt with. That is the provision with respect to treason at the end of Article III, a most instructive curiosity that has not been properly noticed and hence thought about by most students of the Constitution. But then, it is no longer generally remembered that some of the most serious abuses of the power to punish treason had come in English history at the hands of the Judiciary—and the placement of the treason provision in Article III may emphasize a desire to curb the Judiciary as well as the other branches of government with respect to such abuses.

It should also be noticed that counterfeiting was once considered a form of treason. Did the severe limitations placed in Article III upon the power to punish treason suggest to the cautious draftsmen of the Constitution that the Congressional power to punish counterfeiting should not be left (by way of the Necessary and Proper Clause) only as an implication of the Congressional power to coin money? Here, as elsewhere, we can see that the Framers of the Constitution knew what they were doing, however mistaken they may have been in their expectations about what precisely their successors across the centuries would continue to understand about the Anglo-American constitutional tradition.

VI

That constitutional tradition can provide guidance toward understanding much else in Article I, Section 8. How many of the powers listed there are collected thus not only in order to make sure that they exist for the General Government but also in order to make sure who (among the officers of that government) did and did not have primary control over them? It is with respect to this that there are suggested, in Appendix F of this volume, the bracketings of the pre-Constitution character of the powers enumerated in Article I, Section 8.

All seventeen of the powers collected in Section 8 can plausibly be considered "legislative," a designation reinforced by their placement here; the "judicial" bracketing includes not only the eighth and ninth powers but also the sixth, the counterfeiting-related power we have noted (correcting thereby the version of the Appendix F chart I have provided in *The Constitution of 1787*). Another way of putting this is to say that curbs were thus placed upon what today are regarded as "activist" judges. One can wonder whether the Framers would have said something to head off

Judicial Review of Acts of Congress, or at least to restrict it within narrow limits, if its eventual emergence in the form we have it had been anticipated by them.

But the bracketings I have suggested for "Executive" claims, which can be extended into the first few lines of the seventeenth power, suggest that the greatest risk to the intended Legislative dominance would come from the Executive, not from the Judiciary. Central to these powers is the power to "constitute Tribunals inferior to the Supreme Court," denying thereby the centuries-old prerogatives claimed by the monarch (as is evident even in the Magna Carta grievances) with respect to establishing and controlling the Judiciary. We can see in recent developments the tendency of the Executive (as commander-in-chief) to set up "anti-terrorism" tribunals on his own, tribunals in support of powers assumed by the Executive following upon his disregard of still another provision, which is that Congress is to declare war.

VII

Chance influences no doubt affected what was done by the Constitutional Convention. These included not only the effects of the workings of government pursuant to the Articles of Confederation, but also the economic conditions in the Country at the time that the Convention happened to be called. There must have been still other factors that we are never likely to discover, reflecting thereby the inevitable limitations of political life.

The chance influences upon the Framers included as well the great Revolutionary War issues. Particularly to be noticed is the insistence that there be no taxation without representation, something that can be traced back (as we have seen) even to Magna Carta. This, too, is a recognition of Legislative dominance in any proper constitutional government, something challenged so dramatically (however covertly) by the Iran arms/Contra aid usurpation in the 1980s by the Executive.

It can even be seen as a matter of chance that the enumeration in Section 8 of Article I should have come to be regarded as almost the sole source of Congressional power instead of as in large part an effort to protect the general Congressional power from Executive and Judicial aggrandizement. But, on the other hand, the Necessary and Proper Clause has been used to make sure that Congress would indeed have the power that an effective General Government would need. This kind of substitution of one part of the Constitution for another, under the pressure of events, might be considered "natural," even when seen in so bizarre a case as *Missouri* v. *Holland* (1920).

VIII

The student of the Constitution, in order to begin to think properly about these matters, must know not only the particulars of this document but also *what* is *where*. It bears repeating that it also helps to know what preceded the Constitution, including what is said in the Declaration of Independence about the powers of all independent states. We have seen that it was evident, under the Articles of Confederation and thereafter under the Constitution of 1787, that even the original thirteen States of the Union were never fully, or truly, independent states, considering that three of the four great powers accruing to such states were explicitly denied them.

The constitutional insistence upon the appropriate Congressional prerogatives can remind us of the appropriate prerogatives of the Judiciary. The terseness of the Judicial Article, I have suggested, reflects the understanding that little had to be said about the national judiciary because it was to be very much like the long-relied-upon British judiciary—and this meant, among other things, that it should have significant powers for helping to shape the common law of the Country. There is, however, little if any indication that our judges today, and the constitutional scholars who minister to them, are aware of the considerations with respect to these matters sketched out in these *Reflections.*

Reminders of how the Constitution should be read are provided both by the Chief Justice (John Marshall) who could (in 1819) distinguish between the terms "necessary" and "absolutely necessary" and by the learned Justice (Joseph Story) who could (in 1842) look back to the English judges and to Roman and other jurists in an effort to discover what the common law should be in a variety of circumstances. Especially to be guarded against by Congress, Section 8 of Article I can be taken to caution us, are usurpations of Legislative powers by both the Executive and the Judiciary, while similar misconduct on the part of Congress is more easily corrected by the People at large. Particularly troubling, from time to time, is the failure of Congress to insist upon its prerogatives, which it should have done, it bears repeating, in the controversy dealt with in a highly improper way by the Judiciary in *Bush* v. *Gore* (2000).

IX

The instructive inquiry into the principle of order, which has been illustrated on this occasion by an examination of Section 8 of Article I of the Constitution, may be found elsewhere as well in our constitutional documents. The most obvious instance is in the very arrangement of the seven articles of the Constitution of 1787. The progression there—through the three branches of the General Government, then to the resulting status of the States, and then to amendments, and finally to implementation—can seem almost natural.

Less obvious, perhaps, is how the Declaration of Independence is organized. Critical to that arrangement is how, in that 1776 assault upon a monarch, the longstanding, even decisive, grievances against Parliament are buried as war is looming. After all, as we have noticed, these Revolutionaries did intend to have, once effectively independent, legislatures modeled somewhat on that of Great Britain.

More obvious is how the Bill of Rights of 1791 is organized, for we can see, in the dozen amendments originally proposed, a sequence that "tracks" the ordering of the first four articles of the Constitution of 1787. We can be again reminded of the sometimes obscure lessons of history in these matters when we notice that the order of the Bill of Rights we now have was anticipated by where its various provisions would have been placed if the original plan had been followed of placing amendments within the body of the Constitution of 1787. One argument for not including amendments within the original document *should* have been that such changes in the document itself could eventually make it even harder than it might otherwise be for citizens to notice and to be guided by the remarkable overall order of the Constitution of 1787.

Part Two

1. Realism and the Study of Constitutional Law

I

One can hear intelligent law students insist these days that all that really matters, in their law school careers, is their class rank. Everything they do, in class and out, is evidently regarded by some of them as done only with a view to the grades they will receive. Perhaps many, if not most, students have always felt this way—but it is now more fashionable than it may ever have been to talk this way.

Contributing to this state of mind may be the emphasis placed, throughout the career of a prelaw student, upon one standardized test after another, culminating in the LSAT. Attention is directed during this process to the numerical results achieved, not to what is learned and is thereafter to be thought about. It can even seem naive to suggest that there are things worth studying and learning for their own sake.

If one is so old-fashioned as to dare to suggest that it is simply awful that one misses the opportunity—perhaps one's last serious opportunity—to study important things for their own sake, one can be calmly informed that potential employers are not interested in what one knows but rather in where one stands in one's class, whatever that may signify. If one thereupon suggests that one should not want to work for such employers, one can be treated as an amiable idiot, someone who is perhaps harmless if simply ignored. Such are some of the forms that realism can take these days.

II

One can wonder, of course, whether the lawyers developed in accordance with such mechanized standards can comprehend the law in its enduring significance. This concern applies, in particular, to one's grasp of constitutional law. One can wonder, indeed, whether employers, including law firms, who conduct themselves in so mechanical a manner can secure, nurture, and retain the better lawyer.

Superficiality tends to be encouraged by the "realistic" approach. This may be related—as cause or as effect—to the turnover these days in the personnel of even the better law firms. When my law school classmates joined Chicago law firms a half-century ago, it was with the reasonable expectation that they *could* spend their careers there.

Does the very volatility of legal careers today undermine that sense of steadiness upon which a reliable system of law depends? Symptomatic of this is what may be seen in the willingness of judges to return to much more lucrative private practices, a movement that once seemed to be rare. Such a development may be related to what has also happened to the numbers willing to dedicate themselves to the demands of the priesthood.

III

I have long wondered whether the development of ever-more-mammoth law firms has been healthy. The objectives and tone of all legal practice can be adversely affected by the considerable influence of prominent firms that "have" to be run like businesses if they are to "prosper." It is not surprising, therefore, when such enterprises come to rely upon the market-like calculations of class ranks and the like.

It is bad enough when mechanical approaches are used in the hiring of young lawyers. It becomes even worse when such approaches are relied upon for research into the law itself, as may be seen in the uses routinely made these days of electronic devices. The researcher is discouraged, if not even prevented, from studying the issues that had once engaged the lawyers and judges who had developed the leading cases governing any matter under consideration.

All this becomes still worse when the matter at issue turns upon constitutional principles. Such principles depend, even more than the law usually does, upon the venerable and the enduring. Constitutionalism can come to seem irrelevant, if not annoyingly obstructive, to those "realistic" lawyers who want to "get down to business."

IV

A more serious form of the realism issue may be seen in the insistence by some that only that is effectively law which is backed up by recognizable sanctions. To place such an emphasis upon sanctions seems consistent with, if not even required by, a market-oriented approach to the law. It can become difficult in these circumstances to question the severity of whatever sanctions may be believed necessary "to get the job done."

It can also become difficult to determine what one is truly entitled to. In a sense, it can be assumed that no one is entitled to anything which cannot, in practice, be secured by the use of sanctions. This is something that the typical citizen cannot readily grasp, whatever law students may be led to believe from time to time.

One ominous consequence of a sanctions-oriented approach to the law is the implication that one is virtually entitled to whatever one can get away with. Yet we all know, when we stop to think about it, that the healthy community depends to a considerable extent upon a self-policing citizen-body. Many of these comments bear as well on how exactly the law is to be regarded, especially by the kind of community that realists tend to disparage.

V

Another way of putting these questions is to ask whether it is *might* alone which makes *right*. It is obvious enough that power can be influential—but must not *might* itself be ultimately in the service of what is *right* if the community is not to lose control of what it is doing? After all, in the final analysis, *might* alone is senseless and can be ultimately self-defeating.

Critical here is the status of what is known as natural law or, better still perhaps, as natural right. It is this which can provide guidance to the law school graduate who takes the bar exam or who is confronted with an unfamiliar situation in practice: that is, it should be of help to recognize that the law, by and large, favors that resolution of a dispute which is consistent with what seems to be right. It can be deeply realistic, that is, not to settle for a shallow realism.

Vital to the dictates of natural right (or natural law) is an awareness of what makes for a fulfilling life. The greatest lawyers, whatever it may be fashionable to say from time to time, have at least sensed the moral foundations upon which a sound community depends. This is related to their ability to tell stories that make sense, including moral sense, in "the situations" they are repeatedly depended upon to deal with.

VI

A reminder of the comprehensive goodness that Constitutionalism aims at is provided by the Preamble to the Constitution of the United States. We have noticed that that statement of purposes tends to be neglected by jurists and constitutional scholars today. But it does remind us of the scope of legitimate governmental concerns, concerns that every healthy community must deal with one way or another.

A vital concern here is as to what kind of citizen-body seems to be presupposed by the Constitution of 1787. Both the character and the competence of that citizen-body seem to be taken for granted. It also seems to be taken for granted that both character and competence have to be sustained and reinforced by appropriate governmental measures.

The measures that are required very much depend upon the circumstances of the day. Thus, for example, how the Commerce Power of Congress should be used from time to time can be influenced by changes worldwide in social, economic, and other conditions. The current thrust of globalization cannot help but challenge the general government in any country that does not resign itself to being at the mercy of international pressures and movements.

VII

Chance can very much affect what form challenges take from time to time. This could be seen, during and since the Second World War, in the ever-growing importance of race relations worldwide and hence in the United States. Of course, such relations have been of critical concern among us since well before the Civil War, but the Cold War made them seem even more critical.

Explicit racial discrimination, whether required or sanctioned by law, is obviously suspect in the United States—and has been so for several decades now. But what may and should be done, by affirmative action programs and otherwise, to remedy the effects of prior discrimination? That and like questions remain to be addressed by us in an authoritative manner.

Sexual relations are also subject these days to redefinition, as may be seen in the controversies about abortion and same-gender unions.

Such matters, along with race relations, are addressed by the United States Supreme Court periodically. It is instructive to notice, however, that fundamental changes in the official handling of sexual relations (for better or for worse) are happening worldwide, independent of what any court in this Country or elsewhere may chance to say from time to time.

VIII

Fundamental changes should be distinguished in these matters from dramatic developments that may be far less critical than they may at times seem. It is still not generally appreciated, for example, how much of a fluke the "success" of the September Eleventh organizers was. Nor is it generally appreciated how much of a disservice the actions of those men have been to whatever legitimate causes they believed themselves to be serving.

One consequence of the growing unilateralist responses by our current national Administration to the terrorists of our day has been to call into question various long-accepted opinions about the reach and efficacy of international law. This can be seen, for example, in the concerns expressed, here as well as abroad, about the use and abuse of preventive military measures. These concerns become acute wherever it may seem that nuclear-armed countries consider themselves seriously threatened by their neighbors.

Fundamental to relations among nations, as well as to relations among persons within any nation, can be the meaning and reach of the rule of law. These two realms can be brought together whenever a nation undertakes to hold indefinitely "enemy combatants" who owe their allegiance elsewhere. Again and again in these matters, the meaning and very foundations of the law can become vital questions.

IX

The development of the rule of law by one people after another, as well as in relations among the peoples of the world, depends upon the considered opinion that *might* alone cannot make *right*. All this bears upon what is done with the considerable influence, if not even the power, with which the student of law is destined to be entrusted. That is, the thoughtful practitioner is again and again confronted with the question, "What is law?"

An early answer is suggested, in the tradition of the English-speaking peoples, by Magna Carta, an answer on a grand scale. Much more modest, but also far-reaching, is the kind of inquiry pursued in *Langbridge's Case* of 1345. That inquiry, which does pose a constant challenge to the would-be realist, culminated in the insistence by a jurist on that occasion, "Law is that which is right."

The challenge here extends to our understanding of constitutional law. After all, the constitution of a people—whether or not written—is for them *the Law* of laws. And, to return to the personal decisions that the law student makes in taking advantage of the dearly bought opportunity to study law in a good law school, there does remain the question of what understanding of one's professional career is most apt to contribute to a properly productive and hence a truly happy life.

2. The Challenges of Skepticism for the Constitutionalist

I

A challenge put to us from time to time should be examined, for it is always with us. It takes the form of the suggestion that one needs to know everything if one is *to be sure of* (that is, if one is *to know*) anything. There is something to this reservation about what is usually believed to be known.

And yet we do sense (if not even "know") that "knowing everything" is, at least in our circumstances, highly improbable, if not simply impossible. This challenge is an aspect of the fashionable emphasis these days on "realism." The skepticism that is encouraged thereby may, in some circumstances, promote Nihilism, especially with respect to moral discipline and ethical judgments, which can mean that all that is then likely to be left to guide us are the pleasures we happen to be attracted by.

The foundations of all political, as well as moral, reasoning can also be called into question by the skeptic's challenge. The soundness of legal reasoning is thereby called into question as well. On the other hand, it would be irresponsible to allow it to be believed that it is difficult, if not even impossible, to talk sensibly about the things that matter most to us.

II

The sources of systematic skepticism have long been "known." They were drawn on by distinguished thinkers in ancient Greece. They seem to have been drawn on as well, on the other side of the world, as in the speculations of the Taoist school of thought in ancient China.

The considerable variety in the appearances, languages, and customs among the peoples of the earth reinforces the tendency there may be toward skepticism about any reliable access by us to unchanging universals. Observations of this kind can make it seem unlikely, if not impossible, that there should be enduring standards for human conduct reasonably apparent to all. How serious, then, *is* this kind of argument?

Skepticism does have its frivolous aspects. But it has sober aspects as well, which help account for its intermittent appeal. What is enduring about skepticism, however, may suggest that there *is* available to us something not subject to the skeptic's devastating critique.

III

It should be further recognized, before a proper critique of skepticism can in turn be attempted, what its causes include. We do see, from time to time, how far off the mark we can be, even when we feel most certain. And this is with respect both to the world of action and to the world of speculation.

Consider, for example, our experience with the First World War. Western Civilization was traumatized by a four-year catastrophe that was astonishing in the outlandishness of the judgments that were relied upon. Indeed, one can reasonably wonder, "Did *anyone* 'in charge' know what he was doing?"

Consider, also, our experience with the notions we have had from time to time about the relation of the earth to the sun and to the other planets. When we consider what astrophysicists tell us today about the enormous reaches in time and space that they have recently discovered, we can well wonder where and when *we* are. We may even be driven to wonder whether we truly exist, at least in any knowable sense.

IV

One fashionable form that skepticism takes, at least among us, is the insistence upon a fundamental distinction between *facts* and *values*. Only facts, we are told, can truly be known, if anything can. Values, on the other hand, can be considered as no more than the cherished opinions that diverse peoples, regions, or associations happen to hold.

This attitude toward values has affected how the law has come to be regarded. It has had a particularly unsettling effect upon how the common law is regarded, making it seem much more an expression of power than a dictate of reason. This shift is evident, for example, in the century-long movement in United States Supreme Court adjudication from *Swift* v.

Tyson to *Erie Railroad Company* v. *Tompkins* (1842–1938) that is glanced at more than once in these *Reflections*.

The fact-value distinction may have had its most respectable appeal to intellectuals during the opening decades of the twentieth century. But the Nazi experience in Europe, reinforced by what the Stalinists did in Russia and elsewhere, made it much more difficult for sensible people to argue that all "values" are equally valid—or, at least, to argue that no set of "values" could be considered objectively inferior to any others. Atrocities were confronted that could not be satisfactorily comprehended if what was horrible (and indeed simply unbelievable) about them could not be recognized for what it was, suggesting that there are (at least at the extremes) objectively recognizable differences between good and evil.

V

These revelations have proven to be a sobering experience for intellectuals of a radically skeptical turn of mind. This has contributed, furthermore, to a more serious examination (by teachers such as Leo Strauss) of what skepticism depends upon. It can be suspected, for example, that the arguments for skepticism themselves depend upon certainties that are implicitly repudiated by the skeptic.

The radical skeptic, we recall, insists that nothing can be known until *all* is known. This is an article of faith with him, it seems. But how can even *that* be regarded as known by him before his own knowledge itself becomes comprehensive?

Does the skeptic sense that he has enough of a grounding in the way things truly are to be justified in making the arguments he does? Whatever the merits of the skeptic's arguments, does his reliance upon "a grounding in the way things truly are" testify to his awareness of that *nature of things* that human beings may somehow be equipped to grasp? Is there, that is, a guide provided by nature, at least with respect to the premises that we intuit, which can help us distinguish the truly desirable from the undesirable and the harmful?

VI

What guidance *does* nature provide the typical human being? What can we sense, if not even know, about the promptings and guidance of nature with respect to how we should conduct ourselves? *Is* there a moral sense that may have some grounding in nature?

It can be useful to recall here Aristotle's observation about the degree of certainty appropriate for each kind of inquiry. Thus, one should not expect in practical deliberations the precision properly expected in mathematics. It might even be said that it would be unnatural not to distinguish the varying requirements of such pursuits.

Aristotle also indicates that there is a natural hierarchy among the pursuits that human beings have access to. Is it nature which teaches us that it is better *to know* than it is *to act,* that (as Socrates, Plato, and Aristotle all believed) the life of the mind is superior to the life of action? Is there not a sense in which the skeptic agrees with such a teaching, particularly insofar as skepticism considers all evaluating and choosing (that is, all acting) to be subordinate to understanding, at least to the extent that understanding calls into question the ends that we believe ourselves to know reliably enough to have them serve as objects of choice?

VII

However all this may be, skepticism is supported somewhat by our awareness that chance can very much affect what premises we happen to become aware of and to accept. Some "self-evident truths" can seem more obvious at one time than they do at another. Such variability *can* seem to some to support the conclusion that nothing can truly be known.

But it does not seem to be merely a matter of chance that we *want* some standards to be reliable. Nor does it seem a matter of chance that there is something in us that can induce us, or at least many of us, to identify some standards (or premises) as reliable, and others as unreliable. Thus, something permits us to "appreciate" (that is, at least to feel the sense in) the stories we hear about the choices made by others even in distant times and places.

In this and other ways we are persuaded that there is a reliability in the workings of human nature, whatever the chance influences may have been across the ages that may have helped shape the human species as we know it. Such an awareness may well be implicit in the sense that peoples have of the Divine. It may be implicit as well in the confident judgments that can be made about the justice of systems of law in quite different times and places.

VIII

Human beings somehow learn, early on, that standards of proof do vary from discipline to discipline. Thus, the reasoning relied upon in the law cannot be of the rigor relied upon in, say, physics. Even so, it can be salutary to be reminded, from time to time, of the things that the scientific reasoner must (sometimes without recognizing it) simply take for granted as well.

Be all this as it may, we can come to see that there are standards appropriate to each pursuit. Our Constitution is properly regarded as fundamental to our political/legal system. It is surely for us the Law of laws.

And yet, consider again the implications of the fact that the Constitution may be amended at any time. This fact points to other facts, including the fact that there are "values" or standards that are recognized elsewhere, standards by which even our much-esteemed Constitution, as well as the constitutions or ways of life of other peoples, may be compared and judged. We look especially to the Declaration of Independence for guidance as to what those enduring standards have to be.

IX

These, then, are considerations that bear on how the instructive challenges of skepticism can begin to be addressed. These challenges oblige us—not all the time, but now and then, here and there—to consider *what* we can truly know *and how.* I say "not all the time" because we can sense that practical considerations may require us to deal with "situations" pretty much as they happen to seem to us from time to time.

Constitutional inquiries are not the highest activity of which reason is capable. But neither are they trivial or insignificant. In fact, the very highest of our activities—moral, intellectual, or spiritual—may usually require a sound political order, and hence a reliable constitutional system, if they are to be secured.

Implicit in much that we say or do—even when we call into question our ability either to know or to teach anything—is an awareness of an enduring goodness that we have and that we expect others to have, if properly guided. Our opinions may be woefully mistaken from time to time, just as our dreams may be mistaken for "reality." But do we not naturally sense, perhaps even *in* our dreams, that there is available to us something more enduring and hence more reliable than dreams?

3. Constitutionalism and the Common Law: The *Erie* Problem Reconsidered

I

What *is* law? This is a question that applies to all forms of law, ranging from a village rule to that Law of laws, the Constitution. What, if anything, do such laws have in common?

The traditional account of what law is may be found in Thomas Aquinas's *Summa Theologica.* He collects there, in Question 90 of his *Treatise on Law,* the elements of law. That description is summed up in this fashion: "Law is an ordinance of reason, for the common good, promulgated by those who have the care of the community."

One of Thomas's four elements is apt to be emphasized today in some quarters. That is the promulgation—the act of directing what is to be done. It seems to suit the modern taste for *realism* that much should be made here, as elsewhere, of the significance of the evident *exercise* of power.

II

The old-fashioned sense of law may be detected in how the Anglo-American common law was regarded for centuries. That law, developed by lawyers, judges, and scholars, is generally presupposed by the Constitution of the United States. It is even referred to explicitly in the Seventh Amendment to the Constitution (drafted in 1789 and ratified in 1791).

Justice Joseph Story, perhaps the most learned Justice ever to sit on the United States Supreme Court, described in the 1842 case of *Swift* v. *Tyson* how the common law should be regarded. It is concerned, he observed, with "questions of a more general nature, not at all dependent upon local statutes or local usages of a fixed and permanent operation." And, he added, when "questions of general commercial law [are addressed in litigation], where the State tribunals are called upon to perform the like functions as ourselves [in the Courts of the United States]," judges are obliged "to ascertain, upon general reasoning and legal analogies, what is the true exposition of the contract or instrument, or what is the just rule furnished by the principles of commercial law to govern the case."

Thus, Justice Story insists, the common law, even when applied to matters arising in a particular State, should not be restricted to what the judges of that State might say it is. When, for example, something like the treatment of a negotiable instrument is at issue, guidance is sought by judges from the best authorities that may be available. Thus, in *Swift* v. *Tyson*, Justice Story drew (we have seen in Essay Seven of Part One of these *Reflections*) upon the guidance provided by Cicero and by Lord Mansfield, among others.

III

The rhetorical campaign against the traditional kind of approach to what the law is was led in the twentieth century (in this Country) by Oliver Wendell Holmes Jr. This campaign culminated, a century after *Swift* v. *Tyson*, in the much-celebrated case of *Erie Railroad Company* v. *Tompkins* (1938). Justice Brandeis spoke for the Court on that occasion, very much relying on the Dissenting Opinions of Justice Holmes in *Kuhn* v. *Fairmont Coal Company* (1910) and the *Black and White Taxicab Case* (1928).

The doctrine relied upon in *Swift* v. *Tyson*, Justice Brandeis argued, "rests upon the assumption that there is [and here he quotes Justice Holmes] 'a transcendental body of law outside of any particular State but obligatory within it unless and until [it is] changed by statute.'" It is a doctrine, he goes on to say, which assumes "that federal courts have the power to use their judgment as to what the rules of common law are; and that in the federal courts 'the parties are entitled to an independent judgment on matters of general law.'" But, he also goes on to say, "law in the sense in which courts speak of it today does not exist without some definite authority behind it."

This is what the Holmesian (if not even the Hobbesian) repudiation of anything "transcendental" means in practice (quoting again from Justice Holmes):

The common law so far as it is enforced in a State, whether called common law or not, is not the common law generally but the law of that State existing by the authority of that State without regard to what it may have been in England or anywhere else. . . . [T]he authority and only authority is the State, and if that be so, the voice adopted by the State as its own [whether it be of its Legislature or of its Supreme Court] should utter the last word.

Thus, it is in effect argued by Justices Holmes and Brandeis, what is critical on any occasion is not the cogency of the rule that is applied, but rather the authority of the body pronouncing the rule. To depend upon cogency is to look to considerations of justice; to depend upon authority is to defer to the power, if not even to the force, of an authoritative body.

IV

To respect *force* in this way reflects the critical place of calculations of forces in modern physics, a form of science which seems to support (and not only in its technology) a productive realism. The kind of question about how the rules of the common law are developed is addressed in similar ways in other contemporary disciplines. This became evident to me in the course of a conversation I had with an archaeologist who was organizing a conference on the origins of writing, particularly in the Ancient Near East.

One question that I raised with him was as to why writing proceeds in the direction it does in the Western World if not also in the Near East— usually from left to right, but sometimes from right to left. I wondered whether the dominant (that is, the natural?) right-handedness of human beings (as of other animals on earth) made it more likely that writing would go from left to right, especially if this meant that one's hand would not interfere either with one's writing or with one's view of that writing. I gathered from him that this has not been discussed in the relevant literature.

My archaeologist tended to discount my suggestion, explaining that the choice of direction may have been ultimately arbitrary in each instance. Indeed, he went on to say, the choice of direction was probably, if not even certainly, the result of *an edict* by someone in authority. Presumably, that might also be said about the choices of the symbols (or letters or characters) settled upon in one written language after another, as well as about departures from what nature is inclined to prefer.

V

All this leaves us, however, with a critical question, a question similar to that which we can ask when we are told that the law is what the judges say it is. What, we may well wonder, determines what someone in authority may say on any occasion? What, that is, bears on the choices made by the powerful?

A related question may be as to what determines who is in authority. Or should we assume, consistent with what some particle physicists seem to argue these days, that there is a radical indeterminancy at the core of things? What, for example, does determine whether one stays in authority?

One suspects that those who issue edicts usually like to be obeyed, and hence to remain (or at least to seem to remain) in control. Is that more likely if the edict issued somehow conforms to what people generally sense to be called for in the circumstances that they confront? Does, in such matters, the apparent sensibleness of an authoritative pronouncement make an enduring compliance more likely?

VI

We can return explicitly now to the *Erie* problem. What moves the powerful—a judge or a legislator—to say what he does? Is not some sense of justice apt to be invoked by him, whatever he may personally feel?

Certainly, it is rare for someone in authority (other than an exasperated parent) to justify an edict only with the explanation, "Because I say so!" Equities and expectations may be talked about, with the likely consequence (personal or social) suggested. The *Erie* doctrine does not deny that common law adjudication in State courts may still draw on such considerations.

One odd feature of the *Erie* doctrine is the insistence that Federal judges are to be the only ones involved in common law adjudications who are *not* expected, or even permitted, to reason their way to the judgments they render. They must, instead, limit themselves (*at least in appearance*) to what State court judges have said about the issues before them, no matter how much more competent than State court judges they are generally taken to be. Thus, the edicts that Federal judges may issue, in *Erie*-type cases, are supposed to be no more than echoes of what the relevant State courts have said.

VII

Chance circumstances, therefore, can very much affect what a Federal judge may say and do. In fact, he can rule this way one day and quite a different way the next day, with respect to the same issue, depending upon the State court system that chanced to be deemed relevant on each occasion. And, on each occasion, would he nevertheless be expected to speak persuasively of what a *just* ruling called for?

Does such a reliance upon chance make it more likely that *power,* rather than *reason,* will indeed be considered critical in human affairs? Chance can make passing whims or desires seem more important—and that can seem in turn to be power-at-work. But is one truly powerful if one depends primarily upon chance either for one's pronouncements or for one's effectiveness?

One problem that moderns face, with their emphasis upon the power that those in authority happen to have, is that this could make human existence seem, if not even be, meaningless. Existentialism and other modern movements have tried to cope with an account of things that denies the authoritativeness of any supposed guidance provided either by Nature or by the Divine. The desperation evident here is suggested by the attempted recourse to the *acte gratuite* that intrigued André Gide four-score years ago.

VIII

Arbitrariness in human affairs is likely to be minimized if *reasons* are given for the rules laid down from time to time. When that happens, the truly human is more apt to be in control. Or, at least, the *knower*—one who understands—may be of some influence.

One who understands can recognize the usefulness of the precedents he inherits, even as he recognizes their limitations. Precedents and the other materials of the law are most apt to be put to good use when it is generally sensed (as in *Langbridge's Case* [1345]) that "Law is that which is right." It is then that law can become most powerful, for it encourages conformity to it even when no one in authority is watching.

The rule of law may be, in the final analysis, a kind of self-rule. This, to be effective over the long-term, depends upon a properly trained (or deeply inspired?) citizen-body. A proper Constitutionalism can thus be understood as prudence institutionalized.

IX

The common law, as traditionally understood, depended upon systematic reasoning in the service of justice. It is generally obvious to us that sound reasoning may help one reach whatever goal is aimed at. What is not as obvious to many is the fact that reasoning may help one determine what is truly good.

We can be reminded by these observations that there may be an intimate relation among the good, the true, and the beautiful. At the highest level these may even blend together. Such considerations are hardly compatible with the sophisticated realism (if not even the determined skepticism) of the *Erie* doctrine, a doctrine which implicitly rejects not only traditional Anglo-American jurisprudence but also the philosophical system in which that jurisprudence was grounded.

The highest reasoning, then, is *not* that which directs us to the finest actions we are capable of in our circumstances. However important that may be, an even higher form of reasoning is that which permits us to make the best of our souls. Thus, the highest looks to *being* rather than to *doing*—and hence not to acting, but rather to understanding.

4. The Confederate Constitution (1861–1865)

I

Our primary interest in this volume of *Reflections* is in the reading of the Constitution of 1787. The circumstances of its drafting can help us notice features of that instrument. It can also help us if we understand the language of the Constitution, which language is, in effect, another set of relevant circumstances.

It could perhaps help as well if we had drafts of the document. But we are pretty much limited here to records of provisions agreed upon, from time to time in Philadelphia, between May and September of 1787. We also have some discussions, and consequent modifications, of the draft submitted to the Convention for adoption, discussions which were developed and recorded in far more detail in some of the subsequent State Ratifying Conventions.

The circumstances of the 1787 drafting include the Framers' experience with earlier constitutional documents, documents that anticipate and contribute to the Constitution itself. An immediate source for the Framers was the authoritative Declaration of Independence, followed immediately by that early attempt at Constitution-making for the United States known as the Articles of Confederation. In the background, of course, are Magna Carta and other English documents of note, where there can be found features that show up in the Constitution of 1787 and in its Bill of Rights of 1791.

II

These and like materials are supplemented, for the student of the Constitution, by the Confederate Constitution of 1861 (set forth, with its new language underlined, in Appendix I of this volume). This is, in effect, a subsequent draft, almost a century later, which throws light back on the Constitution of 1787. The 1861 document could be prepared fairly quickly because it had the 1787 "draft" to work from.

The two documents look, at least from a distance, pretty much alike.

There *are* differences in capitalization of substantives (far less of that by 1861) and occasionally of spelling and of punctuation. But the divisions into Articles and Sections are parallel, which permits ready noticing of differences between them.

My own count—and here I modify what I have said in my *Commentary* on the Amendments to the Constitution—is that more than seventy-five percent of the 1861 document may be found (word for word) in the 1787 document. It is obvious that the changes made in 1861 reflect an awareness of how various 1787 passages had been read and applied for decades. Of course, some of the 1861 changes undertook to correct what some Southerners had long regarded as lamentable misreadings by Northerners of key 1787 provisions.

III

Thus we see from the outset something which is indicated again and again in the 1861 document: the Confederates *did not* want to recognize the existence and authority of the people of any country as a whole. This is evident in the language of their 1861 Preamble. And it is evident as well in how the Ninth and Tenth Amendments are modified when they are incorporated by the Confederates in Article VI of their 1861 document.

The changes in the 1861 Preamble, where more than one-third of its sixty words are new, alert us as to what is to come. Critical to the change is the christening of the association of "seceding" States as a Confederation instead of as a Union, with the term "federal" introduced, whereas it had never been used in the 1787 document. This is reinforced by something never seen in the 1787 document, the invocation of Divine favor.

Also anticipated in the 1861 Preamble is the deliberate repudiation thereafter (as in Article 1, Section 8) of any Confederation-wide dedication to the *general welfare.* This shift is reinforced by limitations placed upon efforts by the new Congress to promote commerce. A different (if not even old-fashioned and genteel, but not truly English) notion about the purpose of government seems to have been drawn upon in 1861.

IV

One prominent feature of the 1861 Constitution is its reinforcement of the place of the States in the overall system. The stature of the States is markedly enhanced. This is evident from the opening lines of the Preamble.

One can be reminded here of the Federal-minded Articles of Confederation. This 1861 association is to be a "confederation," definitely not a "union." One is also reminded of where the ultimate control is to rest when one notices the provision, in Article V, for amendments that are to be controlled entirely by the States, a provision in which Congress is assigned no more than a minor ministerial role.

Other provisions also reflect the deference felt for the integrity, and the ultimate authority, of the States. This may be seen in the powers recognized in the States to initiate the impeachment of some officers of the Confederate government. It may be seen as well in the power that States have to manage the rivers that they share.

V

At the heart of the differences between the 1787 and the 1861 constitutions is the status in each of the institution of slavery. The 1787 Constitution can be understood to have done no more than tolerate slavery, refusing even to call it by name. The 1861 Constitution repeatedly provides for the explicit protection, perhaps even for the extension, of slavery.

One way of characterizing what was done in 1861 is to say that the controversial 1857 *Dred Scott* decision, which had been bitterly resented by the opponents of slavery, is repeatedly reaffirmed in the Confederate Constitution, dramatizing thereby how important it had seemed to the South. Indeed, it is, upon reading the 1861 Constitution, difficult to understand how anyone could doubt (as some scholars evidently do) the central place of the slavery controversy among the causes of the Civil War. One can even suspect that no other issue (except, perhaps, that of "honor") truly mattered, at least for those most anxious to secede.

This is not to deny that the dominant concern in the North was, in the beginning of the war, a determination to save the Union, not to abolish slavery. But the Unionists saw during the first years of the war how critical slavery was for what the Secessionists were trying to do. That recognition found decisive expression in the Emancipation Proclamation of January 1, 1863, and eventually in the Thirteenth Amendment.

VI

After all, the primacy of the slavery question is repeatedly evident in the history of the United States in the years leading up to the Civil War. It may be seen in the roster of the States that attempted to secede in 1860–1865: only slaveholding States were interested in this "exercise" (however serious the grievances of New England disunionists might have been earlier in the century). The primacy of the slavery question may also be seen in how slavery matters show up in the new language of the 1861 Constitution (where more than ten percent of that new language is clearly about slaves and their handling).

The slavery issue was so critical that the authority of the Declaration of Independence could itself be called into question in some quarters. Particularly threatening, of course, was the insistence "that all Men are created equal." It had been this authoritative insistence which had helped legitimate abolitionist passions during the decades leading up to the Civil War.

But it was not only the Declaration that proved threatening. For, after all, there had been a venerable constitutional tradition which had permitted the Declaration itself to emerge and to have the remarkable effect that it did. This meant, among other things, that sensitive Southerners could not help but be deeply divided, in their own souls, about what they considered themselves obliged to defend.

VII

One consequence of the 1861 move is that these Southerners, unlike their ancestors, could no longer date their political existence from 1776. In fact, looking all the way back to 1776 had long seemed to some of them to concede too much to those Unionists who saw a nation emerge at that time. It might even be worth considering whether the partial repudiation in 1861 of the Declaration of Independence, the 1776 document anticipated for some by the antislavery *Somerset* precedent of 1771–1772, required, as a substitute, that a greater emphasis be placed upon the religion of the day.

Thus, it can be suggested, there was a shift among the Secessionists from reliance upon the political religion of the Declaration of Independence (with its separation-of-powers-style organization of the Divine) to the actual religion(s) of the day. This was particularly attractive for those who could find in the Bible justifications for the institution of slavery. Whether this was truly in the spirit of the Bible could, of course, be questioned, as it was by abolitionists such as John Brown.

It may have been somewhat a matter of chance what the religious and other doctrines were that could be used by Secessionists in their desperation. Also accidental may have been the effects of various innovations in the 1861 Constitution, such as the incorporation (virtually unchanged) of the first eight amendments of the 1791 Bill of Rights in its Article I, Section 9. One consequence of this—and one can well wonder whether anyone was aware of this at the time—was to undermine further the argument unsuccessfully advanced in *Barron* v. *Baltimore* (1833), the argument that (as we shall see further on in these *Reflections*) depended, in effect, upon the proposition that all of the great rights of the English-speaking peoples were naturally to be respected by all governments in the United States.

VIII

Slavery was the most dramatic feature of the way of life for which the Secessionists sacrificed themselves. It was to be a genteel way of life, under the new Constitution, in which manufactures and commerce were to be denied all subsidies. Even the postal service was required to be self-supporting by March 1863.

We can wonder, however, whether it was generally recognized among the Secessionists how much one "industry," slavery itself, was to be subsidized under the 1861 Constitution. The costs of the protections mandated for slaveholders would have eventually been substantial. Even during the Civil War, the Confederacy seems to have been seriously hobbled because of the resources that the Secessionists were obliged to devote to policing their slaves.

It could be instructive to inventory and assess how the day-to-day workings of a slavery-connected legal system (aside from the demands for means for recovering fugitive slaves) affected traditional Southern assumptions about property, civil liberties, and family relations. We have noticed that Article III (the Judiciary Article) was the least changed in 1861 from what it had been in 1787 (with only two dozen new words among its three hundred and fifty-three). One suspects that there must have been constant unease among those truly professional judges in the South who wanted to continue doing what judges had "always" done.

IX

There were, in the 1861 Constitution, innovations that deserve a respectful assessment. It might even be of use to try to determine what the experience was with these innovations during the Civil War. It would be unfortunate if the Secessionists' sponsorship of various of these innovations tended to discredit them ever after, innovations which have to some extent come to be respected nationwide, at least in part.

These innovations include the limitation of one's service as President to a single six-year term (which has taken the form for us of a limitation to two four-year terms), as well as the provision of a line-item veto. Another innovation was the option provided to members of the President's Cabinet to participate in discussions, on the floor of the two Houses of Congress, of matters affecting their departments (something that does take place routinely today in Congressional hearings). Still another innovation was the power given to the President to dismiss nonjudicial officers he has appointed, something which had been a matter of debate in the First Congress and which is now routinely accepted.

That is, there *were* things in the 1787 Constitution that could seem to experienced political men to be in need of adjustment. But it is hard for us to believe that the precarious state of slavery was something that had to be ministered to as it was in 1861. Thus, the Secessionists (about whom much more should be said in my forthcoming volume of reflections on slavery and the Constitution) may have had to be saved from themselves, permitting them (or at least their descendants) to return to that Anglo-American constitutional heritage in which they had long shared, a heritage which they had come to regard as an intermittent threat instead of as the reliable and even precious guide that it truly was.

5. *The Japanese Relocation Cases* (1943, 1944)

I

The treatment of West Coast residents of Japanese descent during the Second World War can be instructive in assessing what has been done by us in response to the attacks on the East Coast of September 11, 2001. One can be reminded also of what was done, with far more harmful long-term effects, to North American Indians for more than a century. One can be reminded as well of what was done, in a considerably less rigorous manner, to Americans of German descent (as in Milwaukee) during the First World War.

The situation in this Country after the Pearl Harbor and related attacks by Japan in December 1941 was far more serious than it was after the monstrous September Eleventh attacks. For one thing, much of our Pacific Fleet had been destroyed overnight by a formidable enemy. And it was an enemy that had, as its principal ally, a country which had already conquered much of Europe.

It remains to be seen just how sensible our domestic security measures have been since September Eleventh. It is to be noticed that civil liberties in this Country were less restricted, *for the population at large,* after September Eleventh than they were during the early years of the Cold War. A quite different assessment has to be made of what was evidently routinely done by the United States to its prisoners at Guantanamo Bay and elsewhere.

II

It is against this backdrop—of official conduct both before and after the Japanese relocation measures—that we can better see what happened in 1942–1944 on the West Coast. First, there were the nightlong curfews for all West Coast people of Japanese ancestry, curfews that were upheld by a unanimous United States Supreme Court in the 1943 *Hirabayashi Case.* Then, there were the relocation and internment of the same people, upheld (by a deeply divided Court) in the 1944 *Korematsu Case.*

The rationale in support of these measures was fairly simple: it was that of "military necessity." Not much of a record was made; little if any evidence was provided either of misconduct or of improper plans on the part of the people dealt with. It did not matter whether the persons thus treated, if they resided on the West Coast, were natural-born citizens of the United States.

It can sometimes seem, in such controversies, that legal and constitutional arguments do not matter much. In fact, an occasional Supreme Court Justice can even be heard to counsel that it would be prudent for the Court not to pretend that it can effectively second-guess claims of "military necessity." The Court, by participating in these activities, can seem to legitimate what it can rarely effectively supervise.

III

The difficulty faced here by the Court can be expected whenever an effort is made to resist the sustained passions of the day. The Pearl Harbor attack *did* inflame public opinion for years in this Country. It was not surprising that there was little, if any, significant public outcry as the anti-Japanese policies were developed here as well as abroad.

It did not matter, it seemed, that the implementation of our domestic policies could be described as it was by Justice Robert H. Jackson at the outset of his Dissenting Opinion in *Korematsu*. He put it thus:

> Korematsu was born on our soil, of parents born in Japan. The Constitution makes him a citizen of the United States by nativity and a citizen of California by residence. No claim is made that he is not loyal to this country. There is no suggestion that apart from the matter involved here he is not law-abiding and well disposed. Korematsu, however, has been convicted of an act not commonly a crime. It consists merely of being present in the State whereof he is a citizen, near the place where he was born, and where all his life he has lived.

These facts were not disputed.

Deep anti-Japanese passions continued in this Country to the end of the war. They culminated, of course, in the dropping of atomic bombs upon two Japanese cities in August 1945. Such ferocious attacks did not seem to trouble most Americans at the time, particularly after it became generally known how viciously prisoners of war and conquered peoples had been treated by the Japanese Army, reinforcing thereby the animosity that the Japanese Navy had earned at Pearl Harbor and elsewhere.

IV

One can wonder whether the Japanese government ever worried about the effects its foreign policy might have on the fortunes of people of Japanese ancestry living abroad. It seems not. But then, that government was not sensible either in what it expected would happen in the United States because of the Pearl Harbor attack.

I do not recall that there was ever any serious doubt, among our public at large, about the fate of Japan during the war. Indeed, within the first year of the war the fateful Battle of Midway was fought, leaving Japan thereafter permanently on the defensive. It did not seem that what was done to Japanese Americans made much difference in how effectively the war was prosecuted by the United States.

It *was* recognized by the responsible officials, including by the President of the United States, that "concentration camps" had been established in the United States. But, it should be noticed, there was no systematic killing in those camps, however severe the loss of property and other deprivations for the people of Japanese descent thus affected may have been. It should also be noticed that the judicial critics of those measures could dare to insist publicly that they should be attributed to racial prejudice.

V

It is perhaps significant that nothing is said, in the West Coast orders regulating the West Coast Japanese, about people of mixed blood. It seems that intermarriage between Japanese and Caucasians was rare at that time. This reflects the relative isolation, and perhaps the related vulnerability, of people of Japanese descent in this Country.

It might even be suggested that the unjust way the West Coast Japanese were treated contributed to their well-being in the long run, forcing them out of the enclaves to which they had become accustomed. Particularly important here was the military record, in Italy, of a Japanese American unit, which was said to be one of the most decorated units in the American Army during the Second World War. These men were able to provide lessons in patriotism and sacrifice for their more fortunate fellow-citizens.

All this is in marked contrast to the long-term consequences of another Second World War relocation program, that initiated by Josef Stalin against the Chechyans in 1944. The repercussions of that brutal campaign, which followed upon centuries of Tsarist oppressiveness, continue to plague the Russians sixty years later. And there is no civilized end in sight, which suggests something healthy both about the American regime and about Japanese Americans.

VI

A grim parallel to the capacity of Japanese Americans to turn calamity into redemption may be seen in the experience of European Jews during and after the Second World War. Those Jews were treated far worse than were Japanese Americans or, for that matter, even the much-abused Chechyans. Furthermore, the Germans, in doing what they did to the Jews, markedly weakened their own military capacity.

It seems, however, that what was done to the Jews, in so horrific and sustained a manner, did contribute to the emergence of Israel as an independent state. Some have even been inclined to see all this, despite the resulting tensions in the Middle East, as part of a Divine plan. In what sense, if at all, can the establishment of Israel be said to have been worth the unbelievable sacrifices of the concentration camps?

Does a solution at all like this await the Chechyans? Perhaps not—but what about the Kurds of Iraq? Are they destined to become the Japanese Americans, if not the Israelis, of the Muslim world?

VII

It seems that Justice Black, to the very end of his long career on the Supreme Court, was troubled by the Opinion he wrote for the Court in *Korematsu*. It also seems that his response on that occasion may have been in large part due to the accidents of his personal friendships with President Roosevelt and the commanding general primarily responsible for the West Coast measures. Perhaps, however, all this (which I glance at both in the Preface and in Essay 1 of Part Two of *Reflections on Freedom of Speech and the First Amendment*) made him even more vigorous thereafter in his defense of civil liberties.

Chance, it can also be said, contributed to the opportunities given to others to redeem themselves for what they had helped do to Japanese Americans during the Second World War. Particularly to be noticed is Earl Warren, who had been an important California politician advocating Relocation. He came to regret what he had done to Japanese Americans, perhaps even to advance his political career.

Earl Warren did distinguish himself as the Chief Justice who presided over the Supreme Court during its most ambitious years as a champion of civil liberties in this Country. The *Korematsu Case* offered Justice Frank Murphy the opportunity to write perhaps his most distinguished dissent. Another *Korematsu* dissenter, Justice Robert H. Jackson, served thereafter as the chief American prosecutor of the surviving Nazi leaders during the landmark Nuremberg Trials, where he could learn firsthand how much worse things could become once the kind of measures used on the West Coast were experimented with, the kind of intensified measures from which American Indians in this Country and Gypsies (or the Roma people) in Europe are evidently not yet equipped to recover.

VIII

The invocation of military necessity in justification of our West Coast measures is, as we have seen, difficult (if not, usually, impossible) for Courts to counter. But there *was* a test, proposed by Justice Murphy, that should have been taken more seriously than it was. He argued, in effect, that if matters were as serious (say, on the West Coast) as it was said, then martial law should have been imposed as a precondition to the other restrictive measures resorted to.

This is somewhat like the recognition that civil liberties, such as the freedom of speech, should be recognized wherever conditions are *not* considered bad enough to warrant suspending the writ of *habeas corpus*. Requiring such suspension is comparable to our suggesting to our political and military leaders that they should not initiate any wars to which they are not willing to send their own children as soldiers. There are, that is, readily apparent tests for "seriousness."

After all, "necessity" can be discerned in some places, while it is not noticed in other (even more dramatic) places. Thus, although there was a far greater proportion of residents of Japanese descent in Hawaii than there was on the West Coast, no Relocation program was resorted to there, perhaps partly because it would have been so disruptive. This forbearance, especially since there *were* more suspicious activities on behalf of Japan alleged in Hawaii, does suggest that racial prejudice and even a calculating greediness may have *helped* shape what was done on the West Coast to the Japanese and their property.

IX

Perhaps, also, sober second thoughts about what was done to the West Coast Japanese contributed to the unanimity of the Supreme Court a decade later in *Brown* v. *Board of Education*. This was under the leadership of a Chief Justice who did come to regret the part he had played in the Relocation program. It can be salutary to be reminded, from time to time, of the burdens that one, because of supposedly necessary compromises, can be saddled with, sometimes for years thereafter.

Particularly to be celebrated are those Japanese Americans who rose above the abuse to which their people had been subjected by unduly fearful leaders. Two of these were University of Chicago Law School classmates of mine. One of them became a Justice of the Hawaii Supreme Court, and the other became a leading Member of the United States House of Representatives.

Indeed, perhaps the greatest honor paid this late Congresswoman was given her, in effect, during the 2004 Olympic Games. It had been her championing of the Title IX program for educational institutions that seems to have been a major factor in the successes of so many American women during the games in Athens. The late Fred Korematsu, too, was able to transform the abuse of his people into a badge of honor.

6. *Calder* v. *Bull* (1798);
Barron v. *Baltimore* (1833)

I

Calder v. *Bull* provides venerable authority for the proposition that *ex post facto* prohibitions refer only to criminal matters. Some State constitutional provisions do provide for this explicitly. The language in Sections 9 and 10 of Article I of the Constitution of 1787, however, is not limited, in its *language,* to criminal matters.

Even so, such a limitation does make sense. That is, an attempt to limit retroactivity with respect to legislation about civil matters invites conscientious attempts to circumvent it. And, as George Mason warned the Constitutional Convention, such necessary circumvention could undermine general fidelity to the Constitution.

The Justices in *Calder* found support for their *ex post facto* limitation in the argument that extension of the provision to civil matters would make superfluous the accompanying Contracts Impairments Clause in Section 10 of Article I (as that Clause is generally understood). A sound rule of constitutional interpretation is thereby invoked. That is, any reading of a well-crafted document is suspect which has to regard part of it as unnecessary.

II

It can be instructive to notice what *has* been done with the Contracts Clause for two centuries now. It is understood to apply to contracts already entered into. That is, we are told, it is only the obligations of such contracts that States cannot impair by their legislation.

It can also be instructive to notice what has *not* been done with the Contracts Clause. For example, it is not generally noticed that whatever is bad about the forbidden governmental impairment relates only to the doings of State Governments, just as is the case (for example) with respect to the granting of Letters of Marque and Reprisal. The Congress does not have any Contracts Clause limitation accompanying *its own ex post facto* prohibition in Section 9 of Article I.

One explanation (rarely used) for this discrepancy is the suggestion that what the States are kept from doing is to weaken in any way the obligations of contracts, especially through changes in commercial law. This explanation (examined by William W. Crosskey) can be reinforced by the suggestion that a comprehensive Commerce Power is assumed throughout the Constitution for the General Government, a power that that Government exercises more and more. All this leaves open the possibility, therefore, that the *ex post facto* prohibitions *were* originally intended to apply to civil as well as to criminal matters, a possibility that has been foreclosed (as a practical matter) by what the Supreme Court did in *Calder* and thereafter.

III

Another possibility that seems to have been foreclosed by the Supreme Court in *Calder* and elsewhere is that of subjecting legislation to the test of "natural justice." Justice James Iredell considers, and seems to rule out, the use by the Court of standards of what we know as natural law or natural right. Of course, markedly offensive legislation might well stimulate Justices to scrutinize legislation closely for other imperfections.

It is also likely, if not even expected, that judges will generally be guided by considerations of natural justice in developing and applying the common law. It is obvious that legislators, as well as citizens at large, are expected to take enduring standards of right and wrong, of good and bad, into account in making the choices they do. But it is not likely that judges were ever expected, as a routine matter, to pass moral judgment on all the State *statutes* that come before them.

But what about passing *political* judgment? Is not this assumed by the requirement (rarely invoked) that a Republican Form of Government be guaranteed by the General Government to each State in the Union? Can it—should it—be said that serious affronts to natural justice, especially if extensive and sustained, pose a threat to republican government?

IV

It is several times noticed in the *Calder* Opinions that the Constitution was made by the People of the United States. There is not *here* the kind of insistence upon State autonomy found, later, in the Confederate Constitution. And the People, it can be expected, are open to appeals grounded in natural justice.

Important in any effort to deal realistically with the requirements of a proper Constitutionalism is the provision in the Constitution for amendments. This reminds us that there *are* standards outside of the Constitution that can be drawn upon to improve the Constitution itself. Such standards can be moral as well as political.

It seems to be taken for granted throughout the *Calder* Opinions that the Courts of the United States can declare State statutes to be void. The Supremacy Clause in Article VI seems to authorize such interventions when State actions are involved, but that cannot be readily extended to apply to Congressional enactments. Perhaps the Federal Courts *are* empowered to invalidate, or at least to disregard, those Acts of Congress which attempt to get courts to do things that judges simply should not do, such as presiding over prosecutions dependent on *ex post facto* criminal legislation.

V

The criteria to be drawn upon in assessing the Constitution itself are implicit in that set of standards and objectives which can be regarded as a Super-Constitution. Such standards can be thought of as drawn upon in Magna Carta and the Declaration of Independence. But the drafters of those now-sacred documents themselves looked to something even higher.

Critical here can be the relation between the old (if not even the ancient) and the good. There *is* something to be said for the proposition that that which is long-established, at least among a civilized people, has likely been "certified" by nature as somehow good. It is this expectation that makes precedents attractive.

A respect for venerable precedents is expected in judicial proceedings. Even so, we should be reminded of the fact that relatively little of what the community and its legislatures do can ever be reviewed, either for their constitutionality or for their good sense, by the Courts of the United States (the Federal Courts). Much depends, therefore, upon the insight and integrity of the People at large, if the system is to work as it should.

VI

Barron v. *Baltimore* encourages us to consider further whether restraints upon governments depend upon explicit constitutional provisions. It is evident in the *Barron Case* that a jury believed that there had been a good case against the City of Baltimore. We might well wonder whether the city, while conducting this litigation, ever offered compensation for the harm evidently done by it to the Barron wharf.

The United States Supreme Court did not pass on whether the city had been at fault, but only on whether the Fifth Amendment (and especially its Takings Clause) applied to the States. It can usefully be wondered what those bringing this case to the Supreme Court believed about the "reach" of the 1791 Bill of Rights, and why this was believed. It can be wondered, that is, whether the issues here were as simple as Chief Justice Marshall made them out to be in his Opinion for the Court.

It is instructive to watch the Chief Justice at work, especially as he explains what the repetition of Section 9 prohibitions in Section 10 of Article I says about the limited scope of what would otherwise seem a universal application of those prohibitions in Section 9. But this argument cuts two ways: why should not the prohibitions in the Fifth Amendment be considered universal (that is, encompassing the States as well as the United States) if there should not be the kind of juxtaposition seen in Sections 9 and 10 of Article I of the Constitution? Indeed, might not the use of "Congress" in the First Amendment even suggest that the remaining articles of the Bill of Rights are *not* similarly limited to the General Government?

VII

What the Chief Justice ultimately relies upon is history, not constitutional interpretation, recalling in his quite short Opinion that the primary agitation in the late 1780s had been to have more restraints placed on the General Government, not on the State Governments. And this, of course, is how James Madison's Bill of Rights proposal (in June 1789) began in the House of Representatives: most of those restraints would have been so placed in Article I as clearly to apply only to the General Government (just as was later done in the Confederate Constitution). There *was* one set of restraints, in Madison's June 1789 proposal, explicitly applicable to the States, by way of contrast.

But it can be wondered what the (perhaps accidental) effect was of dropping the States-connected restraints altogether *and* of adding all of the amendments to the end of the Constitution, which meant that only one of the proposed amendments that were ratified was explicitly limited to Congress. Did the others become, however inadvertently, applicable against the States as well? And if that one had not been ratified, then the amendments would have appeared almost entirely general in application.

Would this make too much of chance factors? The Chief Justice, no doubt, would have suggested that common sense should be used in moderating the extremes to which applying the rules might take one, something which I consider further in my *Reflections on Freedom of Speech and the First Amendment.* Or, as it was once suggested, "The Sabbath was made for man, not man for the Sabbath."

VIII

Still, what *should* be made of the arguments advanced by quite respectable people during the Ratification Campaign that no Bill of Rights was really needed? After all, it was insisted (by men pushing for immediate ratification of the proposed Constitution) that the great rights to be included in such a Bill would exist, whether or not incorporated explicitly in the Constitution. In fact, these rights had long been routinely exercised and depended upon by Americans.

This argument is reinforced by the Ninth Amendment, which recognizes rights that may not be explicitly referred to in the Bill of Rights. If such rights had always been part of the heritage of the People of the United States and their forebears, why should they not be routinely applicable against the States? And, it might be added, would not these rights, or at least some of them, be critical to that Republican Form of Government to be guaranteed by the General Government to every State in the Union?

But even if all this is granted, there does remain the question of whether the Judiciary should be the body primarily responsible for protecting such rights. This question becomes particularly acute when a request is made to correct abuses by State Governments. Is this the sort of thing best left to the State courts, especially when the operations of the General Government are not threatened?

IX

However all this may be, it is possible that *Calder* and *Barron* were rightly decided, but not for the principal reasons given on each occasion by the United States Supreme Court. Thus, the challenged actions of the State legislature in *Calder* could properly be considered Judicial, not Legislative, and thereby not raising any *ex post facto* issue. Thus, also, the actions of the City of Baltimore litigated in *Barron* may not have been a "taking," however questionable such actions may be.

Care should be taken, in any event, lest virtually every governmental action come to be regarded as a "taking" if anyone should be harmed thereby. Much legislation would thus be converted into a prelude to litigation. Care should also be taken lest judicial activity be systematically converted into a form of legislation.

With the passage of time, the specific *Calder* problem has receded, inasmuch as State legislatures have pretty much given up their judicial activities. As for the *Barron* problem, there has been the long-term effect of the Civil War to reckon with. That war's Fourteenth Amendment has meant that that which the plaintiffs in *Barron* took for granted has come to be recognized—that is, that the States, too, are properly bound by the great rights inherited by the People of the United States in 1776.

7. *Corfield* v. *Coryell* (1823) and the Privileges and Immunities Puzzles

I

"The importance of [United States Supreme Court] Justice Bushrod Washington's *Circuit Court* opinion [in *Corfield* v. *Coryell* (1823)] [we are told by the *Encyclopedia of the American Constitution*] derives from the fact that it contains the only judicial exposition of Article IV, Section 2 [of the Constitution of 1787], prior to the adoption of the Fourteenth Amendment, that also uses the phrase 'Privileges and Immunities.'" That Clause in Article IV declares, "The Citizens of each State shall be entitled to all Privileges and Immunities of Citizens in the several States." "*Corfield* arose," the *Encyclopedia* continues, "because the plaintiff's vessel had been condemned under a [New Jersey] law forbidding nonresidents to take shell fish from State waters; in his trespass action, the plaintiff relied upon the privileges and immunities clause."

The Privileges and Immunities Clause, in Article IV, is immediately preceded by the Full Faith and Credit Clause, which provides that "the public Acts, Records, and Judicial Proceedings" of one State will be properly deferred to in other States. The Privileges and Immunities Clause, which provides in effect that citizens of each State will be duly recognized in other States than their own, is immediately followed by the requirement that a fugitive from justice will be returned to the State demanding him. That, in turn, is followed by the provision mandating the return of fugitive slaves.

Thus, there are addressed here questions of how the arrangements or residents of one State are to be considered in the other States. Justice Washington, in *Corfield*, observes, "The inquiry is, What are the privileges and immunities of citizens in the several States?" His immediate answer is: "We feel no hesitation in confining these expressions to those privileges and immunities which are, in their nature, fundamental, which belong, of right, to the citizens of all free governments, and which have, at all times, been enjoyed by the citizens of the several States which compose this Union, from the time of their becoming free, independent, and sovereign."

II

Justice Washington then explains, "What these fundamental principles are, it would perhaps be more tedious than difficult to enumerate." But he does venture to suggest, "They may, however, be all comprehended under [various] general heads." The first of these general heads is "Protection by the government."

We can see here the primacy, at least in the English-speaking tradition, of what has been identified as the right of self-preservation. Life itself is at the outset of the "Life, Liberty, and the Pursuit of Happiness" trinity acclaimed by the Declaration of Independence. Whether everything else should be sacrificed to the maintenance of one's life does remain a question, bearing as it does on the other "fundamental principles" that can illuminate what makes human existence meaningful.

It should be noticed that there does not seem to be any question, in Justice Washington's approach, about whether the fundamental rights of citizens *can* be vindicated as against a State in the Courts of the United States. In *Corfield,* a grand right is invoked with respect to trespass litigation. We can be reminded of the attempt made a decade later in *Barron* v. *Baltimore* (about which I shall say more further on than I already have).

III

Justice Washington continues his enumeration of the general heads of "fundamental principles." Following immediately upon "protection by the government" are these: "the enjoyment of life and liberty, with the right to acquire and possess property of every kind, and to pursue and obtain happiness and safety, subject nevertheless to such restraints as the government may justly prescribe for the general good of the whole." Are these expansions of that "protection by the government" with which he had begun his enumeration?

There can be heard here echoes of John Locke's property-oriented account of the founding and perpetuation of the political order. Here, too, there are phrases that remind us once again of the seminal status for the United States of the Declaration of Independence. We can be reminded as well of the respect to be shown for the legitimate powers of government, powers essential for the effective possession and enjoyment by citizens of various rights.

It is evident, here as elsewhere, how critical "the right to acquire and possess property of every kind" is to our constitutional regime. Life itself, it can be said, depends upon access to various kinds of property; and, it can also be said, a good life depends in large part upon how that property is used. It is not noticed here, however, how much the very existence of property—its identification and allocation—depends upon the doings of governments, something which may not be given due weight by those among us who somehow assume that they have most, if not all, of their property independent of any governmental activity, activity which they tend to see only as intermittent threats to the enjoyment of "their" property.

IV

Justice Washington, after having noted the general heads of his subject, mentions "some of the particular privileges and immunities of citizens," which, he says, "are clearly embraced by the general description of privileges, deemed to be fundamental." The first of these particular privileges is "[t]he right of a citizen of one State to pass through, or to reside in any other State, for purposes of trade, agriculture, professional pursuits, or otherwise." We can detect here ramifications of the other provisions in Article IV which anticipate problems developing because of the movements of human beings among the States.

It remains a challenge to us to determine the basis on which the Justice selected the particulars that he did. The first of them can be said to draw upon Magna Carta. An emphasis seems to be placed here, if not also several times elsewhere, upon the human being as acquisitive.

This right, it seems, recognizes what it can mean for many human beings *to live*. It could even be identified, in its comprehensives, as *Legislative* in character. The other particular privileges and immunities can be understood as somehow reinforcing the exercise of the first one listed here.

V

The second particular privilege and immunity can be considered a response to questionable *Executive* conduct. It is "the right of a citizen [of one State] to claim the benefit [in another State] of the writ of habeas corpus." I mention, in passing, that this too seems to question the *Barron* v. *Baltimore* principle.

This particular privilege and immunity is, it seems, one of the few, if not the only one, explicitly provided for in the body of the Constitution of 1789. How is it related to the guarantee (in Article IV of the Constitution) of a Republican Form of Government in every State in the Union? Are there other provisions similarly related to this guarantee?

Nothing more is said in *Corfield* about the *habeas corpus* assurance being in the Constitution. Did it matter? We can be again reminded of the *Barron* problem by wondering what the status is, both as privileges and immunities which are good against the States and as elements of a Republican Form of Government, of the rights enumerated in the Bill of Rights of 1791.

VI

Justice Washington's next particular is "[t]he right of a citizen . . . to institute and maintain actions of any kind in the courts of the State" to which he goes. This can be considered a critical privilege if the visiting citizen is to have useful access to the *Judiciary* wherever he is. It remains uncertain, however, how many of the assured privileges and immunities were to be vindicated in the courts.

Here, too, we have a right that can be traced back to Magna Carta. But, we must wonder, when it is said that an "action of any kind" may be maintained in the courts of a State, whether "any kind" is to be taken literally. Is the reference here to the actions of "any kind" which are available to the visitor only those actions which citizens of that State also have?

With this question we can recognize the possibility that the Privileges and Immunities Clause in Article IV may not have the scope either of the Republican Form of Government Guarantee or of the Bill of Rights. That is, the rights assured for the visitor may be limited to those that citizens of the visited States themselves have independent of the Constitution of the United States. But there does remain the requirement that States can be obliged, one way or another, to demonstrate that they are indeed extending to everyone else the privileges and immunities that they recognize for their own citizens.

VII

It may be that the enforcement of various rights depends, in large part, upon the demands of public opinion in a State, not primarily upon any government actions. Among the principles respected by public opinion are those that encourage and protect the acquisition and use of property. It comes as no surprise, then, that Justice Washington recognizes "[t]he right of a citizen . . . to take, hold, and dispose of property, either real or personal."

Precisely what property one does have can be very much a product of chance. But however property is acquired or identified, it is to be treated with considerable, if not even with the utmost, respect. The status of property is such that it can be made much of by Justice Washington both among his "general heads" and among "the particular privileges and immunities."

Also to be identified, one way or another, are the rights to which citizens are considered to be entitled. No limits seem to be anticipated as to the amount of property one might accumulate. Are there limits, however, to the rights that one may have consistent with the cohesiveness of a community and with the effectiveness of its governments?

VIII

Be this as it may, it is not assumed that one may retain forever all the property that one accumulates. After all, it *is* assumed that taxes may be levied. But one is likely to be protected here by the uniformity of the levying that is done.

This is evident enough among the citizens of a particular State. But it is critical as well for the sake of anyone from another State. He is assured of "an exemption from higher taxes or impositions than are paid by . . . citizens of the State."

One can be reminded here of the issues considered in *M'Culloch* v. *Maryland* (1819). One can also be reminded, once again, of the spirit of Magna Carta. That is, one can see again and again how common sense can be reinforced by a sense of fairness, and vice versa.

IX

All of these reassurances, it is said by Justice Washington in *Corfield*, "may be mentioned as some of the particular privileges and immunities of citizens." These are said by him to be "clearly embraced by the general description of privileges deemed to be fundamental." And then there comes something which appears almost as an afterthought, surprisingly so, for it is said by the Justice that there "may be added [to all the privileges and immunities that have been enumerated], the elective franchise, as regulated and established by the laws or constitution of the State in which it is to be exercised."

More is made here than was made earlier in the enumeration of the differences in regulations by the various States, something we are familiar with because of Electoral College–related differences among the States. This can mean, among other things, that the nonresident cannot simply show up in a State on election day and expect to participate in its balloting, just as (it turns out) the nonresident cannot simply show up and expect to fish when and where he wishes. Likewise today, we are told, the nonresident cannot expect to enjoy at once the tuition rates at State universities that tax-paying residents are entitled to.

Justice Washington's enumeration had begun with the right that one has to "[p]rotection by the government"; it ends with "the elective franchise," part of the process by which legitimate governments are established in this Union. It seems to be recognized, that is, that all one's rights, including those associated with property, depend upon governments that are properly organized and employed. Thereupon it can be recognized that there are "many other" "particular privileges" that "are, strictly speaking, privileges and immunities," the enjoyment of which "by the citizens of each State, in every other State, was manifestly calculated (to use an expression in the Preamble of the corresponding provision in the old Articles of Confederation), 'the better to secure and perpetuate mutual friendship and intercourse among the people of the different States of the Union.'"

8. *The Slaughter-House Cases* (1872): A False Start?

I

When I first came to Chicago to go to school in Hyde Park after the Second World War, one could, from time to time, smell the stockyards a few miles to the northwest. The city was then one of the principal sites in this Country for the slaughter of livestock. New Orleans, although much smaller, similarly dominated the livestock market in Eastern Louisiana in the late nineteenth century.

Our experience in Chicago could remind us that the collecting and slaughtering of animals can be the concern of the community at large, reaching far beyond those immediately engaged in such operations. Concerns of this kind were addressed in an Act passed by the Louisiana legislature in 1869 "granting to a corporation, created by [the Act], the exclusive right, for twenty-five years, to have and maintain slaughter-houses, landings for cattle, and yards for inclosing cattle for sale or slaughter" within three parishes (counties) of that State, and principally that in which New Orleans is located. It was held by the United States Supreme Court, the reporter of the *Slaughter-House Cases* tells us, "that this grant of exclusive right or privilege, guarded by proper limitation of the prices to be charged, and providing the duty of providing ample conveniences, with permission to all butchers to slaughter at those places, was a [proper] police regulation for the health and comfort of the people."

The parties bringing this suit, who included various butchers and associations of butchers in the New Orleans area, are described by the Supreme Court as having "relied upon, and asserted throughout the entire course of the litigation . . . that the grant of privileges in the charter . . . , which they are contesting, was a violation of the most important provisions of the [Thirteenth and Fourteenth Amendments]." Further on the Court reports, "This statute is denounced not only as creating a monopoly and conferring odious and exclusive privileges upon a small number of persons at the expense of the great body of the community of New Orleans, but it is [also] asserted that it deprives a large and meritorious class of citizens—the whole of the butchers of the city—of the rights to exercise their trade . . . ; and that the unrestricted exercise of the business of butchering is necessary to the daily subsistence of the population of the city." The Court then adds, "But a critical examination of the act hardly justifies these assertions."

II

There *were,* it seems, legitimate health concerns in the New Orleans area related to the operations of the slaughter-houses. Such concerns had been addressed theretofore in other cities as well, with various restrictions placed on where and how slaughter-house operations might be conducted, just as there are licenses provided for or restrictions routinely placed on the operations of public utilities. We can be reminded by these observations that there *is* usually, if not even always, something to be said for each position in a continuing controversy.

One of the dissenting Justices speaks of the favoritism shown, in the 1869 charter, toward a few. It was suspected, of course, that a minority of butchers profited substantially, because of their political connections, at the expense of all the others. Such favoritism could be resented as the commercial equivalent of the official titles of nobility prohibited by the Constitution of the United States.

A related issue here is whether the improper favoritism alleged with respect to the trade of butchering resulted in higher prices being charged to the consumers of meat products. This is the kind of concern that Congress, later in the nineteenth century, addressed as it developed an antitrust policy. The emphasis in 1873, however, is upon the alleged deprivations suffered by the butchers not empowered by the challenged charter, butchers who argued (for the most part) that their privileges and immunities had been abridged by the State, contrary to the assurances given in the Fourteenth Amendment.

III

The challenge in the *Slaughter-House Cases* is led by a former Justice of the United States Supreme Court who had served, during the Civil War, in the Government of the Confederate States of America. The conspiracy-minded might wonder what *he* as counsel was really after, especially when it is recognized that one result of this litigation was that the Country ended up, at least for a half-century thereafter, with a severely limited Fourteenth Amendment. But, in such matters, the long-run consequences should be distinguished from the kind of short-run advantage that can eventually be self-defeating.

The challengers of the 1869 Louisiana statute could draw upon centuries of suspicions of monopolies in the Anglo-American legal tradition. There had been a serious political crisis late in the reign of Elizabeth I because of the abuses of grants of monopolies, abuses which were eventually addressed comprehensively during the reign of her successor, James I. The recourse thereafter of Charles I to the revenues to be gotten from the grant of monopolies—a way of collecting revenues that avoided any royal dependence upon a balky Parliament—can be said to have contributed to the revolution which cost him his head.

This history was known, of course, to the *Slaughter-House* Justices. It can even be said that the Constitution, with its provisions for copyrights and patents (for *limited* terms) tacitly rules out the kinds of privileges once dispensed by the English monarchs. Reservations about the empowerment of a few at the expense of the many may already be seen in Magna Carta, something which can again remind us of how much of the political history of the English-speaking peoples bears on our constitutional developments.

IV

The *Slaughter-House* majority, in rejecting the challenges to the 1869 charter, severely limits the reach of the Privileges or Immunities Clause of the Fourteenth Amendment. An emphasis is placed on the primary (if not the virtually exclusive) concern of the Fourteenth Amendment being the welfare of the newly emancipated slaves. The rights that are recognized by this Court as of general application—such as the right to travel to the nation's capital—can seem to limit severely the extent of "privileges or immunities."

This *is* an odd way of dealing with the matter, considering how extensive the list of "Privileges and Immunities" was in the discussion of the matter by Justice Washington in *Corfield* v. *Coryell* (1823), a discussion of the Article IV Privileges and Immunities Clause several times referred to with approval by the *Slaughter-House* Justices. But then, Justice Washington himself had not found any "Privileges and Immunities" problem in the matter *he* had assessed. In fact, little has ever been *done* with the "Privileges and/or Immunities" language either in Article IV or in the Fourteenth Amendment.

Why this should be so remains a mystery. Perhaps the scope of this language is intimidating, providing no limits to the restraints that may be placed upon State governmental efforts. A list of particular privileges and immunities, such as in the 1791 Bill of Rights, can seem less threatening, except for the "open-ended" provision in its Ninth Amendment, which is somewhat like the two Privileges and/or Immunities Clauses.

V

Even so, one can sometimes wonder what the Civil War *was* all about. That a defense of slavery was critical, from its outset, to the Secession movement was obvious enough. But it also became obvious that the Unionist victors developed a determination to place severe limitations upon the scope of State sovereignty.

The extent of State sovereignty presupposed by the Secessionists is indicated by the States' Rights recognized in the Confederate Constitution of 1861. The Unionists, on the other hand, came to believe that there was no good reason why the Governments of the States should not be obliged to be as respectful of long-established rights (such as those enumerated in the 1791 Bill of Rights) as the General Government had to be. This kind of thinking had been anticipated by the approach taken by those who brought the case of *Barron v. Baltimore* (1833).

It should be remembered that a serious argument *could* be made, during the Ratification Campaign, that a bill of rights was not really needed, inasmuch as the rights that would be listed there were already possessed and exercised by the People of the United States. If such rights already bound the General Government, why should they not bind also the State Governments? This kind of argument could be reinforced by the observation that the General Government did have the duty to guarantee to each State in the Union a Republican Form of Government.

VI

The four dissenting Justices in the *Slaughter-House Cases* protested, in effect, that the Court was acting as if the Civil War had been of limited effect, constitutionally. But it was obvious enough that this was not so. This could even be seen in the composition of the Louisiana legislature that had enacted the 1869 statute under review: it was, at least for awhile, a racially integrated (Reconstruction-era) legislature.

One consequence of litigation such as that in the *Slaughter-House Cases* is that the relevant issues can be dramatized. A judicial decision can seem to "settle" the issues, at least for the immediate parties. But, it can once again be said, fundamental issues are not settled until they are "settled right."

And, it might also be said, the *Slaughter-House* issues were not properly settled until the People had had *their* say. This took the form of the repeal of the relevant *Slaughter-House* statute a few years after the decision in this litigation. In some situations, it seems, the political correction is more effective than whatever judges may provide, something that may be seen, for example, in the difficulties encountered when the Executive goes to war without the explicit Legislative authorization (with all the facts "on the table") that anticipates and legitimates, in effect, the sacrifices that will be needed.

VII

It can be partly a matter of chance what constitutional provisions and what arguments are effective from time to time. Sometimes the official language that is promulgated can seem to take on a life of its own, no matter what may have been originally intended. This may be seen in the influence, for more than seven hundred years now, of key provisions in Magna Carta.

This may be seen as well in what has happened with the Declaration of Independence, the document recognized in one of the *Slaughter-House* Dissenting Opinions as fundamental to the American regime. One consequence of this in the United States, partly in response to the troubling expansion of slavery, may have been a shift in emphasis from *liberty* to *equality* as vital to the meaning of our regime. Is it this that seems to have contributed to the growing passion for unregulated gun ownership in this Country, with firearms becoming particularly attractive as "equalizers"?

There can be unpredictable factors and consequences in such developments. Thus, it may well be that one condition for upholding the *Slaughter-House* statute was the then-prevailing opinion about the limited scope of the Commerce Clause. But when technology and an ever-more-complicated world economy made it seem necessary that Congress should be recognized as having a quite broad Commerce Power, it could be expected that State efforts to dole out economic privileges would fall into disfavor, or would even be ultimately futile, as would be the judicial Opinions and the scholarship crafted for another era.

VIII

However all this may be, it should have been expected, as a long-term consequence of the Civil War, that most if not all of the traditional rights that can be invoked against the General Government should eventually be applicable against State Governments as well. The then-recent rebellious conduct of the Governments of a dozen slave States testified to the need for their supervision by a superior authority, the People of the United States or that People's General Government. Such supervision included, it has turned out, the insistence that the State Governments would be obliged to respect virtually all, if not even all, of the rights that the General Government had long been bound to respect.

The simplest way to have done this would probably have been through the use of the Privileges or Immunities Clause of the Fourteenth Amendment. But the *Slaughter-House* Court, having "legislated" a quite limited scope for that Clause, made that way of proceeding difficult. Another path to have taken would have been by way of the Republican Form of Government Guarantee, but that would have been rather awkward, inasmuch as that guarantee had barely been used before the Civil War—and it must have seemed that the war (despite President Lincoln's invocation of the guarantee) had not sufficiently invigorated it.

What has been done instead, by a piecemeal method extending over more than a half-century, is the "incorporation" of virtually all of the Bill of Rights provisions, as applicable against the States, by using the Due Process Clause of the Fourteenth Amendment. And thus we have what is known as "substantive due process," which means, among other things, that the Fourteenth Amendment "due process" language must be read quite differently from identical language in the Fifth Amendment. This can seem peculiar— but what the Supreme Court has done thereby is to manipulate language that serves as the practical equivalent of the "Privileges or Immunities" language that had been denied its intended scope by that Court.

IX

There can be said about the scope of the Fourteenth Amendment what can also be said about the scope of the Commerce Clause, that sensible judges and legislators will accommodate constitutional interpretations to modern circumstances, one way or another. Sometimes, because of earlier misconstructions, this has to be done at the expense of a disciplined reading of the Constitution. However useful, if not even necessary, these accommodations can be in the short run (because of earlier false steps), they *can* undermine an enduring respect for constitutional principles.

We can wonder to what extent misreadings of the Constitution may even have contributed to the Civil War. But whatever the causes of that war, it did contribute to the eventual empowerment of the opinion that all who live in the United States should be free, at least so long as they behave themselves. Considerable effort continues to be required to determine what should be included in the "freedom" to which all are now said to be entitled.

The easiest part of this process of determination has been accomplished. That is, there *is* now the insistence that all governments in the United States are obliged to respect most of the traditional rights (the "Privileges or Immunities") of the English-speaking peoples, with no discrimination permitted that singles out any law-abiding segment of the population for adverse treatment. It remains to be seen, however, whether newly fashioned (or, perhaps it would be better to say, newly discovered) rights, such as those associated with the desire for privacy or with the desire for sexual fulfillment, can properly (some might even say, naturally) be discovered in a Constitution that has such provisions as the Ninth Amendment to reckon with.

9. *The Civil Rights Cases* (1883);
Plessy v. *Ferguson* (1896): More False Starts?

I

The Civil Rights Act of 1875 was declared by a near-unanimous United States Supreme Court, in 1883, to be unconstitutional. Section 1 of the Act provided: "That all persons within the jurisdiction of the United States shall be entitled to the full and equal enjoyment of the accommodations, advantages, facilities, and privileges of inns, public conveyances on land or water, theaters, and other places of public amusement." Thus, the activities covered are in the more or less public associations for which people are likely to pay something.

It is also likely that those providing the services involved here were licensed, or at least carefully monitored, by State or local officials wherever they operated. Today we might even talk of these operators as having a quasi-public status. Certainly, even then, a State could have made "full and equal enjoyment" as a condition of the activities licensed or otherwise supervised by the State.

The concern of Congress is evident in the language that follows the passage which I have quoted from Section I of the 1875 Civil Rights Act: "subject only to the conditions and limitations established by law, and applicable alike to citizens of every race and color, regardless of any previous condition of servitude." It is evident, that is, that this measure represented an effort, a decade after the Civil War, to help the recently emancipated slaves begin to be integrated into the public life of the communities in which they lived. Congress can be understood to have taken the position that such efforts, affecting social relations in this Country, were needed if the provisions of the Thirteenth and Fourteenth Amendments were to be effective in securing the liberty of the freedmen.

II

The Supreme Court, in invalidating the Civil Rights Act of 1875 with respect to the challenged regulations, argued that only "State action" can be controlled by the use of the powers provided to Congress in the Fourteenth Amendment. The Tenth Amendment was invoked by the Court. Virtually all that the Civil War did, by way of the post–Civil War amendments, the Court suggested, was to emancipate the slaves.

This means that offensive "private" actions, with respect to race relations, are not within the domain of Congress to control. Otherwise, it was feared, the State legislatures could eventually be replaced by Congress. However traumatic the Civil War may have been, the Court argued, it did not make so fundamental a change in constitutional relations in this Country.

But since the Congress had not gone *that* far, the Court could at least have said that the various commercial enterprises covered by the Civil Rights Act depended upon access to the police power of the State for secure and successful operations. And, the Court could have added, "State action" is relied upon by such enterprises in order to enforce any racially discriminatory policies. But the Court was not inclined thus to find a way which would permit this 1875 Act of Congress to pass constitutional muster.

III

A reconsideration of what "State action" means is called for here, assuming that that is indeed required to make the Thirteenth and Fourteenth Amendments applicable. Suppose there are two States, side by side geographically and with similar distributions therein of racial groups. And suppose further that the operators of their inns, public conveyances, and theaters discriminate racially, at least to the extent of providing separate but equal facilities.

The activities we can see in the two States would be comprehensible to those who know the makeup and the history of each of these States. Should it matter, in assessing what is happening, if one State has a law explicitly mandating such discrimination while the other does not? Is it not highly likely that the law in the former State merely confirms, or testifies to, the quite similar social pressures (or unwritten laws) that account for the discrimination evident in both States?

A dose of realism is called for here as we look behind the mask. That is, the laws on the books in such circumstances often do no more than confirm the community opinions and forces which are ultimately responsible for the obvious discrimination. This, it can be said (but not by the 1883 Court), is what Congress recognized in 1875 when it decided (like Captain Ahab?) to strike through the mask at the forces that dictated the proscribed conduct.

IV

An odd feature of the Court's Opinion in the *Civil Rights Cases* is its concession that perhaps a different result (with respect to the constitutionality issue) would have been called for if another provision of the Constitution, such as the Commerce Clause, had been invoked by the defenders of the Act of Congress. Why should not the Court itself have made certain (even by calling for briefs on this subject) that there was *no* provision in the Constitution that permitted Congress to do what it had done? Does not the unwillingness of the Court to do this tend to turn constitutional litigation into a game?

It should be remembered that there is nothing in the Constitution which requires Congress to designate the Constitutional provision it is relying upon when it passes a Bill. If the Congress is to be required to *cite* authority for its actions, should not the Supreme Court be likewise required? After all, we have noticed that there is nothing in the Constitution that explicitly authorizes the Supreme Court to review Acts of Congress for their constitutionality.

Of course, the Commerce Clause did come to be used by Congress, almost a century after the *Civil Rights Cases,* to do what the 1875 Congress had tried to do. One dubious consequence of this has been to make more of an economic rationale than of a moral rationale, obscuring thereby what the sacrifices of the Civil War had been about. The full force of the educative power of the law is dissipated when this is the way that high principles are substituted for.

V

Perhaps the most remarkable feature of the *Civil Rights Cases* and of *Plessy* v. *Ferguson* is how Justice John Marshall Harlan (a vigorous champion of property rights) dissented in both cases. His responses can seem even more impressive when it is recalled that he had been, back in Kentucky, a slaveholding Unionist who had opposed ratification of the Thirteenth Amendment. On the other hand, the rulings by his colleagues in these two cases have long been repudiated, having been no more than unseemly delaying actions.

That is, it can be said of Justice Harlan that he recognized, as a judge, the profound consequences of the Civil War, a war which included for him the commendable contributions made by men of African descent who fought to preserve the Union. Particularly telling were his observations, in his *Civil Rights Cases* dissent, that the Court should permit Congress to find, in the Thirteenth and Fourteenth Amendments, as much authority to minister to the freedmen as the Court had permitted Congress to find authority, in the Fugitive Slave Clause (of Article IV), to help owners to recover their fugitive slaves. This was indeed a Solomon come to judgment.

Justice Harlan could also attempt to make use, on behalf of the emancipated slaves, of the Republican Form of Government Guarantee. The Justice's heroic efforts here are to be contrasted to the questionable efforts by his successors on the United States Supreme Court on behalf of "federalism" in our own time. Furthermore, the original (or genuine) John Marshall Harlan would surely never have argued, as was done in the revealing case of *Cohen* v. *California* (1971), that "one man's vulgarity is another's lyric."

VI

The Supreme Court had insisted in the *Civil Rights Cases* that "State action" was required to permit Congress to do what it had tried to do in 1875. In the *Plessy* case, a decade after the *Civil Rights Cases,* there *was* State action involved. This was the 1890 Louisiana legislation which required "that all railway companies carrying passengers in their coaches in this state, shall provide equal but separate accommodations for the white and colored races by providing two or more passenger coaches for each passenger train, or by dividing the passenger coaches by a partition so as to secure separate accommodations."

The question here, according to the Court, was not whether there had been State legislation, but rather whether it discriminated against freedmen. Nor did it seem to matter to the Court whether there had been Congressional legislation attempting to suppress such practices. The question was, instead, whether the Thirteenth and Fourteenth Amendments invalidated the State legislation relied on here.

The Court recognized that racial prejudices may have contributed to this State legislation. But, it argued, such prejudice is beyond the power of government to eliminate. We can suspect, however, that once private actions are immunized by a "State action" requirement (as in the *Civil Rights Cases*), then it is likely that the prejudice thereby protected will find expression in legislation designed to keep the disfavored race "in its place."

VII

We can see, in the series of cases that chanced to develop from *Slaughter-House* to *Plessy* and beyond, what changes in circumstances can do to Supreme Court doctrines. Particularly critical here is the passage of time that there had been since the Civil War. The passions of the war receded as people at large settled into their private pursuits.

One feature of the post–Civil War developments was the depreciation of the Commerce Clause power of Congress, a depreciation promoted by vigorous business interests. This continued the depreciation that the proslavery interests had promoted before the war. It was not until the late 1930s that circumstances had changed enough to induce the Supreme Court to recognize *once again* the original extent of the Commerce Clause that had been recognized by Chief Justice Marshall and his colleagues a century earlier.

The waning of Civil War passions did make the Supreme Court, and thereafter the Congress, less inclined to insist upon proper treatment of the freedmen. Indeed, the Court could even protest that people freed from slavery should (by that time [1896]) be able to stand on their own without support from governments. That protest can seem, more than a century later, to have been naively premature—but this sort of defensive maneuver can perhaps be expected when passions have been excruciating.

VIII

The "separate but equal" approach had, by the time of *Plessy*, already been relied upon in public schools. Whether truly equal facilities are objectionable can be argued, especially if the group cordoned off is fairly confident of its superiority in critical respects. But, as a practical matter, it must be rare that separate facilities *remain* equal, inasmuch as those in control of budgets are highly likely to favor "their own."

Consider how W.E.B. Du Bois, in his 1903 book *The Souls of Black Folk,* describes the conditions that develop. First, there is a recognition (in his account of a train trip across the South) of the plight of others besides the freedmen and their descendants:

> But we must hasten on our journey. This that we pass as we leave Atlanta is the ancient land of the Cherokees,—that brave Indian nation which strove so long for its fatherland, until Fate and the United States drove them beyond the Mississippi.

Then he adds:

> If you [as a white man] wish to ride with me you must come into the "Jim Crow Car." There will be no objection,—already four other white men, and a little white girl with her nurse, are in there. Usually the races are mixed in there, but the white coach is all white.

Thus, we can see, it is difficult to retain the equality of separate facilities: one of the railroad cars is strictly policed, while the other car is not. Then Du Bois notices:

> Of course, this [nonwhite] car is not so good as the other, but it is fairly clean and comfortable. The discomfort lies chiefly in the hearts of those four black men yonder—and in mine.

In short, sustained forced separation, however it is explained and justified, is likely to be resented by the spirited among those *treated* as inferior, something which is reflected in Du Bois's determination (in 1961, two years before his death at age ninety-five) to leave the United States for Ghana, where he renounced his American citizenship (after becoming a citizen of Ghana).

IX

However that may be, the condition of racial minorities does seem to have improved substantially during the past half-century. The Second World War contributed to this development, especially as more than ten million young Americans were shown the world in the course of their military service. Then there came the Cold War, during which it became expedient for the United States plausibly to display itself to the rest of the world as rising above its longstanding racial prejudices.

When circumstances changed as radically as they have for us since the Great Depression, it was likely that the Supreme Court, among others, would come to recognize how broad the powers of Congress were originally intended to be. We can see that movement in what the pressures of economic globalization have been doing to judicial readings of the Commerce Clause. That is, it can become "obvious" what "has" to be done by *some* government in the United States.

Fortunately, the Framers of the Constitution did so arrange matters as to permit our General Government to be recognized as having powers comparable to those of the governments of other modern States. What they did *not* provide is a wide-ranging power in the United States Supreme Court to nullify Acts of Congress as "unconstitutional," whatever that Court may properly do to protect its own powers and to guarantee the integrity of its processes. Still, it is salutary to acknowledge that the Court *has* contributed to the promotion of racial justice and economic well-being in the United States during the past seven decades, abandoning thereby the presumptuous and crippling dogmas of its judicial predecessors for almost a century.

10. *Shelley* v. *Kraemer* (1948); *Brown* v. *Board of Education* (1954, 1955)

I

Changes in race relations in the United States were "in the wind" after the Second World War. Racial segregation was still very much in evidence in much of the South, something which could disturb Northern servicemen stationed in that part of the Country during the war. Additional challenges to racial segregation came from around the world as the United States developed its Cold War foreign policies.

Such challenges drew, in large part, on widely accepted opinions both about human decency and social justice and about an effective use of resources. Less salutary were the challenges to segregation that questioned the right and the duty of a community to promote *any* standard of morality, not only those standards grounded in racial prejudice. But such challengers, who can make much of an advocacy of an unbridled individualism, do not appreciate that the most enduring repudiation of segregation depends upon the moral sense of a properly trained community.

The training provided by a community, both "officially" and "unofficially," is likely to be reflected in the language that is used by the People at large. Thus we can hear, over a century, shifts in how our most obvious minority is called by well-wishers, ranging from "Colored" (as in the "National Association for the Advancement of Colored People"), to "Negro" (as in the "Negro Baseball League"), then to "Black" (with which there *are* problems), and now to "African American." Instructive controversies can develop as to what the most respectful name is, as may be heard as well when an attempt is made to identify those peoples who lived on this continent before 1492.

II

The first of the cases to be noticed here is *Shelley* v. *Kraemer,* the 1948 litigation that invalidated racially restrictive covenants, at least so far as they depend upon judicial proceedings to enforce their provisions. Such judicial proceedings are now regarded as instances of those "State actions" which are properly subject to review pursuant to Section 1 of the Fourteenth Amendment. A significant shift in the general opinion is suggested by the recognition that similar recognition of "State action" could have been discovered by the United States Supreme Court in such litigation as the *Civil Rights Cases* of 1883.

After all, the segregation practices in 1883 of transportation companies, theaters, and the like were reinforced by the recognition that law enforcement officers could be summoned by proprietors encountering members of any excluded minority who insisted upon being treated like the rest of the paying public. This is aside from whatever "State action" is implicit in the licensing and other regulations that there may be for such publicly oriented facilities. This is also aside from any question there may be about whether Section 1 of the Fourteenth Amendment does in fact limit Congress to the regulation only of "State actions."

However all this may be, *Shelley* v. *Kraemer* was a significant step in the process of demolishing officially recognized racial discrimination in this Country. But neither it nor *Brown* v. *Board of Education* (six years later) was as much of a break with the past as it may have seemed. The student of law was familiar, well before 1948, with a line of cases, reaching back two decades, if not even more, that anticipated what was done in *Shelley* and *Brown*.

III

Shelley v. *Kraemer* threatened to undermine measures that promoted residential segregation. Would this, in turn, tend to undermine racial segregation in schools, especially in the lower grades? Also difficult to maintain are separate publicly funded school systems that remain substantially equal in the resources devoted to them, especially since people are naturally inclined to favor their own.

We have seen, in quotations from W.E.B. Du Bois's 1903 account, how inconvenient it could be to attempt to police strict separation of the races in this Country. A half-century later, it had become generally evident that separateness meant an inequality in the resources available to the weaker contenders in the struggle for public funds. Then there were the disturbing effects on those who were being told, in effect, that they were not good enough to associate (even as youngsters) with the dominant race in the Country.

The most remarkable feature of *Brown* v. *Board,* therefore, was *not* that the Court ruled as it did. Rather, it was that Chief Justice Earl Warren managed to get all of the Court to agree to one Opinion, with no concurrences, something that his recently deceased predecessor probably would not have been able to do. This is even more remarkable when it is remembered that Earl Warren had not, as a California State official, conducted himself properly during the development of the Japanese Relocation Program, something that he did come to regret.

IV

There were, of course, compromises that had to be made to secure unanimity in *Brown,* something that became evident during the following decades as the Supreme Court fashioned the remedies appropriate for its invalidations of the "separate but equal" systems, invalidations which steadily reached beyond education. The first of these efforts was seen in *Brown* v. *Board of Education II,* in which the famous language, "with all deliberate speed," can be found. The Court concluded, that is, that conditions so varied throughout the Country that no single remedy was available, or at least no remedy that could be readily implemented.

This was in marked contrast to the greater progress made during the 1950s in the integration of the armed forces following upon an Executive Order to that effect. It took a generation after *Brown* before political men and women in various parts of the Country could "afford" to stand politically for racial integration, however segregated many school systems have remained (or have once again become) in practice. Politicians were encouraged to endorse racial integration, of course, once the Voting Rights Act of 1965 added significant numbers of African Americans to the election rolls.

The most critical effect of the Supreme Court, in cases such as *Brown,* was not what it "did" to invalidate segregation laws and provide for their replacement. Important as that was, it was far more important that the Court had *said* what it did, however inelegantly. That is, legally mandated racial segregation came generally to be thought of as "unthinkable," promoting thereby the development of a new generation of citizens who would "know better" than their parents and grandparents, thereby making it easier in the future for the community to try to do the right thing, something that post–Civil War Congresses had tried to do before encountering resistance from the Supreme Court and others.

V

The lessons learned by the community at large are not apt to be the most refined that are available. This was seen during a Presidential Debate in October 2004 when an eminent politician made a hash of *Dred Scott* (1857) and its reading of the Constitution—and could do so without others recognizing it. One should not expect too much in such situations.

But then, the Supreme Court's own reading of the Constitution is not always reliable. Thus, even as the Court maintained an anti-segregation line in the 1950s, it did not distinguish itself during that same period in its responses to the security-minded repressiveness that tended to cripple the political processes of this Country, perhaps contributing thereby to our Vietnam debacle. That is, the First Amendment tended to be neglected even as the racial policy of the Fourteenth Amendment came to be recognized somewhat as its framers intended.

We can again be reminded by all this of the tension in the American regime between *liberty* and *equality.* This can be understood as the tension between an aspiration for *excellence,* on the one hand, and the pursuit of *justice,* on the other. It is justice that a judicial system can properly be expected to favor when these two worthy objectives are placed in opposition to each other.

VI

It is today once again a time when security concerns can override liberty interests, however much it can be argued that an enduring security, at least among us in this Country, depends upon a disciplined liberty. It *is* politically difficult to make the argument that our security concerns are exaggerated. Thus, one does not hear suggestions, at least from politicians concerned about their careers, that the September Eleventh attacks were not as serious as they have been made out to be, that most of the subsequent damage that we suffered was self-inflicted.

Such timidity upon the part of practicing politicians is not altogether undesirable. After all, it tends to make for a healthier society among us that no prominent politician today dares to stand for racial segregation, whatever he may personally believe. But timidity may also keep the ambitious from suggesting, at least for awhile, that many of our recent security measures have been ill-conceived.

Another way of putting all this is to say that there is "a lot of ruin" in a well-founded regime. It can eventually right itself, when it goes off course, so long as fundamental principles can be intelligently invoked—now and then, here and there—by a few in the community. It is this that was done, for two centuries, by those who opposed systematic racial discrimination (beginning with slavery)—it is this that was done, that is, by those who insisted (sometimes recklessly) that Americans were obliged to respect the proposition that "all Men are created equal."

VII

We can be reminded of how much circumstances may affect constitutional adjudication when we notice the unanimity, or near-unanimity, of the Supreme Court in cases as diverse as *Shelley* v. *Kraemer* and *Brown* v. *Board,* on the one hand, and the *Civil Rights Cases* and *Plessy* v. *Ferguson,* on the other. The modern Court was evidently affected by the battles that had had to be fought against the deadly racism of the Nazis during the Second World War. It was this challenge which had found Americans disregarding their prejudices as they allied themselves (in 1938) with Joe Louis against Max Schmeling.

The Cold War was more complicated in its effects. It did encourage the United States, in its appeal to the peoples of the world against the blandishments of the Soviet Union, to stand for racial equality at home. But at the same time it also made it seem dangerous to rely, as much as we once had, upon First Amendment freedoms.

But however we understand the "forces" that move nations and their institutions, we should not exaggerate the powers of courts. Louis Fisher, for example, has observed:

> What finally turned the tide [against racial discrimination in the United States] were a series of Legislative enactments: the Civil Rights Act of 1964; the Voting Rights Act of 1965; and the Fair Housing Act of 1968. The struggle against racial discrimination

required the conscientious effort of all three branches [of the Government of the United States].

Still, it should be added that although Congress is, at least on paper, the dominant branch in the Government provided for in the United States Constitution, its Members, like the public at large, *can* be influenced by the salutary lessons that the Supreme Court chances to teach from time to time.

VIII

The limitations of Courts are suggested, curiously enough, in *Bolling* v. *Sharpe* (1954), the companion case to *Brown* v. *Board of Education I. Bolling* challenged the segregation practices then routine in the public schools of the District of Columbia. It must have seemed to the Supreme Court that it would be politically impossible for it to invalidate State segregation practices without doing the same for District of Columbia practices.

And yet, the Equal Protection Clause of the Fourteenth Amendment, which had been relied upon in *Shelley* and *Brown,* obviously did not address the Congressional authority upon which District segregation depended. So the Court looked to the Due Process Clause of the Fifth Amendment to justify its invalidation of District of Columbia segregation practices. But if "due process" could be understood and used thus, then the Fourteenth Amendment, which has its own Due Process Clause, had not needed its Equal Protection Clause.

Should Congress have been relied upon to correct practices in the District of Columbia, once the Court had spoken as it did in *Brown?* On the other hand, considering the size and complexity of the Country, should not someone (that is, the General Government) be left empowered to segregate on occasion? These and like questions probably did not much interest the Court—and so (once again?) it set rigor in constitutional interpretation aside as it bowed to what it probably considered the political necessities of the moment, however questionable a lesson it provided thereby in constitutional interpretation.

IX

Still another dubious lesson is provided by the authorities relied upon by the Supreme Court in *Brown* v. *Board of Education I.* Modern arguments and authorities are invoked to support the Court's use of the Four-teenth Amendment. This is in the course of its insistence that *separate* can never be *equal*.

Whether this is so can be questioned. Indeed, it has even been questioned by some minority spokesmen who argue that their children may need schools of their own if they are to overcome the damage long done by society at large in their communities. But, aside from all this, there *is* the problem left by the *Brown* Court's relying as much as it did upon the findings of social science (as in its much-commented-on Note 11) to bolster its conclusions in 1954.

Still, it is not so much what was used that can be troubling, but rather what was ignored in the process. It is astonishing that the Declaration of Independence, with its invocation of an intrinsic equality among human beings, should have been neglected. All this is not to deny, however, that *Brown* v. *Board of Education* has had a profound effect, generally for the good; but it *is* to wonder whether it could have done even more good if its authors (or rather, *their* teachers) had been more soundly grounded in the enduring principles of the American regime.

11. Affirmative Action and the Fourteenth Amendment

I

Practice, as well as guidance, is needed for an effective *observation* of the things that are routinely *seen* by us that bear on race relations in this Country. Consider, for example, what can be learned upon noticing the complexion of the crowds evident these days on television screenings of baseball, basketball, and football games. It can seem that those crowds are ninety-nine percent white.

The same can be said, of course, about the adults in attendance at art museums, symphony halls, opera houses, and (except for the presence of "Asians") the more prestigious universities. But the sporting events are significantly different and hence revealing in that the athletes observed, unlike the crowds in attendance, draw heavily on the racial minorities among us. This should remind us of the considerable interest in such sports in those communities.

The scarcity of people of a darker hue in our sports crowds is probably due, in part, to financial disabilities. But those disabilities themselves reflect the relative inability of some groups among us to develop and market the (nonathletic) talents they may be born with. And this in turn reflects, even as it perpetuates, the separate paths, or ways of life, still followed by diverse groups in this Country.

II

Although racial separation is no longer required by law, the consequences of centuries-long separation seem to remain with us. This may be observed, for example, in the restaurants we visit: there is usually no color-bar that keeps out anyone who has the money and is well-behaved. Even so, those seated at any particular table will typically be of one "color," as is likely to be true as well in churches, college dining rooms, and other institutions.

Ever since the Civil War, efforts have been made from time to time by governments in this Country to help, first, the emancipated slaves and, thereafter, their descendants to develop and use their talents. This has been done for the sake both of such people and of the community at large. Similar efforts are also made by the often-troubled Bureau of Indian Affairs and by the Veterans Administration (with the post–Second World War provision of "G.I. Bill" benefits being one of the most successful government programs in our history).

The partisans of our minorities-enhancement programs prefer to speak of them as "affirmative action." Critics, on the other hand, are likely to disparage them as "quotas" and even as "reverse discrimination." All parties to the relevant controversies here (however diverse their objectives) do seem to be agreed, upon reflection, that it can be hard to determine what "works" (and for how long) when social engineering is undertaken.

III

The suspicion of "quotas" is evident in the first major race-related "affirmative action" case in modern times, *Regents of the University of California Board* v. *Bakke* (1978). We can see there the resentment that can be aroused on behalf of a citizen who has had someone else of inferior technical qualifications preferred instead of him for a coveted privilege. Such resentment may be even more vigorously acted upon when the citizen passed over has been well-served by the "system" theretofore, if only because he has the wherewithal, the sophistication, and the aid of like-minded beneficiaries of the overall system to press his claims.

Medical schools, we are told, are not as able as other professional schools to expand class size on any particular occasion. A good medical school is apt to have many more qualified applicants to choose from than can be accepted. And, as was the situation for the medical school involved in the *Bakke Case*, it was known by the school administration that if applicants were selected solely on the basis of merit as determined by standard grades, tests, and the like, few if any of the *qualified* African American applicants would be admitted—and this led to setting aside a fixed number of the available places for them.

Justice Lewis F. Powell's Opinion in *Bakke*—a Concurring Opinion that proved for decades to be the most authoritative—argued that the *Bakke* arrangement depended on an improper "quota" approach. He recommended instead an approach identified as that relied upon by Harvard University to secure the desired diversity in the student body admitted to its College. But it should not take much sophistication to figure out that the Harvard authorities would adjust the weight given to various factors if they were not getting the desired racial diversity in their College population.

IV

Is the lack of candor in effect endorsed by the Powell Opinion in *Bakke* a form of deception that is politically salutary? Another Powell, as Secretary of State, acknowledged, and endorsed, the affirmative action program that had made possible his distinguished military career. This kind of acknowledgment is something that other distinguished beneficiaries are all too often reluctant to make once they find themselves in high office, with such reluctance reflecting the disrepute associated, from time to time, with something that can be disparaged as "reverse discrimination."

The passions aroused by this issue may well suggest to the moderate citizen that this controversy should be avoided if that can reasonably be done. Certainly, students in the better schools (who are, of course, predominantly white) simply do not want to speak publicly against affirmative action lest they be condemned as racists engaging in a form of Hate Speech. This can include students who feel that they, or others like them (including firemen and policemen), have been "cheated" by a system that does not proceed simply according to the recognized standards of merit.

Still, such students may, when properly instructed, be equipped to recognize how cheated many African Americans often feel when they notice that although their families have been here much longer (sometimes centuries longer) than the families of most of the rest of us, they tend to be significantly less privileged than the late-comers. Even so, African Americans tend to be far better off, at least financially, than descendants of those tribes who have been here even longer. Such observations should encourage us to wonder what policies and consequences are apt to be best, in the long run, for the community at large.

V

Much is to be said, of course, for having the more talented members of the diverse groups in our community be reliably familiar with respectable representatives of all other groups, especially in our racially divided cities. Much is also to be said for making the best possible use of the talents and energy of everyone in the community, and not only in athletics (as was seen in the 2004 Olympics). Both personal safety and social justice should encourage a determined inclusiveness.

Why the problems encountered here should be as chronic as they seem to be remains both a mystery and a challenge, especially when one notices the remarkable successes in this Country of other peoples who have been much imposed upon elsewhere. Perhaps it would be useful to reflect upon the distinction suggested somewhere by Etienne Gilson, in accounting for the differences between St. Augustine and St. Thomas Aquinas—the profound differences between the *freedman* and the *freeman.* Our inquiries and speculations here are bound to take account of our authoritative proposition, that "all Men are created equal."

However all this may be, the high unemployment rate among the young men in our most prominent minority should be troubling—and would be vigorously dealt with by the General Government if that rate were encountered in the population at large. It is a sad state of affairs when the most racially integrated institutions among us are the military, sports teams, and prisons. Perhaps there is hope to be gotten from the growing integration of our Legislative bodies, something much advanced by the Voting Rights Act of 1965.

VI

We can turn now to two cases challenging University of Michigan affirmative action practices that were decided in 2003. If the student body could simply be drawn, by lot, from all *qualified* applicants, then a substantial number of minority members would likely be assembled. But many, perhaps most, of the *very best* in all groups would likely be lost thereby, something that even the affirmative action partisan would be troubled by—for there are contributions we do get from the very best that no one else can provide.

The first of our 2003 Michigan cases, *Gratz* v. *Bollinger,* assesses an admission policy that did permit the very best to be secured, even as it provided minority members enough points to rank higher than they otherwise would. This was seen by the Supreme Court to be, in effect, a race-based quota, and as such in violation of the Equal Protection Clause of the

Fourteenth Amendment. Justice Ruth Bader Ginsburg, in her Dissenting Opinion, suggests that the University of Michigan was being penalized for its candor.

Of course, the radical solution that would avoid the affirmative action measures that are resorted to from time to time would be to develop, early on, the talents of the children of deprived families. Thus, more reliance upon effective Head Start programs can be advocated as an alternative to affirmative action. But that means, among other things, that no substantial racial diversity can be expected for at least another generation, *if then.*

VII

"Everyone" senses that something more is needed immediately. This has led (in Texas and elsewhere) to reliance upon a policy that guarantees the upper rank (say, ten percent) of graduates from a State's high schools automatic admission to the principal State university. Racial diversity is made likely where this arrangement is relied upon.

This mechanical approach does depend, however, upon the existence of a substantially segregated high school system. Such segregation is, of course, no longer required by law. But it does reflect the *de facto* (not any obviously *de jure*) residential segregation.

One consequence of this arrangement, not readily recognized, is that the top rank in an inferior minority-dominated school may not be as well-prepared as minority students well below the top rank in other schools. Thus, a mechanical approach can mean that the best minority students in a State are not the ones selected for *the* university. This is the kind of thing that can happen when reliance upon judgment is ruled out altogether and chance is relied upon instead.

VIII

The other 2003 Michigan case, *Grutter* v. *Bollinger,* dealt with the admissions policy of a first-rate law school. It is recognized that no "automatic ten percent" rule can be relied upon there, inasmuch as the pool of students drawn upon is nationwide. It is also recognized that if a completely color-blind approach should be used, there would be few minority students in the typical class, something that would be politically difficult to justify as well as harmful (it is said) for the education of the students drawn from the dominant population.

Thus, the Court had here something comparable to the *Bakke*-type situation. And (partly because judges *are* apt to know the problems law schools face) the Court looked to the Powell Opinion in *Bakke* for guidance, seeing in the Michigan Law School arrangement a variation of the acceptable "Harvard College" approach. This is the sort of response that Justice Ginsburg can regard as lacking in candor.

A curious feature of the *Grutter Case* is Justice Clarence Thomas's insistence that a twenty-five-year limit has been set by the Court for the Michigan Law School approach. It is an insistence by him (someone who once evidently benefitted, properly enough, from affirmative-action programs) that simply misreads what Justice Sandra Day O'Connor had said in her Opinion for the Court. And it can help us see how much one's prized reliance upon "the original understanding of the Constitution" can appear to be warped by one's passions.

IX

There *are* rules to be respected in a constitutional system. But there are also the enduring objectives that the rules are intended to serve. Thus, the "domestic Tranquility" extolled in the Preamble to the Constitution depends in part on racial harmony, a harmony made more likely if the talents of all are, and also seem to be, conscientiously developed, thereby elevating as well the general competence of the community.

The duty and power here of the General Government should be recognized far more than it is. It should again be noticed, for example, that the General Government is *not* limited by the Fourteenth Amendment. Rather, Congress is empowered to advance the objectives of the Fourteenth Amendment, and this it should be able to try to do by recourse to race-conscious mandates that take account of the ever-changing circumstances of the day.

Congress should be reminded here of Justice Harlan's suggestion in his 1883 *Civil Rights Cases* dissent, that Congress should be permitted to do as much on behalf of emancipated slaves as Congress had once been permitted to do on behalf of slaveowners. It should not be denied that considerable progress has been made in race relations in this Country, even as one is confronted by such recent observations as this 2004 comment by a University of Chicago administrator:

The University of Chicago has done a great job diversifying the student body. When I [first came here more than thirty years ago], it was a very white place and five years ago most of the ethnic students were East Asian. But now I see people from South and Middle Asia, Middle Eastern and Latino students, which is a really wonderful thing. Troublesome, though, is the fact that the number of [African American] students hasn't increased.

It would be salutary if our General Government should at least exhibit itself as troubled by such observations about the condition of this minority group, rather than have its Executive branch file the amicus briefs it did in the Supreme Court questioning the conscientious efforts that the University of Michigan authorities had made in addressing a chronic threat both to insuring our domestic tranquility and to establishing justice among us in a reliable fashion.

12. *San Antonio Independent School District* v. *Rodriguez* (1973)

I

The *Rodriguez* plaintiffs, identified as "Mexican American" parents with children in the San Antonio public school system, complained that their schools had far fewer resources allocated to them than did some other public schools in the area. Those resources were derived primarily from local property taxes, supplemented by some funds from the State treasury. The schools are established pursuant to State law, as are the revenue provisions relied upon.

These Mexican Americans are part of the Latino (or Hispanic) community, which is now said to be the largest minority population in the United States. They seem to make up one-fourth of the population of Texas. There, as elsewhere, their economic circumstances are such that they tend to live pretty much together, at least for a generation or so after their initial settlement here.

This means that their schools, which (like most public schools) are residentially based, are largely segregated, racially, in the makeup of their student bodies. The substantially less public funding for the Mexican American schools was said to lead to significantly lower levels of education in these schools. And this, it was argued, meant that the State ultimately responsible for these schools denied to the children of such schools the equal protection of the laws.

II

The discrepancies in levels of funding among school districts in a State can be quite evident. This reflects the substantial differences in property values among the districts, those values upon which the school taxes are usually levied. Supplements from the State treasury tend to reduce somewhat these differences between school districts.

160

Differences in property values can mean that the poorer districts, even when they tax local property as much as State law permits, may not be able to match the monies collected by the more affluent districts, even when those districts do not tax *their* property as much as State law permits. The substantial reliance upon local property taxes for such public schools is said to be "historic," reflecting the tradition of considerable local governance of precollegiate education in this Country. Questions have been raised, however, about how much local control there usually is, especially in States such as Texas, where the State Government vigorously manages public school operations with respect to such matters as teacher accreditation, calendars, curriculum, and textbook selections.

Other services provided in the community—services also considered vital to the safety and welfare of people at large—may be funded entirely by the State. It is not likely to be argued that the level of funding of *those* services should depend on the wealth of the residents in each community. The opposition to differential funding for education can be reinforced by invocations of whatever *State* constitutional mandates there may be providing for equal funding of all public schools in a State.

III

May there be an issue here, because of what *State* constitutions prescribe, that the Courts of the United States can adjudicate—that is, taking their guidance from *State* constitutional provisions for equal funding? State courts have invoked such provisions. One can imagine circumstances in which the Courts of the United States might rely upon State court rulings, if not also upon State constitutional provisions, in such matters.

But should the Courts of the United States be able to invoke State constitutional provisions when State courts have not done so? Further, may the National Courts even have a *duty* to do this? We may have here variations both of the *Erie* problem and of State legislative reapportionment issues.

Even so, the emphasis in litigation before the United States Supreme Court in these matters has been on the Fourteenth Amendment, not on State provisions, however much it may be noticed that State constitutions and State laws do aim at equality in funding among school districts. The particularly troubling feature of the matters thus brought into the Courts of the United States is that some law-abiding people derive much greater advantage from public funds than other law-abiding people in similar circumstances. This *can* look like an equal protection problem.

IV

One serious objection to judicial interference here is that these matters are too complicated for *any* court, that these are matters better left to legislatures to deal with. State legislatures address public education issues routinely. But what are the powers, if not also the duties, of still another legislature, the Congress, with respect to precollegiate education nationwide?

There are, for example, the so-called War Powers of Congress, which might be invoked to make it more likely that citizens will be adequately equipped by their education to serve in the military if they should be needed. There is also the Commerce Power, which might be used to make it more likely that the education of the people of this Country will equip them to be productively employed. It is significant that a "conservative" national Administration can now make as much as it does of its No Child Left Behind Act—legislation which authorizes unprecedented interference by the General Government with the everyday operations of public schools.

We can, in considering Congressional powers here, return to the Fourteenth Amendment with its Section V empowerment of Congress. May Congress, using its Fourteenth Amendment powers, require the States to provide equal funding of public schools when tax revenues are used, a requirement that may be reinforced by, say, the conditions attached by Congress to grants-in-aid provided for the States? If Congress should thus involve itself, would it be inclined—*should* it be obliged—to promote equality not only within a State but even among the States, subject to accommodations to varying conditions?

V

An underlying question in these and like situations is as to how much money and governmental control really matters. Of course, those who make an effort to get and spend more and more money—whether in affluent school districts or in the Defense Department—do seem to believe that money matters quite a bit. So do those, of course, who work hard to make and to keep ever more money for themselves.

Even so, an instructive parallel is suggested by recent studies of the consequences of felon disenfranchisement in the United States. It can be asked there, reflecting like questions in other fields, whether those apt to become felons are likely to be voters. Does this question provide any guidance, in turn, to how the chronically poor should be regarded by a sensible and compassionate community?

Who are likely to be chronically poor in a highly mobile community such as ours? The champions of the poor should be prepared to deal with the argument that those in poor neighborhoods are apt to be people who are, by and large, not likely to do much better than they would do if their schools *were* better financed. A less controversial, if not also fairer, way of putting this kind of argument is to observe that we all know of institutions (such as the small public high school I attended in a Southern Illinois town sixty years ago) that somehow do much better than their better-financed counterparts elsewhere.

VI

Certainly, people elsewhere, with far fewer resources, have done much better than many among us do who are the beneficiaries of much more affluence. And we know of individuals—if not also of peoples—who are very hard to keep down, while there are others (parents and grandparents can lament) who are very hard to raise up. The discipline available in a community, especially across generations, can be decisive in these matters, something which is evident in vital Hispanic communities in this Country.

However all this may be, there *can* be something obviously questionable about public allocations of resources that seem to benefit some more than others. The apparent unfairness of such discrepancies can become notorious when influence is used, as it was shamelessly used during the Vietnam War by some, to avoid dangerous service in a war that (we have noticed) they were willing to have others conscripted to fight. The affluent will eventually put their own safety at risk if it should come to be generally believed that burdens and privileges are not fairly allocated in the community, encouraging many to doubt whether there is indeed a community to be cherished and sacrificed for.

The grievances dramatized in the *Rodriguez* case are now partially addressed in Texas by that State's "Robin Hood" legislation, whereby the funds of the poorer school districts are supplemented by grants not only from the State treasury but also from the taxes levied in the richer school districts. Thus, political power has evidently been used to begin to do in that State what could not be done through litigation. This, too, should remind the affluent of how vulnerable they can become if the less fortunate consider themselves cheated of a fair share of the wealth somehow generated and protected by the entire community.

VII

The allocation of wealth by "the system" may well seem to some the result primarily of chance, if not also of the workings of improper influence. This kind of opinion can become particularly disruptive, if not even explosive, if the more talented and enterprising among depressed groups do not seem to have "a fair chance" to develop themselves. In such matters appearances can be critical.

On the other hand, it does still seem to be true that people in the United States are less likely than most peoples elsewhere to be trapped by their circumstances. Indeed, Mexican Americans, such as those involved in the *Rodriguez* controversy, are themselves made up, in large part, of enterprising souls who, one way or another, have made their way into this Country from desperate conditions elsewhere. They do seem to be destined, because of their capacity for hard work, to have the political and economic success in this Country that other major contingents of immigrants, such as the Germans, the Irish, and the Poles, have had.

We should notice further the part that chance can play in the circumstances and hence the success of particular school districts. Where the district lines happen to be drawn, and what resources (such as shopping malls) happen to become available, can have unanticipated consequences. But a productive ambition may be discouraged if the opinion should develop among us that many are likely to be permanently trapped by their circumstances, even when those circumstances are significantly better in critical respects than the circumstances of their counterparts left behind in the Old Country.

VIII

It should be evident, in considering both the *Rodriguez*-type controversy and the Affirmative Action controversy, that critical questions of *fairness* are posed, questions implicit in such concepts as "equal protection" and "due process." But there are also here considerations of domestic tranquility and of self-interest for the more affluent among us. Are we not all less secure when there is a permanently depressed class in this Country, a class which makes it likely that there will be breeding grounds for ever more crime, disease, and volatile politics?

That is, people who are not raised properly do not simply go away. We may not be willing to pay for substantially upgraded schools, especially in our inner cities, but we end up paying much more than we otherwise might: the ever-growing annexes to our poorer schools are our prisons, to which vastly more resources are devoted by us than may be seen anywhere else (per capita) in the Western World. All who "work" in our criminal justice system—both the good guys and the bad—tend to be damaged by that system.

It should not be hard to see that there is substantial waste because of the way we use public funds. Our current approach to education, for example, should be contrasted with the generous "G.I. Bill" educational benefits available to veterans of the Second World War. The principal beneficiary of *that* policy was the community, which could draw for a generation upon a remarkably enhanced citizen body and labor force.

IX

It should once again be evident, upon considering the *Rodriguez* issue, that constitutional questions and political issues are intertwined. This "fact of life" can suggest that it is usually better to deal with such matters in legislatures than in courts. One can more easily see the sensibleness of this suggestion in the British system, with its more limited powers for courts.

It is tempting among us to rely, on behalf of depressed classes, more on litigation than on politics. Litigation depends upon a few skilled advocates here and there, while effective politics depends upon broad community organization. But if a community is organized enough to be effective politically, it is not likely that it will be chronically depressed, at least in a Country such as ours.

However all this may be, both the rich and the poor among us have serious failings, with the poor tending toward a crippling resentment and the rich tending toward an unbecoming fearfulness. Resentment can more easily be recognized as harmful than can fearfulness, as we have seen in how our excessive apprehensiveness about the attacks of "terrorists" has been converted into a shortsighted patriotism. This suggests that the most troubling failings of our education system are not limited to our poorer communities.

13. Whose Votes Count for What—and When?

I

It was apparent, by the middle of the twentieth century, that the allocations of seats in many State legislatures did not reflect the considerable urbanization of this Country since 1900. Thus, a Concurring Justice, in the revolutionizing case of *Baker* v. *Carr* (1962), noted that "37% of the voters of Tennessee elect 20 of the 33 Senators [in the State legislature] while 40% of the voters elect 63 of the 99 members of the [Tennessee] House." It was evident that such disparities, all over the Country, would become ever greater if no changes were made in the drawing of long-established electoral district lines.

The periodic reallocation of seats in State legislatures, taking account of changes in population distribution, is usually done by the members of each legislature. It was evident, however, that many members of State legislatures nationwide were determined *not* to make the required changes that would, in effect, deprive them of their seats. They were also reluctant to authorize other initiatives (such as a population-based State constitutional convention or a Statewide referendum) that would deal with apportionment problems.

The Governor of a State, typically chosen by a Statewide constituency, would find himself unable to influence State legislators to make the personal sacrifices that reapportionment required of them. The legislators' own constituents could, in turn, easily persuade themselves that they were entitled to their substantially enhanced representation in the State legislature that they had long profited from. The people at large, in the absence of access to a Statewide referendum option that did not depend upon legislative approval, could (unless they relocated themselves) expect to improve their influence in the State legislature only by contributing to political campaigns in the privileged districts.

II

The only other practical remedy in a State seemed to be recourse to the Courts, but the United States Supreme Court indicated in *Colegrove* v. *Green* (1946) that it was reluctant to step into that "political thicket." The State courts, by and large, took their lead here from the United States Supreme Court. When the Supreme Court changed its mind about these issues, however, it did not much matter what the State courts thought or did thereafter.

That is, the district allocations had become so grotesque in some States that the United States Supreme Court was finally moved to inter- vene. Once this happened in one of the more notorious States, it soon led to substantial redistricting in virtually all of the States. Chief Justice Earl Warren could speak of the *Reapportionment Cases* as the most important litigation during his tenure on the Supreme Court.

There is a lesson here for lawyers in ordinary practice. If one insists upon a questionable advantageous arrangement, one is asking for trouble, as happened with proponents of the Articles of Confederation. Thus, def- erence to considerations of justice and fair play may be more realistic than the hardball approach that it is so often fashionable to advocate.

III

The United States Supreme Court did face warnings that it should not involve itself in "political questions." The Opinion by the Court in *Baker* v. *Carr* left things uncertain, but only apparently so. Once the District Court in that case was empowered to assess the Tennessee arrangement, the considerable equity powers of a trial court came into play.

It was obvious to most observers that the Tennessee arrangement, and similar arrangements elsewhere, did not make sense. The presumption in favor of the equality proclaimed by the Declaration of Independence and reinforced by the Fourteenth Amendment was very much in evidence in the doctrine that was developed in the *Reapportionment Cases*. Within a few years, dozens of State legislatures had had their electoral districts re- drawn under judicial supervision, invalidating thereby generations-old favoritism.

The "one person, one vote" standard took hold—and it was applied in a more or less mechanical fashion. It is, after all, the standard used, every decade, in allocating seats among the States in the United States House of Representatives. Of course, partisan considerations continue to influence precisely where boundaries will be drawn from time to time, with gerrymandering techniques very much in evidence, techniques which reflect an acute awareness by professional politicians of who lives where.

IV

A less mechanical approach might have been used if the Republican Form of Government Guarantee, instead of the Fourteenth Amendment, had been relied upon by the Courts. But the Supreme Court has generally held that the Guarantee Clause cannot provide the basis for litigation. Besides, there is something to be said for a more or less mechanical approach, in that it seems to leave less play for the political sympathies of the judges.

We should be aware, however, of the costs usually associated with the more mechanical approach. Thus, there may be seen in *Lucas* v. *Forty-Fourth General Assembly* (1964) the inability of the majority of the people of Colorado to allow, subject to periodic reconsiderations by Statewide referenda, more influence for the western part of the State than numbers alone would warrant. This is an arrangement that might have been more readily approved by the Court if it had relied primarily on the Guarantee Clause.

There may be seen in the *Reapportionment Cases* of the 1960s the extent of the equity powers of the Courts, powers which can even threaten the very existence of Legislative bodies as constituted. A critical threat posed by Courts in reapportionment controversies is an order for an at-large election of all members of a State legislature, something which could leave the majority of the population Statewide in control of *all* seats in both houses of the Legislature. On the other hand, efforts were made, by constitutional amendment, to strip the Federal Courts of any jurisdiction to consider State legislative apportionment—but the rate of change in the makeup of State legislatures, pursuant to judicial decrees, was faster than the rate of development of a call (either in Congress or among the States) for a relevant constitutional amendment, a call which the newly reapportioned State legislatures could not be expected to support.

V

Congress, of course, could have used its Guarantee Clause powers to promote the reforms in State legislative reapportionment that had obviously long been needed, with the arrangements for the General Government in the United States Constitution providing one model for a Republican Form of Government. In addition, Congress could have experimented with the powers provided it in Section V of the Fourteenth Amendment. Congressional involvement in these matters would probably have led to a more "political," a less "mechanical," arrangement.

Although the Supreme Court continues to abjure reliance on the Guarantee Clause, there is in the Opinions of the Justices in the *Reapportionment Cases* considerable talk about that Clause. Indeed, it can sometimes seem that the Court attempted to apply in those cases the *spirit* of the Guarantee Clause. In this way, the Guarantee Clause is used, if only tacitly, to reinforce what is done explicitly by the Supreme Court with the Equal Protection Clause.

We can be reminded, by our experience with *Bush* v. *Gore* (2000), of how dubious it can appear when the Supreme Court does what Congress would likely have done, in identifying the duly elected President of the United States. Far less dramatic is what the Supreme Court has done (as we have seen) in the "burdens on interstate commerce" litigation, undertaking thereby to make assessments and to lay down rules that Congress is better equipped than judges to develop. And then there has been the Supreme Court's substantial involvement in the abortion controversy, not allowing the political process to resolve this volatile issue, as has happened in much of the Western World, with far less disruption elsewhere than here of the politics of the national community.

VI

However all this may be, a deep-rooted egalitarianism in this Country does seem to promote a "one person, one vote" arrangement in our political life. That the Senate of the United States is an exception here is recognized by the provision in the United States Constitution that makes the Senatorial allocation virtually unamendable. The only other provision similarly protected is the 1808 slave-trade provision, which also offended our egalitarian sensibilities.

The abolition of slavery itself came with the end of a wrenching Civil War. An effective "correction" of the Senate problem came with the development of political parties in this Country. Thus, the principal alignment of Senators is now along party lines, far less than before according to differences between the smaller and the larger States (although the smaller States do remain more influential in the Senate than in the House of Representatives).

Differences between the smaller and the larger States still figure as well in discussions of the Electoral College system used in the selection of the President. Fashions change, from time to time, in sophisticated Opinions about which States are particularly benefitted by this system. Concerns are repeatedly expressed as to the efficiency and fairness of the system, with some of the arguments used here resembling those brought to bear upon the reapportionment issue a half-century ago.

VII

It is obvious that the Electoral College system is in large part due to chance, depending upon the political experience and expectations, as well as upon the level of technology, in 1787. Certainly, we would not devise such an arrangement today if we were starting from scratch. Even so, much more can be said on behalf of this arrangement than is usually heard today: among its merits is its promotion (in the typical situation) of a prompt identification of the winner, and this partly because of its discouragement of widespread fraud.

But all this is not to deny that public opinion does seem to be turning against the Electoral College arrangement, at least in its winner-take-all form. This turn is evident upon reviewing major editorials on this subject in the *New York Times* (November 6, 2004) and in the *Chicago Tribune* (November 7, 2004), quite influential newspapers that can agree on *this* subject even though they had differed in their 2004 Presidential endorsements. It is generally believed, however, that a relevant constitutional amendment would be hard, if not impossible, to secure at this time.

The principal practical course, for the advocates of immediate change here, looks to inducing the States to abandon the winner-take-all approach, applying instead the kind of allocation of Electoral College votes used in Maine. If this were done—and it could be done without any constitutional amendment—it would make it even more likely than it already is that the Electoral College victory would rarely go to the candidate who ran second in the popular vote. The prospect of the popular-vote runner-up winning the Presidency does trouble people, even though it has happened only three (or perhaps only two) times in more than two centuries.

VIII

It is difficult to persuade the public at large that the total vote does not now mean what it would mean if only the total vote counted. To make as much as we now do of the total vote is something like judging baseball teams by the total number of runs scored during a season or during a World Series rather than by the total number of games won. It is hard to predict what changes in campaigning, including in allocations of political expenditures, would be made if the Maine-type system should be generally instituted in this Country, encouraged perhaps by grants-in-aid from Congress.

It is also hard to predict, on any particular occasion, which political party would be benefitted by such a "reform." I suggest that a comprehensive change might more easily be brought about, assuming that it *is* desirable, by arranging that it should come into effect during, say, three Presidential elections from now. Who would presume to know now which candidate or party would be favored then by whatever arrangement is made now?

Certainly, it is often easier to act in a statesmanlike fashion when one's immediate interests do not seem to be threatened. In any event, something *is* to be said for deferring somewhat to public opinion, even when that opinion is not as well-informed as it should be. Public opinion *is* inclined to make more than it should of the total vote in Presidential elections, even though it is not yet inclined to make as much as it should of the total amount of money spent in such elections, especially if we allow television to continue to be used as much as it is in political campaigns.

IX

There are, I have indicated, unpredictable consequences of a nationwide reliance on the Maine-style (Congressional districts-oriented) arrangement for allocation of Electoral College votes. For example, would this tend to make the General Government more like a parliamentary system, at least in making it highly likely that one party would control both the Congress and the Presidency during the first half of a President's term? The critical issues here have yet to be identified and discussed properly.

But whatever is done with the Electoral College, it is virtually certain that there will always be an identifiable President or Acting President at hand. This is assured by the elaborate line of succession that exists for the replacement of a sitting President. Courts, too, can be readily replaced— that is, within days (or at least weeks)—if anything should happen to any of them.

But it is a different matter with the Congress, and particularly with the House of Representatives (since vacancies in the membership of the Senate can usually be filled overnight by the Governors in the several States). Similar powers of appointment to House seats can be given to the Governors, by amendment of the United States Constitution, powers to be exercised only when, say, a majority of the House of Representatives (needed for a quorum) is incapacitated. Pending such an amendment, Congress could plausibly provide for emergency powers to be exercised in specified contingencies, powers to be exercised by the Senate and the President together and subject to suspension if not ratified within, say, a month after the reestablishment of a properly constituted Congress, with the Members of each House properly grounded by then in their designated constituencies.

Appendix A

Magna Carta (1215)

Magna Carta

John, by the Grace of God, King of England, Lord of Ireland, Duke of Normandy and Aquitaine, and Earl of Anjou, to his Archbishops, Bishops, Abbots, Earls, Barons, Justiciaries, Foresters, Sheriffs, Governors, Officers, and to all Bailiffs, and his faithful subjects,—Greeting.

Know ye, that We, in the presence of God, and for the salvation of our own soul, and of the souls of all our ancestors, and of our heirs, to the honour of God, and the exaltation of the Holy Church and amendment of our Kingdom, by the counsel of our venerable fathers, Stephen Archbishop of Canterbury, Primate of all England, and Cardinal of the Holy Roman Church, Henry Archbishop of Dublin, William of London, Peter of Winchester, Joceline of Bath and Glastonbury, Hugh of Lincoln, Walter of Worcester, William of Coventry, and Benedict of Rochester, Bishops; Master Pandulph our Lord the Pope's Subdeacon and familiar, Brother Almeric, Master of the Knights-Templars in England, and of these noble persons, William Mareschal Earl of Pembroke, William Earl of Salisbury, William Earl of Warren, William Earl of Arundel, Alan de Galloway Constable of Scotland, Warin Fitz-Gerald, Hubert de Burgh Seneschal of Poictou, Peter Fitz-Herbert, Hugh de Nevil, Matthew Fitz-Herbert, Thomas Basset, Alan Basset, Philip de Albiniac, Robert de Roppel, John Mareschal, John Fitz-Hugh, and others our liegemen:

[1] [We] have in the First place granted to God, and by this our present Charter, have confirmed, for us and our heirs for ever: That the English Church shall be free, and shall have her whole rights and her liberties inviolable; and we will this to be observed in such a manner, that it may

Sources: See Richard Thomson, *An Historical Essay on the Magna Carta of King John* (London: John Major and Robert Jennings, 1829). See also, George Anastaplo, *The Amendments to the Constitution: A Commentary* (Baltimore: Johns Hopkins University Press, 1995), 239, 244–55.

appear from thence, that the freedom of elections, which was reputed most requisite to the English Church, which we granted, and by our Charter confirmed, and obtained the Confirmation of the same, from our Lord Pope Innocent the Third, before the rupture between us and our Barons, was of our own free will: which Charter we shall observe, and we will it to be observed with good faith, by our heirs for ever.

We have also granted to all the Freemen of our Kingdom, for us and our heirs for ever, all the underwritten Liberties, to be enjoyed and held by them and by their heirs, from us and from our heirs.

[2] If any of our Earls or Barons, or others who hold of us in chief by military service, shall die, and at his death his heir shall be of full age, and shall owe a relief, he shall have his inheritance by the ancient relief; that is to say, the heir or heirs of an Earl, a whole Earl's Barony for one hundred pounds: the heir or heirs of a Baron for a whole Barony, by one hundred pounds; the heir or heirs of a Knight, for a whole Knight's Fee, by one hundred shillings at most: and he who owes less, shall give less, according to the ancient custom of fees.

[3] But if the heir of any such be under age, and in wardship, when he comes to age he shall have his inheritance without relief and without fine.

[4] The warden of the land of such heir who shall be under age, shall not take from the lands of the heir any but reasonable issues, and reasonable customs, and reasonable services, and that without destruction and waste of the men or goods, and if we commit the custody of any such lands to a Sheriff, or any other person who is bound to us for the issues of them, and he shall make destruction or waste upon the ward-lands we will recover damages from him, and the lands shall be committed to two lawful and discreet men of that fee, who shall answer for the issues to us, or to him to whom we have assigned them. And if we shall give or sell to any one the custody of any such lands, and he shall make destruction or waste upon them, he shall lose the custody; and it shall be committed to two lawful and discreet men of that fee, who shall answer to us in like manner as it is said before.

[5] But the warden, as long as he hath the custody of the lands, shall keep up and maintain the houses, parks, warrens, ponds, mills, and other things belonging to them, out of their issues; and shall restore to the heir when he comes to full age, his whole estate, provided with ploughs and other implements of husbandry, according as the time of Wainage shall require, and the issues of the lands can reasonably afford.

[6] Heirs shall be married without disparagement, so that before the marriage be contracted, it shall be notified to the relations of the heir by consanguinity.

[7] A widow, after the death of her husband, shall immediately, and without difficulty have her marriage and her inheritance; nor shall she give any thing for her dower, or for her marriage, or for her inheritance, which her husband and she held at the day of his death: and she may remain in her husband's house forty days after his death, within which time her dower shall be assigned.

[8] No widow shall be distrained to marry herself, while she is willing to live without a husband; but yet she shall give security that she will not marry herself without our consent, if she hold of us, or without the consent of the lord of whom she does hold, if she hold of another.

[9] Neither we nor our Bailiffs, will seize any land or rent for any debt, while the chattels of the debtor are sufficient for the payment of the debt; nor shall the sureties of the debtor be distrained, while the principal debtor is able to pay the debt; and if the principal debtor fail in payment of the debt, not having wherewith to discharge it, the sureties shall answer for the debt; and if they be willing, they shall have the lands and rents of the debtor, until satisfaction be made to them for the debt which they had before paid for him, unless the principal debtor can shew himself acquitted thereof against the said sureties.

[10] If any one hath borrowed any thing from the Jews, more or less, and die before that debt be paid, the debt shall pay no interest so long as the heir shall be under age, of whomsoever he may hold; and if that debt shall fall into our hands, we will not take any thing except the chattel contained in the bond.

[11] And if any one shall die indebted to the Jews, his wife shall have her dower and shall pay nothing of that debt; and if children of the deceased shall remain who are under age, necessaries shall be provided for them, according to the tenement which belonged to the deceased: and out of the residue the debt shall be paid, saving the rights of the lords [of whom the lands are held]. In like manner let it be with debts owing to others than Jews.

[12] No scutage nor aid shall be imposed in our kingdom, unless by the common council of our kingdom; excepting to redeem our person, to make our eldest son a knight, and once to marry our eldest daughter, and not for these, unless a reasonable aid shall be demanded.

[13] In like manner let it be concerning the aids of the City of London. And the City of London should have all it's ancient liberties, and it's free customs, as well by land as by water. Furthermore, we will and grant that all other Cities, and Burghs, and Towns, and Ports, should have all their liberties and free customs.

[14] And also to have the common council of the kingdom, to assess and aid, otherwise than in the three cases aforesaid: and for the assessing of scutages, we will cause to be summoned the Archbishops, Bishops, Abbots, Earls, and great Barons, individually, by our letters. And besides, we will cause to be summoned in general by our Sheriffs and Bailiffs, all those who hold of us in chief, at a certain day, that is to say at the distance of forty days [before their meeting], at the least, and to a certain place; and in all the letters of summons, we will express the cause of the summons: and the summons being thus made, the business shall proceed on the day appointed, according to the counsel of those who shall be present, although all who had been summoned have not come.

[15] We will not give leave to any one, for the future, to take an aid of his own free-men, except for redeeming his own body, and for making his eldest son a knight, and for marrying once his eldest daughter; and not that unless it be a reasonable aid.

[16] None shall be distrained to do more service for a Knight's-Fee, nor for any other free tenement, than what is due from thence.

[17] Common Pleas shall not follow our court, but shall be held in any certain place.

[18] Trials upon the Writs of *Novel Disseisin*, of *Mort d'Ancestre* [Death of the Ancestor], and *Darrien Presentment* [Last Presentation], shall not be taken but in their proper counties, and in this manner: We, or our Chief Justiciary, if we are out of the kingdom, will send two Justiciaries into each county, four times in the year, who, with four knights of each county, chosen by the county, shall hold the aforesaid assizes, within the county on the day, and at the place appointed.

[19] And if the aforesaid assizes cannot be taken on the day of the county-court, let as many knights and freeholders, of those who were present at the county-court remain behind, as shall be sufficient to do justice, according to the great or less importance of the business.

[20] A free-man shall not be amerced for a small offence, but only according to the degree of the offense; and for a great delinquency, according to the magnitude of the delinquency, saving his contenement: a Merchant

shall be amerced in the same manner, saving his merchandise, and a villain shall be amerced after the same manner, saving to him his Wainage, if he shall fall into our mercy; and none of the aforesaid amerciaments shall be assessed, but by the oath of honest men of the vicinage.

[21] Earls and Barons shall not be amerced but by their Peers, and that only according to the degree of their delinquency.

[22] No Clerk shall be amerced for his lay-tenement, but according to the manner of the others as aforesaid, and not according to the quantity of his ecclesiastical benefice.

[23] Neither a town nor any person shall be distrained to build bridges or embankments, excepting those which anciently, and of right, are bound to do it.

[24] No Sheriff, Constable, Coroners, nor other of our Bailiffs, shall hold pleas of our crown.

[25] All Counties, and Hundreds, Trethings, and Wapontakes, shall be at the ancient rent, without any increase, excepting in our Demesne-manors.

[26] If any one holding of us a lay-fee dies, and the Sheriff or our Bailiff, shall shew our letters-patent of summons concerning the debt which the defunct owed to us, it shall be lawful for the Sheriff or our Bailiff to attach and register the chattels of the defunct found on that lay-fee, to the amount of that debt, by the view of lawful men, so that nothing shall be removed from thence until our debt be paid to us; and the rest shall be left to the executors to fulfil the will of the defunct; and if nothing be owing to us by him, all the chattels shall fall to the defunct, saving to his wife and children their reasonable shares.

[27] If any free-man shall die intestate, his chattels shall be distributed by the hands of his nearest relations and friends, by the view of the Church, saving to every one the debts which the defunct owed.

[28] No Constable nor other Bailiff of ours shall take the corn or other goods of any one, without instantly paying money for them, unless he can obtain respite from the free will of the seller.

[29] No Constable [Governor of a Castle] shall distrain any Knight to give money for castle-guard, if he be willing to perform it in his own person, or by another able man, if he cannot perform it himself, for a reasonable cause: and if we have carried or sent him into the army, he shall be excused from castle-guard, according to the time that he shall be in the army by our command.

[30] No Sheriff nor Bailiff of ours, nor any other person shall take the horses or carts of any free-man, for the purpose of carriage, without the consent of the said free-man.

[31] Neither we, nor our Bailiffs, will take another man's wood, for our castle or other uses, unless by the consent of him to whom the wood belongs.

[32] We will not retain the lands of those who have been convicted of felony, excepting for one year and one day, and then they shall be given up to the lord of the fee.

[33] All kydells [fish-weirs] for the future shall be quite removed out of the Thames, and the Medway, and through all England, excepting upon the sea-coast.

[34] The writ which is called *Præcipe,* for the future shall not be granted to any one of any tenement, by which a free-man may lose his court.

[35] There shall be one measure of wine throughout all our kingdom, and one measure of ale, and one measure of corn, namely the quarter of London; and one breadth of dyed cloth, and of russets, and of halberjects, namely, two ells within the lists. Also it shall be the same with weights as with measures.

[36] Nothing shall be given or taken for the future of the Writ of Inquisition of life or limb; but it shall be given without charge, and not denied.

[37] If any hold of us by Fee-Farm, or Socage, or Burgage, and hold land of another by Military Service, we will not have the custody of the heir, nor of his lands, which are of the fee of another, on account of that Fee-Farm, or Socage, or Burgage; nor will we have the custody of the Fee-Farm, Socage, or Burgage, unless the Fee-Farm owe Military Service. We will not have the custody of the heir, nor of the lands of any one, which he holds of another by Military Service, on account of any Petty-Sergeantry which he holds of us by the service of giving us daggers, or arrows, or the like.

[38] No Bailiff, for the future, shall put any man to his law, upon his own simple affirmation, without credible witnesses produced for that purpose.

[39] No freeman shall be seized, or imprisoned, or dispossessed, or outlawed, or exiled, or in any way destroyed; nor will we condemn him, nor will we commit him to prison, excepting by the legal judgment of his peers, or by the law of the land. [In the Latin original: *Nullus liber homo capiatur, vel imprisonetur, aut disseisiatur, aut utlagetur, aut exuletur, aut*

aliquo modo destruatur, nec super eum ibimus, nec super eum mittemus, nisi per legale judicium parium suorum vel per legem terre.]

[40] To none will we sell, to none will we deny, to none will we delay right or justice.

[41] All Merchants shall have safety and security in coming into England, and going out of England, and in staying and in travelling through England, as well by land as by water, to buy and sell, without any unjust exactions, according to ancient and right customs, excepting in the time of war, and if they be of a country at war against us: and if such are found in our land at the beginning of a war, they shall be apprehended without injury of their bodies and goods, until it be known to us, or to our Chief Justiciary, how the Merchants of our country are treated who are found in the country at war against us; and if ours be in safety there, the others shall be in safety in our land.

[42] It shall be lawful to any person, for the future, to go out of our kingdom, and to return, safely and securely, by land or by water, saving his allegiance to us, unless it be in time of war, for some short space, for the common good of the kingdom: excepting prisoners and outlaws, according to the laws of the land, and of the people of the nation at war against us, and Merchants who shall be treated as it is said above.

[43] If any hold of any escheat, as of the Honour of Wallingford, Nottingham, Boulogne, Lancaster, or of other escheats which are in our hand, and are Baronies, and shall die, his heir shall not give any other relief, nor do any other service to us, than he should have done to the Baron, if that Barony had been in the hands of the Baron; and we will hold it in the same manner that the Baron held it.

[44] Men who dwell without the Forest, shall not come, for the future, before our Justiciaries of the Forest on a common summons; unless they be parties in a plea, or sureties for some person or persons who are attached for the Forest.

[45] We will not make Justiciaries, Constables, Sheriffs, or Bailiffs, excepting of such as know the laws of the land, and are well disposed to observe them.

[46] All Barons who have founded Abbies, which they hold by charters from the Kings of England, or by ancient tenure, shall have the custody of them when they become vacant, as they ought to have.

[47] All Forests which have been made in our time, shall be immediately disforested; and it shall be so done with Water-banks, which have been taken or fenced in by us during our reign.

[48] All evil customs of Forests and Warrens, and of Foresters and Warreners, Sheriffs and their officers, Water-banks and their keepers, shall immediately be inquired into by twelve Knights of the same county, upon oath, who shall be elected by good men of the same county; and within forty days after the inquisition is made, they shall be altogether destroyed by them never to be restored; provided that this be notified to us before it be done, or to our Justiciary, if we be not in England.

[49] We will immediately restore all hostages and charters, which have been delivered to us by the English, in security of the peace and of their faithful service.

[50] We will remove from their bailiwicks the relations of Gerard de Athyes, so that, for the future, they shall have no bailiwick in England; Engelard de Cygony, Andrew, Peter, and Gyone de Chancell, Gyone de Cygony, Geoffrey de Martin, and his brothers, Philip Mark, and his brothers, and Geoffrey his nephew, and all their followers.

[51] And immediately after the conclusion of the peace, we will remove out of the kingdom all foreign knights, cross-bow-men, and stipendiary soldiers, who have come with horses and arms to the molestation of the kingdom.

[52] If any have been disseised or dispossessed by us, without a legal verdict of their peers, of their lands, castles, liberties, or rights, we will immediately restore these things to them; and if any dispute shall arise on this head, then it shall be determined by the verdict of the twenty-five Barons, of whom mention is made below, for the security of the peace. Concerning all those things of which any one hath been disseised or dispossessed, without the legal verdict of his peers by King Henry our father, or King Richard our brother, which we have in our hand, or others hold with our warrants, we shall have respite, until the common term of the Crosiaders, excepting those concerning which a plea had been moved, or an inquisition taken, by our precept, before our taking the Cross; but as soon as we shall return from our expedition, or if, by chance, we should not go upon our expedition, we will immediately do complete justice therein.

[53] The same respite will we have, and the same justice shall be done, concerning the disforestation of the forests, or the forests which remain to be disforested, which Henry our father, or Richard our brother, have afforested; and the same concerning the wardship of lands which are in another's fee, but the wardship of which we have hitherto had, occasioned by any of our fees held by Military Service; and for Abbies founded in any

other fee than our own, in which the Lord of the fee hath claimed a right; and when we shall have returned, or if we shall stay from our expedition, we shall immediately do complete justice in all these pleas.

[54] No man shall be apprehended or imprisoned on the appeal of a woman, for the death of any other man than her husband.

[55] All fines that have been made by us unjustly, or contrary to the laws of the land; and all amerciaments that have been imposed unjustly, or contrary to the laws of the land, shall be wholly remitted, or ordered by the verdict of the twenty-five Barons, of whom mention is made below, for the security of the peace, or by the verdict of the greater part of them, together with the aforesaid Stephen, Archbishop of Canterbury, if he can be present, and others whom he may think fit to bring with him: and if he cannot be present, the business shall proceed, notwithstanding, without him; but so, that if any one or more of the aforesaid twenty-five Barons have a similar plea, let them be removed from that particular trial, and others elected and sworn by the residue of the same twenty-five, be substituted in their room, only for that trial.

[56] If we have disseised or dispossessed any Welshmen of their lands, or liberties, or other things, without a legal verdict of their peers, in England or in Wales, they shall be immediately restored to them; and if any dispute shall arise upon this head, then let it be determined in the Marches by the verdict of their peers: for a tenement of England, according to the law of England; for a tenement of Wales, according to the law of Wales; for a tenement of the Marches, according to the law of the Marches. The Welsh shall do the same to us and to our subjects.

[57] Also concerning those things of which any Welshman hath been disseised or dispossessed without the legal verdict of his peers, by King Henry our father, or King Richard our brother, which we have in our hand, or others hold with our warrant, we shall have respite, until the common term of the Croisaders, excepting for those concerning which a plea had been moved, or an inquisition made, by our precept, before our taking the Cross. But as soon as we shall return from our expedition, or if, by chance, we should not go upon our expedition, we shall immediately do complete justice therein, according to the laws of Wales, and the parts aforesaid.

[58] We will immediately deliver up the son of Llewelin, and all the hostages of Wales, and release them from their engagements which were made with us, for the security of peace.

[59] We shall do to Alexander King of Scotland, concerning the restoration of his sisters and hostages, and his liberties and rights, according to the form in which we act to our other Barons of England, unless it ought to be otherwise by the charters which we have from his father William, the late King of Scotland; and this shall be by the verdict of his peers in our court.

[60] Also all these customs and liberties aforesaid, which we have granted to be held in our kingdom, for so much of it as belongs to us, all our subjects, as well clergy as laity, shall observe towards their tenants as far as concerns them.

[61] But since we have granted all these things aforesaid, for GOD, and for the amendment of our kingdom, and for the better extinguishing the discord which has arisen between us and our Barons, we being desirous that these things should possess entire and unshaken stability for ever, give and grant to them the security underwritten; namely, that the Barons may elect twenty-five Barons of the kingdom, whom they please, who shall with their whole power, observe, keep, and cause to be observed, the peace and liberties which we have granted to them, and have confirmed by this our present charter, in this manner: that is to say, if we, or our Justiciary, or our bailiffs, or any of our officers, shall have injured any one in any thing, or shall have violated any article of the peace or security, and the injury shall have been shown to four of the aforesaid twenty-five Barons, the said four Barons shall come to us, or to our Justiciary if we be out of the kingdom, and making known to us the excess committed, petition that we cause that excess to be redressed without delay. And if we shall not have redressed the excess, or, if we have been out of the kingdom, our Justiciary shall not have redressed it within the term of forty days, computing from the time when it shall have been made known to us, or to our Justiciary if we have been out of the kingdom, the aforesaid four Barons, shall lay that cause before the residue of the twenty-five Barons; and they, the twenty-five Barons, with the community of the whole land, shall distress and harass us by all the ways in which they are able; that is to say, by the taking of our castles, lands, and possessions, and by any other means in their power, until the excess shall have been redressed, according to their verdict; saving harmless our person, and the persons of our Queen and children; and when it hath been redressed, they shall behave to us as they have done before. And whoever of our land pleaseth, may swear, that he will obey the commands of the aforesaid twenty-five Barons, in accom-

plishing all the things aforesaid, and that with them he will harass us to the utmost of his power: and we publicly and freely give leave to every one to swear who is willing to swear; and we will never forbid any to swear. But all those of our land, who, of themselves, and of their own accord, are unwilling to swear to the twenty-five Barons, to distress and harass us together with them, we will compel them by our command, to swear as aforesaid. And if any one of the twenty-five Barons shall die, or remove out of the land, or in any other way shall be prevented from executing the things above said, they who remain of the twenty-five Barons shall elect another in his place, according to their own pleasure, who shall be sworn in the same manner as the rest. In all those things which are appointed to be done by these twenty-five Barons, if it happen that all the twenty-five Barons have been present, and have differed in their opinions about any thing, or if some of them who had been summoned, would not, or could not be present, that which the greater part of those who were present shall have provided and decreed, shall be held as firm and as valid, as if all the twenty-five had agreed in it: and the aforesaid twenty-five shall swear, that they will faithfully observe, and, with all their power, cause to be observed, all the things mentioned above. And we will obtain nothing from any one, by ourselves, nor by another, by which any of these concessions and liberties may be revoked or diminished. And if any such thing shall have been obtained, let it be void and null: and we will never use it, neither by ourselves nor by another.

[62] And we have fully remitted and pardoned to all men, all the ill-will, rancour, and resentments, which have arisen between us and our subjects, both clergy and laity, from the commencement of the discord. Moreover, we have fully remitted to all the clergy and laity, and as far as belongs to us, have fully pardoned all transgressions committed by occasion of the said discord, for Easter, in the sixteenth year of our reign [i.e., 1215] until the conclusion of the peace. And, moreover, we have caused to be made to them testimonial letters-patent of the Lord Stephen, Archbishop of Canterbury, the Lord Henry, Archbishop of Dublin, and of the aforesaid Bishops, and of Master Pandulph concerning this security, and the aforesaid concessions.

[63] Wherefore, our will is, and we firmly command that the Church of England be free, and that the men in our kingdom have and hold the aforesaid liberties, rights, and concessions, well and in peace, freely and quietly, fully and entirely, to them and their heirs, of us and our heirs, in

all things and places, for ever as is aforesaid. It is also sworn, both on our part, and on that of the Barons, that all the aforesaid shall be observed in good faith, and without any evil intention.

Witnessed by the above, and many others. Given by our hand in the Meadow which is called Runningmead, between Windsor and Staines, this 15th day of June, in the 17th year of our reign [i.e., 1215: the new regal year began on 28 May].

Appendix B

The Declaration of Independence (1776)

In Congress, July 4, 1776.
A DECLARATION
By the REPRESENTATIVES of the
UNITED STATES OF AMERICA,
In GENERAL CONGRESS assembled.

When in the Course of human Events, it becomes necessary for one People to dissolve the Political Bands which have connected them with another, and to assume among the Powers of the Earth, the separate and equal Station to which the Laws of Nature and of Nature's God entitle them, a decent Respect to the Opinions of Mankind requires that they should declare the causes which impel them to the Separation.

We hold these Truths to be self-evident, that all Men are created equal, that they are endowed by their Creator with certain unalienable Rights, that among these are Life, Liberty, and the Pursuit of Happiness—That to secure these Rights, Governments are instituted among Men, deriving their just Powers from the Consent of the Governed, that whenever any Form of Government becomes destructive of these Ends, it is the Right of the People to alter or to abolish it, and to institute new Government, laying its Foundation on such Principles, and organizing its Powers in such Form, as to them shall seem most likely to effect their Safety and Happiness. Prudence, indeed, will dictate that Governments long established should not be changed for light and transient Causes; and accordingly all Experience hath shewn, that Mankind are more dis-

Sources: See *The Declaration of Independence and the Constitution of the United States,* 96th Cong., 1st sess., House Document No. 96-143 (Washington, D.C.: Government Printing Office, 1979). See also, George Anastaplo, *The Constitution of 1787: A Commentary* (Baltimore: Johns Hopkins University Press, 1989), 235, 239–44. See, as well, George Anastaplo, *Abraham Lincoln: A Constitutional Biography* [preferred title, *Thoughts on Abraham Lincoln*] (Lanham, Md.: Rowman & Littlefield, 1999), 1–38.

posed to suffer, while Evils are sufferable, than to right themselves by abolishing the Forms to which they are accustomed. But when a long Train of Abuses and Usurpations, pursuing invariably the same Object, evinces a Design to reduce them under absolute Despotism, it is their Right, it is their Duty, to throw off such Government, and to provide new Guards for their future Security. Such has been the patient Sufferance of these Colonies; and such is now the Necessity which constrains them to alter their former Systems of Government. The History of the present King of Great-Britain is a History of repeated Injuries and Usurpations, all having in direct Object the Establishment of an absolute Tyranny over these States. To prove this, let facts be submitted to a candid World.

He has refused his Assent to Laws, the most wholesome and necessary for the public Good.

He has forbidden his Governors to pass Laws of immediate and pressing Importance, unless suspended in their Operation till his Assent should be obtained; and when so suspended, he has utterly neglected to attend to them.

He has refused to pass other Laws for the Accommodation of large Districts of People, unless those People would relinquish the Right of Representation in the Legislature, a Right inestimable to them, and formidable to Tyrants only.

He has called together Legislative Bodies at Places unusual, uncomfortable, and distant from the Depository of their public Records, for the sole Purpose of fatiguing them into Compliance with his Measures.

He has dissolved Representative Houses repeatedly, for opposing with manly Firmness his Invasions on the Rights of the People.

He has refused for a long Time, after such Dissolutions, to cause others to be elected; whereby the Legislative Powers, incapable of Annihilation, have returned to the People at large for their exercise; the State remaining in the mean time exposed to all the Dangers of Invasion from without, and Convulsions within.

He has endeavoured to prevent the Population of these States; for that Purpose obstructing the Laws for Naturalization of Foreigners; refusing to pass others to encourage their Migrations hither, and raising the Conditions of new Appropriations of Lands.

He has obstructed the Administration of Justice, by refusing his Assent to Laws for establishing Judiciary Powers.

He has made Judges dependent on his Will alone, for the Tenure of their Offices, and the Amount and Payment of their Salaries.

He has erected a Multitude of new Offices, and sent hither Swarms of Officers to harass our People, and eat out their Substance.

He has kept among us, in Times of Peace, Standing Armies, without the consent of our Legislatures.

He has affected to render the Military independent of and superior to the Civil Power.

He has combined with others to subject us to a Jurisdiction foreign to our Constitution, and unacknowledged by our Laws; giving his Assent to their Acts of pretended Legislation:

For quartering large Bodies of Armed Troops among us:

For protecting them, by a mock Trial, from Punishment for any Murders which they should commit on the Inhabitants of these States:

For cutting off our Trade with all Parts of the World:

For imposing Taxes on us without our Consent:

For depriving us, in many Cases, of the Benefits of Trial by Jury:

For transporting us beyond Seas to be tried for pretended Offences:

For abolishing the free System of English Laws in a neighbouring Province, establishing therein an arbitrary Government, and engaging its Boundaries, so as to render it at once an Example and fit Instrument for introducing the same absolute Rule into these Colonies:

For taking away our Charters, abolishing our most valuable Laws, and altering fundamentally the Forms of our Governments:

For suspending our own Legislatures, and declaring themselves invested with Power to legislate for us in all Cases whatsoever.

He has abdicated Government here, by declaring us out of his Protection and waging War against us.

He has plundered our Seas, ravaged our Coasts, burnt our Towns, and destroyed the Lives of our People.

He is, at this Time, transporting large Armies of foreign Mercenaries to compleat the Works of Death, Desolation, and Tyranny, already begun with circumstances of Cruelty and Perfidy, scarcely paralleled in the most barbarous Ages, and totally unworthy the Head of a civilized Nation.

He has constrained our fellow Citizens taken Captive on the high Seas to bear Arms against their Country, to become the Executioners of their Friends and Brethren, or to fall themselves by their Hands.

He has excited domestic Insurrections amongst us, and has endeavoured to bring on the Inhabitants of our Frontiers, the merciless Indian Savages, whose known Rule of Warfare, is an undistinguished Destruction, of all Ages, Sexes, and Conditions.

In every stage of these Oppressions we have Petitioned for Redress in the most humble Terms: Our repeated Petitions have been answered only by repeated Injury. A Prince, whose Character is thus marked by every act which may define a Tyrant, is unfair to be the Ruler of a free People.

Nor have we been wanting in Attentions to our British Brethren. We have warned them from Time to Time of Attempts by their Legislature to extend an unwarrantable Jurisdiction over us. We have reminded them of the Circumstances of our Emigration and Settlement here. We have appealed to their native Justice and Magnanimity, and we have conjured them by the Ties of our common Kindred to disavow these Usurpations, which, would inevitably interrupt our Connections and Correspondence. They too have been deaf to the Voice of Justice and of Consanguinity. We must, therefore, acquiesce in the Necessity, which denounces our Separation, and hold them, as we hold the rest of Mankind, Enemies in War, in Peace, Friends.

We, therefore, the Representatives of the UNITED STATES OF AMERICA, in General Congress, Assembled, appealing to the Supreme Judge of the World for the Rectitude of our Intentions, do, in the Name, and by Authority of the good People of these Colonies, solemnly Publish and Declare, That these United Colonies are, and of Right ought to be, Free and Independent States; that they are absolved from all Allegiance to the British Crown, and that all political Connection between them and the State of Great-Britain, is and ought to be totally dissolved; and that as Free and Independent States, they have full Power to levy War, conclude Peace, contract Alliances, establish Commerce, and to do all other Acts and Things which Independent States may of right do. And for the support of this Declaration, with a firm Reliance on the Protection of divine Providence, we mutually pledge to each other our Lives, our Fortunes, and our sacred Honor.

Signed by Order and in Behalf of the Congress,

JOHN HANCOCK, President

New-Hampshire. { Josiah Bartlett,
Wm. Whipple,
Matthew Thornton.

Massachusetts-Bay. { Saml. Adams,
John Adams,
Robt. Treat Paine,
Elbridge Gerry.

Rhode-Island and
Providence, &c. { Step. Hopkins,
William Ellery.

Connecticut. { Roger Sherman,
Saml. Huntingon,
Wm. Williams,
Oliver Wolcott.

New-York. { Wm. Floyd,
Phil. Livingston,
Frans. Lewis,
Lewis Morris.

New-Jersey. Richd. Stockton,
{ Jno. Witherspoon,
Fras. Hopkinson,
John Hart,
Abra. Clark.

Pennsylvania. Robt. Morris,
Benjamin Rush,
Benja. Franklin,
{ John Morton,
Geo. Clymer,
Jas. Smith,
Geo. Taylor,
James Wilson,
Geo. Ross.

Delaware. { Caeser Rodney,
Geo. Read,
(Tho M:Kean.)

Maryland. { Samuel Chase,
Wm. Paca,
Thos. Stone,
Charles Carroll, of Carrollton.

Virginia. George Wythe,
Richard Henry Lee,
{ Ths. Jefferson,
Benja. Harrison,
Thos. Nelson, jr.
Francis Lightfoot Lee,
Carter Braxton.

North-Carolina. { Wm. Hooper,
Joseph Hewes,
John Penn,
Edward Rutledge.

South-Carolina { Thos. Heyward, junr.
Thomas Lynch, junr.
Arthur Middletown.

Georgia { Button Gwinnett,
Lyman Hall,
Geo. Walton.

Attest: Charles Thomson, Secretary.*

---

*Richard Henry Lee, of Virginia, had introduced in the Continental Congress, on June 7, 1776, the following resolution proposing a declaration of independence and thereafter articles of confederation:

   "*Resolved*, That these United Colonies are, and of right ought to be, free and independent States, that they are absolved from all allegiance to the British Crown, and that all political connection between them and the State of Great Britain is, and ought to be, totally dissolved.

   "That it is expedient forthwith to take the most effectual measures for forming foreign Alliances.

   "That a plan of confederation be prepared and transmitted to the respective Colonies for their consideration and approbation."

Appendix C

The Articles of Confederation and Perpetual Union (1776–1789)

Articles of Confederation

To all to whom these Presents shall come, we the undersigned Delegates of the States affixed to our Names, send greeting.

Whereas the Delegates of the United States of America, in Congress assembled, did, on the 15th day of November, in the Year of Our Lord One thousand Seven Hundred and Seventy seven, and in the Second Year of the Independence of America, agree to certain articles of Confederation and perpetual Union between the States of Newhampshire, Massachusetts-bay, Rhodeisland and Providence Plantations, Connecticut, New York, New Jersey, Pennsylvania, Delaware, Maryland, Virginia, North-Carolina, South-Carolina, and Georgia in the words following, viz. "Articles of Confederation and perpetual Union between the states of Newhampshire, Massachusetts-bay, Rhodeisland and Providence Plantations, Connecticut, New-York, New-Jersey, Pennsylvania, Delaware, Maryland, Virginia, North-Carolina, South-Carolina and Georgia."

Article I. The Stile of this confederacy shall be "The United States of America."

Article II. Each state retains its sovereignty, freedom, and independence, and every Power, Jurisdiction and right, which is not by this confederation expressly delegated to the United States, in Congress assembled.

Article III. The said states hereby severally enter into a firm league of friendship with each other, for their common defence, the security of their Liberties, and their mutual and general welfare, binding themselves to assist each other, against all force offered to, or attacks made upon them,

Sources: See *Documents Illustrative of the Formation of the Union of the American States,* 69th Cong., 1st sess., House Document No. 398 (Washington, D.C.: Government Printing Office, 1927). See also, George Anastaplo, *The Constitution of 1787: A Commentary* (Baltimore: Johns Hopkins University Press, 1989), 235–36, 245–55.

or any of them, on account of religion, sovereignty, trade, or any other pretence whatever.

Article IV. The better to secure and perpetuate mutual friendship and intercourse among the people of the different states in this union, the free inhabitants of each of these states, paupers, vagabonds and fugitives from justice excepted, shall be entitled to all privileges and immunities of free citizens in the several states; and the people of each state shall have free ingress and regress to and from any other state, and shall enjoy therein all the privileges of trade and commerce, subject to the same duties, impositions and restrictions as the inhabitants thereof respectively, provided that such restriction shall not extend so far as to prevent the removal of property imported into any state, to any other state, of which the Owner is an inhabitant; provided also that no imposition, duties or restriction shall be laid by any state, on the property of the united states, or either of them.

If any Person guilty of, or charged with treason, felony, or other high misdemeanor in any state, shall flee from Justice, and be found in any of the united states: he shall, upon demand of the Governor or executive power, of the state from which he fled, be delivered up and removed to the state having jurisdiction of his offence.

Full faith and credit shall be given in each of these states to the records, acts and judicial proceedings of the courts and magistrates of every other state.

Article V. For the more convenient management of the general interests of the united states, delegates shall be annually appointed in such manner as the legislature of each state shall direct, to meet in Congress on the first Monday in November, in every year, with a power reserved to each state, to recal its delegates, or any of them, at any time within the year, and to send others in their stead, for the remainder of the Year.

No state shall be represented in Congress by less than two, nor by more than seven Members; and no person shall be capable of being a delegate for more than three years in any term of six years; nor shall any person, being a delegate, be capable of holding any office under the united states, for which he, or another for his benefit receives any salary, fees or emolument of any kind.

Each state shall maintain its own delegates in a meeting of the states, and while they act as members of the committee of the states.

In determining questions in the united states in Congress assembled, each state shall have one vote.

Freedom of speech and debate in Congress shall not be impeached or questioned in any Court, or place out of Congress, and the members of congress shall be protected in their persons from arrests and imprisonments, during the time of their going to and from, and attendance on congress, except for treason, felony, or breach of the peace.

Article VI. No state, without the Consent of the united states in congress assembled, shall send any embassy to, or receive any embassy from, or enter into any conference, agreement, alliance or treaty with any King prince or state; nor shall any person holding any office of profit or trust under the united states, or any of them, accept of any present, emolument, office or title of any kind whatever from any king, prince or foreign state; nor shall the united states in congress assembled, or any of them, grant any title of nobility.

No two or more states shall enter into any treaty, confederation or alliance whatever between them, without the consent of the united states in congress assembled, specifying accurately the purposes for which the same is to be entered into, and how long it shall continue.

No state shall lay any imposts or duties, which may interfere with any stipulations in treaties, entered into by the united states in congress assembled, with any king, prince or state, in pursuance of any treaties already proposed by congress, to the courts of France and Spain.

No vessels of war shall be kept up in time of peace by any state, except such number only, as shall be deemed necessary by the united states in congress assembled, for the defence of such state, or its trade; nor shall any body of forces be kept up by any state, in time of peace, except such number only, as in the judgment of the united states, in congress assembled, shall be deemed requisite to garrison the forts necessary for the defence of such state; but every state shall always keep up a well regulated and disciplined militia, sufficiently armed and accoutred, and shall provide and constantly have ready for use, in public stores, a due number of field pieces and tents, and a proper quantity of arms, ammunition and camp equipage.

No state shall engage in any war without the consent of the united states in congress assembled, unless such state be actually invaded by enemies, or shall have received certain advice of a resolution being formed by some nation of Indians to invade such state, and the danger is so imminent as not to admit of a delay till the united states in congress assembled can be consulted: nor shall any state grant commissions to any ships or vessels of war, nor letters of marque or reprisal, except it be after a declaration of war by the united states in congress assembled, and then only against the kingdom or state and the subjects thereof, against which war has been so declared, and under such regulations as shall be established by the united states in congress assembled, unless such state be infested by pirates, in which case vessels of war may be fitted out for that occasion, and kept so long as the danger shall continue, or until the united states in congress assembled, shall determine otherwise.

Article VII. When land-forces are raised by any state for the common defence, all officers of or under the rank of colonel, shall be appointed by the legislature of each state respectively, by whom such forces shall be raised, or in such manner as such state shall direct, and all vacancies shall be filled up by the State which first made the appointment.

Article VIII. All charges of war, and all other expences that shall be incurred for the common defence or general welfare, and allowed by the united states in congress assembled, shall be defrayed out of a common treasury, which shall be supplied by the several states in proportion to the value of all land within each state, granted to or surveyed for any Person, as such land and the buildings and improvements thereon shall be estimated according to such mode as the united states in congress assembled, shall from time to time direct and appoint.

The taxes for paying that proportion shall be laid and levied by the authority and direction of the legislatures of the several states within the time agreed upon by the united states in congress assembled.

Article IX. The united states in congress assembled, shall have the sole and exclusive right and power of determining on peace and war, except in the cases mentioned in the sixth article—of sending and receiving ambassadors—entering into treaties and alliances, provided that no treaty of commerce shall be made whereby the legislative power of the respective states shall be restrained from imposing such imposts and duties on foreigners as their own people are subjected to, or from prohibiting the exportation or importation of any species of goods or commodities, whatsoever—of establishing rules for deciding in all cases, what captures on land or water shall be legal, and in what manner prizes taken by land or naval forces in the service of the united states shall be divided or appropriated—of granting letters of marque and reprisal in times of peace—appointing courts for the trial of piracies and felonies committed on the high seas and establishing courts for receiving and determining finally appeals in all cases of captures, provided that no member of congress shall be appointed a judge of any of the said courts.

The united states in congress assembled shall also be the last resort on appeal in all disputes and differences now subsisting or that hereafter may arise between two or more states concerning boundary, jurisdiction or any other cause whatever; which authority shall always be exercised in the manner following. Whenever the legislative or executive authority or lawful agent of any state in controversy with another shall present a petition to congress stating the matter in question and praying for a hearing, notice thereof shall be given by order of congress to the legislative or executive authority of the other state in controversy, and a day assigned for the appearance of the parties by their lawful agents, who shall then be directed to appoint by joint consent, commissioners or judges to constitute a court for hearing and determining the matter in question: but if they cannot agree, congress shall name three persons out of each of the united states, and from the list of such persons each party shall alternately strike out one, the petitioners beginning, until the number shall be reduced to thirteen; and from that number not less than seven, nor more than nine names as congress shall direct, shall in the presence of congress be drawn out by lot, and the persons whose names shall be so drawn or any five of them, shall be commissioners or judges, to hear and finally determine the controversy, so always as a major part of the judges who shall hear the cause shall agree in the determination: and if either party shall neglect to attend at the day appointed, without showing reasons, which congress shall judge sufficient, or being present shall refuse to strike, the congress shall proceed to nominate three persons out of each state, and the secretary of congress shall strike in behalf of such party absent or refusing; and the judgment and sentence of the court to be appointed, in the manner before prescribed, shall be final and conclusive; and if any of the parties shall refuse to submit to the authority of such court, or to appear or defend their claim or cause, the court shall nevertheless proceed to pronounce sentence, or judgment, which shall in like manner be final and decisive, the judgment or sentence and other proceedings being in either case transmitted to congress, and lodged among the acts of congress for the security of the parties concerned: provided that every commissioner, before he sits in judgment, shall take an oath to be administered by one of the judges of the supreme or superior court of the state, where the cause shall be tried, "well and truly to hear and determine the matter in question, according to the best of his judgment, without favour, affection or hope of reward:" provided also, that no state shall be deprived of territory for the benefit of the united states.

All controversies concerning the private right of soil claimed under different grants of two or more states, whose jurisdictions as they may respect such lands, and the states which passed such grants are adjusted, the said grants or either of them being at the same time claimed to have originated antecedent to such settlement of jurisdiction, shall on the petition of either party to the congress of the united states, be finally determined as near as may be in the same manner as is before prescribed for deciding disputes respecting territorial jurisdiction between different states.

The united states in congress assembled shall also have the sole and exclusive right and power of regulating the alloy and value of coin struck by their own authority, or by that of the respective states—fixing the standard of weights and measures throughout the united states—regulating the trade and managing all affairs with the Indians, not members of any of the states, provided that the legislative right of any state within its own limits be not infringed or violated—establishing or regulating post-offices from one state to another, throughout all the united states, and exacting such postage on the papers passing thro' the same as may be requisite to defray the expences of the said office—appointing all officers of the land forces, in the service of the united states, excepting regimental officers—appointing all the officers of the naval forces, and commissioning all officers whatever in the service of the united states—making rules for the government and regulation of the said land and naval forces, and directing their operations.

The united states in congress assembled shall have authority to appoint a committee, to sit in the recess of congress, to be denominated "A Committee of the States," and to consist of one delegate from each state; and to appoint such other committees and civil officers as may be necessary for managing the general affairs of the united states under their direction—to appoint one of their number to preside, provided that no person be allowed to serve in the office of president more than one year in any term of three years; to ascertain the necessary sums of money to be raised for the service of the united states, and to appropriate and apply the same for defraying the public expences—to borrow money, or emit bills on the credit of the united states, transmitting every half year to the respective states an account of the sums of money so borrowed or

emitted,—to build and equip a navy—to agree upon the number of land
forces, and to make requisitions from each state for its quota, in proportion to the number of white inhabitants in such state; which requisition
shall be binding, and thereupon the legislature of each state shall appoint
the regimental officers, raise the men and cloath, arm and equip them in a
soldier like manner, at the expence of the united states; and the officers and
men so cloathed, armed and equipped shall march to the place appointed,
and within the time agreed on by the united states in congress assembled:
But if the united states in congress assembled shall, on consideration of
circumstances judge proper that any state should not raise men, or should
raise a smaller number than its quota, and that any other state should raise
a greater number of men than the quota thereof, such extra number shall
be raised, officered, cloathed, armed and equipped in the same manner
as the quota of such state, unless the legislature of such state shall judge
that such extra number cannot be safely spared out of the same, in which
case they shall raise, officer, cloath, arm and equip as many of such extra
number as they judge can be safely spared. And the officers and men so
cloathed, armed and equipped, shall march to the place appointed, and
within the time agreed on by the united states in congress assembled.

The united states in congress assembled shall never engage in a war,
nor grant letters of marque and reprisal in time of peace, nor enter into
any treaties or alliances, nor coin money, nor regulate the value thereof,
nor ascertain the sums and expences necessary for the defence and welfare
of the united states, or any of them, nor emit bills, nor borrow money on
the credit of the united states, nor appropriate money, nor agree upon the
number of vessels of war, to be built or purchased, or the number of land
or sea forces to be raised, nor appoint a commander in chief of the army
or navy, unless nine states assent to the same: nor shall a question on any
other point, except for adjourning from day to day be determined, unless
by the votes of a majority of the united states in congress assembled.

The congress of the united states shall have power to adjourn to any
time within the year, and to any place within the united states, so that
no period of adjournment be for a longer duration than the space of six
Months, and shall publish the Journal of their proceedings monthly, except such parts thereof relating to treaties, alliances or military operations,
as in their judgment require secrecy; and the yeas and nays of the delegates
of each state on any question shall be entered on the Journal, when it is
desired by any delegate; and the delegates of a state, or any of them, at

his or their request shall be furnished with a transcript of the said Journal, except such parts as are above excepted, to lay before the legislatures of the several states.

Article X. The committee of the states, or any nine of them, shall be authorized to execute, in the recess of congress, such of the powers of congress as the united states in congress assembled, by the consent of nine states, shall from time to time think expedient to vest them with; provided that no power be delegated to the said committee, for the exercise of which, by the articles of confederation, the voice of nine states in the congress of the united states assembled is requisite.

Article XI. Canada acceding to this confederation, and joining in the measures of the united states, shall be admitted into, and entitled to all the advantages of this union: but no other colony shall be admitted into the same, unless such admission be agreed to by nine states.

Article XII. All bills of credit emitted, monies borrowed and debts contracted by, or under the authority of congress, before the assembling of the united states, in pursuance of the present confederation, shall be deemed and considered as a charge against the united states, for payment and satisfaction whereof the said united states, and the public faith are hereby solemnly pledged.

Article XIII. Every state shall abide by the determinations of the united states in congress assembled, on all questions which by this confederation are submitted to them. And the Articles of this confederation shall be inviolably observed by every state, and the union shall be perpetual; nor shall any alteration at any time hereafter be made in any of them; unless such alteration be agreed to in a congress of the united states, and be afterwards confirmed by the legislatures of every state.

And Whereas it hath pleased the Great Governor of the World to incline the hearts of the legislatures we respectively represent in congress, to approve of, and to authorize us to ratify the said articles of confederation and perpetual union, Know Ye that we the undersigned delegates, by virtue of the power and authority to us given for that purpose, do by these presents, in the name and in behalf of our respective constituents, fully and entirely ratify and confirm each and every of the said articles of confederation and perpetual union, and all and singular the matters and things therein contained: And we do further solemnly plight and engage the faith of our respective constituents, that they shall abide by the determinations of the united states in congress assembled, on all questions, which by the said confederation are submitted to them. And that the articles thereof shall be inviolably observed by the states we respectively represent, and that the union shall be perpetual. In Witness whereof we have hereunto set our hands in Congress. Done at Philadelphia in the state of Pennsylvania the ninth day of July, in the Year of our Lord one Thousand seven Hundred and Seventy-eight, and in the third year of the independence of America.

Josiah Bartlett,
John Wentworth, junr
8th, 1778, Hampshire.
} On the part & behalf of the State of New Hampshire.

John Hancock,
Samuel Adams,
Elbridge Gerry,
Francis Dana,
James Lovell,
Samuel Holten,
} On the part and behalf of the State of Massachusetts Bay.

William Ellery,
Henry Marchant,
John Collins,
} On the part and behalf of the State of Rhode-Island and Providence Plantations.

Roger Sherman,
Samuel Huntington,
Oliver Wolcott,
Titus Hosmer,
Andrew Adams,
} On the part and behalf of the State of Connecticut.

Jas Duane,
Fra: Lewis,
Wm Duer,
Gouvr Morris,
} On the part and behalf of the State of New York.

Jno Witherspoon,
Nathl Scudder,
} On the Part and in Behalf of the State of New Jersey, November 26th, 1778.

Robert Morris,
Daniel Roberdeau,
Jon. Bayard Smith,   } On the part and behalf of the State of
William Clingar,   Pennsylvania.
Joseph Reed,
    22d July, 1778,

Thos McKean,
    Febr 22d, 1779,
John Dickinson,   } On the part & behalf of the State of
    May 5th, 1779,   Delaware.
Nicholas Van Dyke,

John Hanson,
    March 1, 1781,   } On the part and behalf of the State of
Daniel Carroll, do   Maryland.

Richard Henry Lee,
John Banister,
Thomas Adams   } On the Part and Behalf of the State of
Jno Harvie,   Virginia.
Francis Lightfoot Lee,

John Penn,
    July 21st, 1778,   } On the part and behalf of the State of
Corns Barnett,   North Carolina.
Jno Williams,

Henry Laurens,
William Henry Drayton,
Jno Mathews   } On the part and behalf of the State of
Richd Hutson,   South Carolina.
Thos Hayward, junr,

Jno Walton,
24th July, 1778,   } On the part and behalf of the State of
Edwd Telfair,   Georgia.
Edwd Langworthy.

Appendix D

The Northwest Ordinance (1787)

An Ordinance for the Government of the Territory of the United States, North-West of the River Ohio

[Section 1.] BE IT ORDAINED by the United States in Congress assembled, That the said territory, for the purposes of temporary government, be one district; subject, however, to be divided into two districts, as future circumstances may, in the opinion of Congress, make it expedient.

[Section 2.] Be it ordained by the authority aforesaid, That the estates both of resident and non-resident proprietors in the said territory, dying intestate, shall descend to, and be distributed among their children, and the descendants of a deceased child in equal parts; the descendants of a deceased child or grand-child, to take the share of their deceased parent in equal parts among them: And where there shall be no children or descendants, then in equal parts to the next of kin, in equal degree; and among collaterals, the children of a deceased brother or sister of the intestate, shall have in equal parts among them their deceased parents share; and there shall in no case be a distinction between kindred of the whole and half blood; saving in all cases to the widow of the intestate, her third part of the real estate for life, and one third part of the personal estate; and this law relative to descents and dower, shall remain in full force until altered by the legislature of the district————And until the governor and judges shall adopt laws as herein after mentioned, estates in the said territory may be devised or bequeathed by wills in writing, signed and sealed by him or her, in whom the estate may be, (being of full age) and attested by three

Sources: See *The Northwest Ordinance 1787: A Bicentennial Handbook* (Indianapolis: Indiana Historical Society, 1987). See also, George Anastaplo, *The Constitution of 1787: A Commentary* (Baltimore: Johns Hopkins University Press, 1989), 236, 258–65. See, as well, George Anastaplo, *Abraham Lincoln: A Constitutional Biography* [preferred title, *Thoughts on Abraham Lincoln*](Lanham, Md.: Rowman & Littlefield, 1999), 39–49, 69–79.

witnesses;—and real estates may be conveyed by lease and release, or bargain and sale, signed, sealed, and delivered by the person being of full age, in whom the estate may be, and attested by two witnesses, provided such wills be duly proved, and such conveyances be acknowledged, or the execution thereof duly proved, and be recorded within one year after proper magistrates, courts, and registers shall be appointed for that purpose; and personal property may be transferred by delivery, saving, however, to the French and Canadian inhabitants, and other settlers of the Kaskaskies, Saint Vincent's, and the neighbouring villages, who have heretofore professed themselves citizens of Virginia, their laws and customs now in force among them, relative to the descent and conveyance of property.

[Section 3.] Be it ordained by the authority aforesaid, That there shall be appointed from time to time, by Congress, a governor, whose commission shall continue in force for the term of three years, unless sooner revoked by Congress; he shall reside in the district, and have a freehold estate therein, in one thousand acres of land, while in the exercise of his office.

[Section 4.] There shall be appointed from time to time, by Congress, a secretary, whose commission shall continue in force for four years, unless sooner revoked; he shall reside in the district, and have a freehold estate therein, in five hundred acres of land, while in the exercise of his office; it shall be his duty to keep and preserve the acts and laws passed by the legislature, and the public records of the district, and the proceedings of the governor in his executive department; and transmit authentic copies of such acts and proceedings, every six months, to the secretary of Congress: There shall also be appointed a court to consist of three judges, any two of whom to form a court, who shall have a common law jurisdiction, and reside in the district, and have each therein a freehold estate in five hundred acres of land, while in the exercise of their offices; and their commissions shall continue in force during good behaviour.

[Section 5.] The governor and judges, or a majority of them, shall adopt and publish in the district, such laws of the original states, criminal and civil, as may be necessary, and best suited to the circumstances of the district, and report them to Congress, from time to time, which laws shall be in force in the district until the organization of the general assembly therein, unless disapproved of by Congress; but afterwards the legislature shall have authority to alter them as they shall think fit.

[Section 6.] The governor for the time being, shall be commander in chief of the militia, appoint and commission all officers in the same, below the rank of general officers; all general officers shall be appointed and commissioned by Congress.

[Section 7.] Previous to the organization of the general assembly, the governor shall appoint such magistrates and other civil officers, in each county or township, as he shall find necessary for the preservation of the peace and good order in the same: After the general assembly shall be organized, the powers and duties of magistrates and other civil officers shall be regulated and defined by the said assembly; but all magistrates and other civil officers, not herein otherwise directed, shall, during the continuance of this temporary government, be appointed by the governor.

[Section 8.] For the prevention of crimes and injuries, the laws to be adopted or made shall have force in all parts of the district, and for the execution of process, criminal and civil, the governor shall make proper divisions thereof—and he shall proceed from time to time, as circumstances may require, to lay out the parts of the district in which the Indian titles shall have been extinguished, into counties and townships, subject, however, to such alterations as may thereafter be made by the legislature.

[Section 9.] So soon as there shall be five thousand free male inhabitants, of full age, in the district, upon giving proof thereof to the governor, they shall receive authority, with time and place, to elect representatives from their counties or townships, to represent them in the general assembly; provided that for every five hundred free male inhabitants there shall be one representative, and so on progressively with the number of free male inhabitants, shall the right of representation increase, until the number of representatives shall amount to twenty-five, after which the number and proportion of representatives shall be regulated by the legislature; provided that no person be eligible or qualified to act as a representative, unless he shall have been a citizen of one of the United States three years and be a resident in the district, or unless he shall have resided in the district three years, and in either case shall likewise hold in his own right, in fee simple, two hundred acres of land within the same:—Provided also, that a freehold in fifty acres of land in the district, having been a citizen of one of the states, and being resident in the district; or the like freehold and two years residence in the district shall be necessary to qualify a man as an elector of a representative.

[Section 10.] The representatives thus elected, shall serve for the term of two years, and in case of the death of a representative, or removal from office, the governor shall issue a writ to the county or township for which he was a member, to elect another in his stead, to serve for the residue of the term.

[Section 11.] The general assembly, or legislature, shall consist of the governor, legislative council, and a house of representatives. The legislative council shall consist of five members, to continue in office five years, unless sooner removed by Congress, any three of whom to be a quorum, and the members of the council shall be nominated and appointed in the following manner, to wit: As soon as representatives shall be elected, the governor shall appoint a time and place for them to meet together, and, when met, they shall nominate ten persons, resident in the district, and each possessed of a freehold in five hundred acres of land, and return their names to Congress; five of whom Congress shall appoint and commission to serve as aforesaid; and whenever a vacancy shall happen in the council, by death or removal from office, the house of representatives shall nominate two persons, qualified as aforesaid, for each vacancy, and return their names to Congress; one of whom Congress shall appoint and commission for the residue of the term; and every five years, four months at least before the expiration of the time of service of the members of council, the said house shall nominate ten persons, qualified as aforesaid, and return their names to Congress, five of whom Congress shall appoint and commission to serve as members of the council five years, unless sooner removed. And the governor, legislative council, and house of representatives, shall have authority to make laws in all cases for the good government of the district, not repugnant to the principles and articles in this ordinance established and declared. And all bills having passed by a majority in the house, and by a majority in the council, shall be referred to the governor for his assent; but no bill or legislative act whatever, shall be of any force without his assent. The governor shall have power to convene, prorogue and dissolve the general assembly, when in his opinion it shall be expedient.

[Section 12.] The governor, judges, legislative council, secretary, and such other officers as Congress shall appoint in the district, shall take an oath or affirmation of fidelity, and of office, the governor before the president of Congress, and all other officers before the governor. As soon as a legislature shall be formed in the district, the council and house, assembled in one room, shall have authority by joint ballot to elect a delegate to Congress, who shall have a seat in Congress, with a right of debating, but not of voting, during this temporary government.

[Section 13.] And for extending the fundamental principles of civil and religious liberty, which form the basis whereon these republics, their laws and constitutions are erected; to fix and establish those principles as the basis of all laws, constitutions and governments, which for ever hereafter shall be formed in the said territory;—to provide also for the establishment of states, and permanent government therein, and for their admission to a share in the federal councils on an equal footing with the original states, at as early periods as may be consistent with the general interest:

[Section 14.] It is hereby ordained and declared by the authority aforesaid, That the following articles shall be considered as articles of compact between the original states and the people and states in the said territory, and forever remain unalterable, unless by common consent, to wit:

Article the First. No person, demeaning himself in a peaceable and orderly manner, shall ever be molested on account of his mode of worship or religious sentiments in the said territory.

Article the Second. The inhabitants of the said territory shall always be entitled to the benefits of the writ of habeas corpus, and of the trial by jury; of a proportionate representation of the people in the legislature, and of judicial proceedings according to the course of the common law; all persons shall be bailable unless for capital offenses, where the proof shall be evident, or the presumption great; all fines shall be moderate, and no cruel or unusual punishments shall be inflicted; no man shall be deprived of his liberty or property but by the judgment of his peers, or the law of the land; and should the public exigencies make it necessary for the common preservation to take any person's property, or to demand his particular services, full compensation shall be made for the same;————and in the just preservation of rights and property it is understood and declared, that no law ought ever to be made, or have force in the said territory, that shall in any manner whatever interfere with, or affect private contracts or engagements, bona fide and without fraud previously formed.

Article the Third. Religion, morality and knowledge, being necessary to good government and the happiness of mankind, schools and the means of education shall forever be encouraged. The utmost good faith shall always be observed towards the Indians; their lands and property shall never be taken from them without their consent; and in their property, rights and liberty, they never shall be invaded or disturbed, unless in just and lawful wars authorized by Congress; but laws founded in justice and humanity shall from time to time be made, for preventing wrongs being done to them; and for preserving peace and friendship with them.

Article the Fourth. The said territory, and the states which may be formed therein, shall forever remain a part of this confederacy of the United States of America, subject to the articles of confederation, and to such alterations therein as shall be constitutionally made; and to all the acts and ordinances of the United States in Congress assembled, conformable thereto. The inhabitants and settlers in the said territory, shall be subject to pay a part of the federal debts contracted or to be contracted, and a proportional part of the expences of government, to be apportioned on them by Congress, according to the same common rule and measure by which apportionments thereof shall be made on the other states; and the taxes for paying their proportion, shall be laid and levied by the authority and direction of the legislatures of the district or districts or new states, as in the original states, within the time agreed upon by the United States in Congress assembled. The legislatures of those districts, or new states, shall never interfere with the primary disposal of the soil by the United States in Congress assembled, nor with any regulations Congress may find necessary for securing the title in such soil to the bona fide purchasers. No tax shall be imposed on lands the property of the United States; and in no case shall non-resident proprietors be taxed higher than residents. The navigable waters leading into the Mississippi and St. Lawrence, and the carrying places between the same shall be common highways, and forever free, as well to the inhabitants of the said territory, as to the citizens of the United States, and those of any other states that may be admitted into the confederacy, without any tax, impost or duty therefor.

Article the Fifth. There shall be formed in the said territory, not less than three nor more than five states; and the boundaries of the states, as soon as Virginia shall alter her act of cession and consent to the same, shall become fixed and established as follows, to wit: The western state in the said territory, shall be bounded by the Mississippi, the Ohio and Wabash rivers; a direct line drawn from the Wabash and Post Vincent's due north to the territorial line between the United States and Canada, and by the said territorial line to the lake of the Woods and Mississippi. The middle state shall be bounded by the said direct line, the Wabash from Post Vincent's to the Ohio; by the Ohio, by a direct line drawn due north from the mouth of the Great Miami to the said territorial line, and by the said territorial line. The eastern state shall be bounded by the last mentioned direct line, the Ohio, Pennsylvania, and the said territorial line; Provided however, and it is further understood and declared, that the boundaries of these three states, shall be subject so far to be altered, that if Congress shall hereafter find it expedient, they shall have authority to form one or two states in that part of the said territory which lies north of an east and west line drawn through the southerly bend or extreme of lake Michigan: and whenever any of the said states shall have sixty thousand free inhabitants therein, such state shall be admitted by its delegates into the Congress of the United States, on an equal footing with the original states in all respects whatever; and shall be at liberty to form a permanent constitution and state government: Provided the constitution and government so to be formed, shall be republican, and in conformity to the principles contained in these articles, and so far as it can be consistent with the general interest of the confederacy, such admission shall be allowed at an earlier period, and when there may be a less number of free inhabitants in the state than sixty thousand.

Article the Sixth. There shall be neither slavery nor involuntary servitude in the said territory, otherwise than in punishment of crimes whereof the party shall have been duly convicted: Provided always, that any person escaping into the same, from whom labor or service is lawfully claimed in any one of the original states, such fugitive may be lawfully reclaimed and conveyed to the person claiming his or her labor or service as aforesaid.

Be it ordained by the authority aforesaid, That the resolutions of the 23d of April, 1784, relative to the subject of this ordinance, be, and the same are hereby repealed and declared null and void.

DONE by the UNITED STATES in CONGRESS assembled, the 13th day of July, in the year of our Lord 1787, and of their sovereignty and independence the 12th.*

*The following Act of the First Congress, approved August 7, 1789, reenacted the Northwest Ordinance as modified to conform to the United States Constitution of 1787:

An Act to provide for the government of the Territory northwest of the river Ohio.

Whereas, in order that the ordinance of the United States in Congress assembled, for the government of the Territory northwest of the river Ohio may continue to have full effect, it is requisite that certain provisions should be made so as to adapt the same to the present Constitution of the United States:

Be it enacted, &c., That in all cases in which, by the said ordinance, any information is to be given, or communication made by the Governor of the said Territory to the United States in Congress assembled, or to any of their officers, it shall be the duty of the said Governor to give such information, and to make such communication to the President of the United States;

and the President shall nominate, and by and with the advice and consent of the Senate shall appoint all officers which by the said ordinance were to have been appointed by the United States in Congress assembled, and all officers so appointed shall be commissioned by him; and in all cases where the United States in Congress assembled might, by the said ordinance, revoke any commission, or remove from any office, the President is hereby declared to have the same powers of revocation and removal.

Sec. 2. *And be it further enacted.* That in case of the death, removal, resignation, or necessary absence of the Governor of the said Territory, the Secretary thereof shall be, and he is hereby authorized and required to execute all the powers and perform all the duties of the Governor, during the vacancy occasioned by the removal, resignation, or necessary absence of the said Governor.

Appendix E

The United States Constitution (1787)

The Constitution of the United States

We the People of the United States, in Order to form a more perfect Union, establish Justice, insure domestic Tranquility, provide for the common defence, promote the general Welfare, and secure the Blessings of Liberty to ourselves and our Posterity, do ordain and establish this Constitution for the United States of America.

Article. I.

Section. 1. All legislative Powers herein granted shall be vested in a Congress of the United States, which shall consist of a Senate and a House of Representatives.

Section. 2. The House of Representatives shall be composed of Members chosen every second Year by the People of the several States, and the Electors in each State shall have the Qualifications requisite for Electors of the most numerous Branch of the State Legislature.

No person shall be a Representative who shall not have attained to the Age of twenty five Years, and been seven Years a Citizen of the United States, and who shall not, when elected, be an Inhabitant of that State in which he shall be chosen.

Representatives and direct Taxes shall be apportioned among the several States which may be included within this Union, according to their respective Numbers, which shall be determined by adding to the whole Number of free Persons, including those bound to Service for a Term of

Sources: See *Documents Illustrative of the Formation of the Union of the American States,* 69th Cong., 1st sess., House Document No. 398 (Washington, D.C.: Government Printing Office, 1927). See also, George Anastaplo, *The Constitution of 1787: A Commentary* (Baltimore: Johns Hopkins University Press, 1989), 236, 266–79. See, on Constitutionalism, George Anastaplo, *The Constitutionalist: Notes on the First Amendment* (Dallas: Southern Methodist University Press, 1971; Lanham, Md.: Lexington Books, 2005).

Years, and excluding Indians not taxed, three fifths of all other Persons. The actual Enumeration shall be made within three Years after the first Meeting of the Congress of the United States, and within every subsequent Term of ten Years, in such Manner as they shall by Law direct. The Number of Representatives shall not exceed one for every thirty Thousand, but each State shall have at Least one Representative; and until such enumeration shall be made, the State of New Hampshire shall be entitled to chuse three, Massachusetts eight, Rhode-Island and Providence Plantations one, Connecticut five, New-York six, New Jersey four, Pennsylvania eight, Delaware one, Maryland six, Virginia ten, North Carolina five, South Carolina five, and Georgia three.

When vacancies happen in the Representation from any State, the Executive Authority thereof shall issue Writs of Election to fill such Vacancies.

The House of Representatives shall chuse their Speaker and other Officers; and shall have the sole Power of Impeachment.

Section. 3. The Senate of the United States shall be composed of two Senators from each State, chosen by the Legislature thereof, for six Years; and each Senator shall have one Vote.

Immediately after they shall be assembled in Consequence of the first Election, they shall be divided as equally as may be into three Classes. The Seats of the Senators of the first Class shall be vacated at the Expiration of the second Year, of the second Class at the Expiration of the fourth Year, and of the third Class at the Expiration of the sixth Year, so that one third may be chosen every second Year; and if Vacancies happen by Resignation, or otherwise, during the Recess of the Legislature of any State, the Executive thereof may make temporary Appointments until the next Meeting of the Legislature, which shall then fill such Vacancies.

No Person shall be a Senator who shall not have attained to the Age of thirty Years, and been nine Years a Citizen of the United States, and who shall not, when elected, be an Inhabitant of that State for which he shall be chosen.

The Vice President of the United States shall be President of the Senate, but shall have no Vote, unless they be equally divided.

The Senate shall chuse their other Officers, and also a President pro tempore, in the Absence of the Vice President, or when he shall exercise the Office of President of the United States.

The Senate shall have the sole Power to try all Impeachments. When sitting for that Purpose, they shall be on Oath or Affirmation. When the

President of the United States is tried, the Chief Justice shall preside: And no Person shall be convicted without the Concurrence of two thirds of the Members present.

Judgment in Cases of Impeachment shall not extend further than to removal from Office, and disqualification to hold and enjoy any Office of honor, Trust or Profit under the United States: but the Party convicted shall nevertheless be liable and subject to Indictment, Trial, Judgment and Punishment, according to Law.

Section. 4. The Times, Places and Manner of holding Elections for Senators and Representatives, shall be prescribed in each State by the Legislature thereof; but the Congress may at any time by Law make or alter such Regulations, except as to the Places of chusing Senators.

The Congress shall assemble at least once in every Year, and such Meeting shall be on the first Monday in December, unless they shall by Law appoint a different Day.

Section. 5. Each House shall be the Judge of the Elections, Returns and Qualifications of its own Members, and a Majority of each shall constitute a Quorum to do Business; but a smaller Number may adjourn from day to day, and may be authorized to compel the Attendance of absent Members, in such Manner, and under such Penalties as each House may provide.

Each House may determine the Rules of its Proceedings, punish its Members for disorderly Behaviour, and, with the Concurrence of two thirds, expel a Member.

Each House shall keep a Journal of its Proceedings, and from time to time publish the same, excepting such Parts as may in their Judgment require Secrecy; and the Yeas and Nays of the Members of either House on any question shall, at the Desire of one fifth of those Present, be entered on the Journal.

Neither House, during the Session of Congress, shall, without the Consent of the other, adjourn for more than three days, nor to any other Place than that in which the two Houses shall be sitting.

Section. 6. The Senators and Representatives shall receive a Compensation for their Services, to be ascertained by Law, and paid out of the Treasury of the United States. They shall in all Cases, except Treason, Felony and Breach of the Peace, be privileged from Arrest during their Attendance at the Session of their respective Houses, and in going to and returning from the same; and for any Speech or Debate in either House, they shall not be questioned in any other Place.

No Senator or Representative shall, during the Time for which he was elected, be appointed to any civil Office under the Authority of the United States, which shall have been created, or the Emoluments whereof shall have been encreased during such time; and no Person holding any Office under the United States, shall be a Member of either House during his Continuance in Office.

Section. 7. All Bills for raising Revenue shall originate in the House of Representatives; but the Senate may propose or concur with Amendments as on other Bills.

Every Bill which shall have passed the House of Representatives and the Senate, shall, before it become a Law, be presented to the President of the United States; If he approve he shall sign it, but if not he shall return it, with his Objections to that House in which it shall have originated, who shall enter the Objections at large on their Journal, and proceed to reconsider it. If after such Reconsideration two thirds of that House shall agree to pass the Bill, it shall be sent, together with the Objections, to the other House, by which it shall likewise be reconsidered, and if approved by two thirds of that House, it shall become a Law. But in all such Cases the Votes of both Houses shall be determined by Yeas and Nays, and the Names of the Persons voting for and against the Bill shall be entered on the Journal of each House respectively. If any Bill shall not be returned by the President within ten Days (Sundays excepted) after it shall have been presented to him, the Same shall be a Law, in like Manner as if he had signed it, unless the Congress by their Adjournment prevent its Return, in which Case it shall not be a Law.

Every Order, Resolution, or Vote to which the Concurrence of the Senate and House of Representatives may be necessary (except on a question of Adjournment) shall be presented to the President of the United States; and before the Same shall take Effect, shall be approved by him, or being disapproved by him, shall be repassed by two thirds of the Senate and House of Representatives, according to the Rules and Limitations prescribed in the Case of a Bill.

Section. 8. The Congress shall have Power

To lay and collect Taxes, Duties, Imposts and Excises, to pay the Debts and provide for the common Defence and general Welfare of the United States; but all Duties, Imposts and Excises shall be uniform throughout the United States;

To borrow Money on the credit of the United States;

To regulate Commerce with foreign Nations, and among the several States, and with the Indian Tribes;

To establish an uniform Rule of Naturalization, and uniform Laws on the subject of Bankruptcies throughout the United States;

To coin Money, regulate the Value thereof, and of foreign Coin, and fix the Standard of Weights and Measures;

To provide for the Punishment of counterfeiting the Securities and current Coin of the United States;

To establish Post Offices and post Roads;

To promote the Progress of Science and useful Arts, by securing for limited Times to Authors and Inventors the exclusive Right to their respective Writings and Discoveries;

To constitute Tribunals inferior to the supreme Court;

To define and punish Piracies and Felonies committed on the high Seas, and Offences against the Law of Nations;

To declare War, grant Letters of Marque and Reprisal, and make Rules concerning Captures on Land and Water;

To raise and support Armies, but no Appropriation of Money to that Use shall be for a longer Term than two Years;

To provide and maintain a Navy;

To make Rules for the Government and Regulation of the land and naval Forces;

To provide for calling forth the Militia to execute the Laws of the Union, suppress Insurrections and repel Invasions;

To provide for organizing, arming, and disciplining, the Militia, and for governing such Part of them as may be employed in the Service of the United States, reserving to the States respectively, the Appointment of the Officers, and the Authority of training the Militia according to the discipline prescribed by Congress;

To exercise exclusive Legislation in all Cases whatsoever, over such District (not exceeding ten Miles square) as may, by Cession of particular States, and the Acceptance of Congress, become the Seat of the Government of the United States, and to exercise like Authority over all Places purchased by the Consent of the Legislature of the State in which the Same shall be, for the Erection of Forts, Magazines, Arsenals, dock-Yards, and other needful Buildings;—And

To make all Laws which shall be necessary and proper for carrying into Execution the foregoing Powers, and all other Powers vested by this

Constitution in the Government of the United States, or in any Department or Officer thereof.

Section. 9. The Migration or Importation of such Persons as any of the States now existing shall think proper to admit, shall not be prohibited by the Congress prior to the Year one thousand eight hundred and eight, but a Tax or duty may be imposed on such Importation, not exceeding ten dollars for each Person.

The Privilege of the Writ of Habeas Corpus shall not be suspended, unless when in Cases of Rebellion or Invasion the public Safety may require it.

No Bill of Attainder or ex post facto Law shall be passed.

No Capitation, or other direct, Tax shall be laid, unless in Proportion to the Census or Enumeration herein before directed to be taken.

No Tax or Duty shall be laid on Articles exported from any State.

No Preference shall be given by any Regulation of Commerce or Revenue to the Ports of one State over those of another: nor shall Vessels bound to, or from, one State, be obliged to enter, clear, or pay Duties in another.

No Money shall be drawn from the Treasury, but in Consequence of Appropriations made by Law; and a regular Statement and Account of the Receipts and Expenditures of all public Money shall be published from time to time.

No Title of Nobility shall be granted by the United States: And no Person holding any Office of Profit or Trust under them, shall, without the Consent of the Congress, accept of any present, Emolument, Office, or Title, of any kind whatever, from any King, Prince, or foreign State.

Section. 10. No State shall enter into any Treaty, Alliance, or Confederation; grant Letters of Marque and Reprisal; coin Money; emit Bills of Credit; make any Thing but gold and silver Coin a Tender in Payment of Debts; pass any Bill of Attainder, ex post facto Law, or Law impairing the Obligation of Contracts, or grant any Title of Nobility.

No State shall, without the Consent of the Congress, lay any Imposts or Duties on Imports or Exports, except what may be absolutely necessary for executing it's inspection Laws: and the net Produce of all Duties and Imposts, laid by any State on Imports or Exports, shall be for the Use of the Treasury of the United States; and all such Laws shall be subject to the Revision and Controul of the Congress.

No State shall, without the Consent of Congress, lay any Duty of

Tonnage, keep Troops, or Ships of War in time of Peace, enter into any Agreement or Compact with another State, or with a foreign Power, or engage in War, unless actually invaded, or in such imminent Danger as will not admit of delay.

Article. II.

Section. 1. The executive Power shall be vested in a President of the United States of America. He shall hold his Office during the Term of four Years, and, together with the Vice President, chosen for the same Term, be elected, as follows

Each State shall appoint, in such Manner as the Legislature thereof may direct, a Number of Electors, equal to the whole Number of Senators and Representatives to which the State may be entitled in the Congress: but no Senator or Representative, or Person holding an Office of Trust or Profit under the United States, shall be appointed an Elector.

The Electors shall meet in their respective States, and vote by Ballot for two Persons, of whom one at least shall not be an Inhabitant of the same State with themselves. And they shall make a List of all the Persons voted for, and of the Number of Votes for each; which List they shall sign and certify, and transmit sealed to the Seat of the Government of the United States, directed to the President of the Senate. The President of the Senate shall, in the Presence of the Senate and House of Representatives, open all the Certificates, and the Votes shall then be counted. The Person having the greatest Number of Votes shall be the President, if such Number be a Majority of the whole Number of Electors appointed; and if there be more than one who have such Majority, and have an equal Number of Votes, then the House of Representatives shall immediately chuse by Ballot one of them for President; and if no Person have a Majority, then from the five highest on the List the said House shall in like Manner chuse the President. But in chusing the President, the Votes shall be taken by States, the Representation from each State having one Vote; A quorum for this Purpose shall consist of a Member or Members from two thirds of the States, and a Majority of all the States shall be necessary to a Choice. In every Case, after the Choice of the President, the Person having the greatest Number of Votes of the Electors shall be the Vice President. But if there should remain two or more who have equal Votes, the Senate shall chuse from them by Ballot the Vice President.

The Congress may determine the Time of chusing the Electors, and the Day on which they shall give their Votes; which Day shall be the same throughout the United States.

No Person except a natural born Citizen, or a Citizen of the United States, at the time of the Adoption of this Constitution, shall be eligible to the Office of President; neither shall any Person be eligible to that Office who shall not have attained to the Age of thirty five Years, and been fourteen Years a Resident within the United States.

In Case of the Removal of the President from Office, or of his Death, Resignation, or Inability to discharge the Powers and Duties of the said Office, the Same shall devolve on the Vice President, and the Congress may by Law provide for the Case of Removal, Death, Resignation or Inability, both of the President and Vice President, declaring what Officer shall then act as President, and such Officer shall act accordingly, until the Disability be removed, or a President shall be elected.

The President shall, at stated Times, receive for his Services, a Compensation, which shall neither be encreased nor diminished during the Period for which he shall have been elected, and he shall not receive within that Period any other Emolument from the United States, or any of them.

Before he enter on the Execution of his Office, he shall take the following Oath or Affirmation:—"I do solemnly swear (or affirm) that I will faithfully execute the Office of President of the United States, and will to the best of my Ability, preserve, protect and defend the Constitution of the United States."

Section. 2. The President shall be Commander in Chief of the Army and Navy of the United States, and of the Militia of the several States, when called into the actual Service of the United States; he may require the Opinion, in writing, of the principal Officer in each of the executive Departments, upon any Subject relating to the Duties of their respective Offices, and he shall have Power to grant Reprieves and Pardons for Offences against the United States, except in Cases of Impeachment.

He shall have Power, by and with the Advice and Consent of the Senate, to make Treaties, provided two thirds of the Senators present concur; and he shall nominate, and by and with the Advice and Consent of the Senate, shall appoint Ambassadors, other public Ministers and Consuls, Judges of the supreme Court, and all other Officers of the United States, whose Appointments are not herein otherwise provided for, and which shall be established by Law: but the Congress may by Law vest the Appointment of such inferior Officers, as they think proper, in the President alone, in the Courts of Law, or in the Heads of Departments.

The President shall have Power to fill up all Vacancies that may happen during the Recess of the Senate, by granting Commissions which shall expire at the End of their next Session.

Section. 3. He shall from time to time give to the Congress Information of the State of the Union, and recommend to their Consideration such Measures as he shall judge necessary and expedient; he may, on extraordinary Occasions, convene both Houses, or either of them, and in Case of Disagreement between them, with Respect to the Time of Adjournment, he may adjourn them to such Time as he shall think proper; he shall receive Ambassadors and other public Ministers; he shall take Care that the Laws be faithfully executed, and shall Commission all the Officers of the United States.

Section. 4. The President, Vice President and all civil Officers of the United States, shall be removed from Office on Impeachment for, and Conviction of, Treason, Bribery, or other high Crimes and Misdemeanors.

Article. III.

Section. 1. The judicial Power of the United States, shall be vested in one supreme Court, and in such inferior Courts as the Congress may from time to time ordain and establish. The Judges, both of the supreme and inferior Courts, shall hold their Offices during good Behaviour, and shall, at stated Times, receive for their Services, a Compensation, which shall not be diminished during their Continuance in Office.

Section. 2. The judicial Power shall extend to all Cases, in Law and Equity, arising under this Constitution, the Laws of the United States, and Treaties made, or which shall be made, under their Authority;—to all Cases affecting Ambassadors, other public Ministers and Consuls;—to all Cases of admiralty and maritime Jurisdiction;—to Controversies to which the United States shall be a Party;—to Controversies between two or more States;—between a State and Citizens of another State;—between Citizens of different States,—between Citizens of the same State claiming Lands under Grants of different States, and between a State, or the Citizens thereof, and foreign States, Citizens or Subjects.

In all Cases affecting Ambassadors, other public Ministers and Consuls, and those in which a State shall be a Party, the supreme Court shall have original Jurisdiction. In all the other Cases before mentioned, the supreme Court shall have appellate Jurisdiction, both as to Law and Fact, with such Exceptions, and under such Regulations as the Congress shall make.

The Trial of all Crimes, except in Cases of Impeachment, shall be by Jury; and such Trial shall be held in the State where the said Crimes shall have been committed; but when not committed within any State, the Trial shall be at such Place or Places as the Congress may by Law have directed.

Section. 3. Treason against the United States, shall consist only in levying War against them, or in adhering to their Enemies, giving them Aid and Comfort. No Person shall be convicted of Treason unless on the Testimony of two Witnesses to the same overt Act, or on Confession in open Court.

The Congress shall have Power to declare the Punishment of Treason, but no Attainder of Treason shall work Corruption of Blood, or Forfeiture except during the Life of the Person attainted.

Article. IV.

Section. 1. Full Faith and Credit shall be given in each State to the public Acts, Records, and judicial Proceedings of every other State. And the Congress may by general Laws prescribe the Manner in which such Acts, Records and Proceedings shall be proved, and the Effect thereof.

Section. 2. The Citizens of each State shall be entitled to all Privileges and Immunities of Citizens in the several States.

A Person charged in any State with Treason, Felony, or other Crime, who shall flee from Justice, and be found in another State, shall on Demand of the executive Authority of the State from which he fled, be delivered up, to be removed to the State having Jurisdiction of the Crime.

No Person held to Service or Labour in one State, under the Laws thereof, escaping into another, shall, in Consequence of any Law or Regulation therein, be discharged from such Service or Labour, but shall be delivered up on Claim of the Party to whom such Service or Labour may be due.

Section. 3. New States may be admitted by the Congress into this Union; but no new State shall be formed or erected within the Jurisdiction of any other State; nor any State be formed by the Junction of two or more States, or Parts of States, without the Consent of the Legislatures of the States concerned as well as of the Congress.

The Congress shall have Power to dispose of and make all needful Rules and Regulations respecting the Territory or other Property belonging to the United States; and nothing in this Constitution shall be so construed as to Prejudice any Claims of the United States, or of any particular State.

Section. 4. The United States shall guarantee to every State in this Union a Republican Form of Government, and shall protect each of them against Invasion; and on Application of the Legislature, or of the Executive (when the Legislature cannot be convened) against domestic Violence.

Article. V.

The Congress, whenever two thirds of both Houses shall deem it necessary, shall propose Amendments to this Constitution, or, on the Application of the Legislatures of two thirds of the several States, shall call a Convention for proposing Amendments, which, in either Case, shall be valid to all Intents and Purposes, as Part of this Constitution, when ratified by the Legislatures of three fourths of the several States, or by Conventions in three fourths thereof, as the one or the other Mode of Ratification may be proposed by the Congress; Provided that no Amendment which may be made prior to the Year One thousand eight hundred and eight shall in any Manner affect the first and fourth Clauses in the Ninth Section of the first Article; and that no State, without its Consent, shall be deprived of it's equal Suffrage in the Senate.

Article. VI.

All Debts contracted and Engagements entered into, before the Adoption of this Constitution, shall be as valid against the United States under this Constitution, as under the Confederation.

This Constitution, and the Laws of the United States which shall be made in Pursuance thereof; and all Treaties made, or which shall be made, under the Authority of the United States, shall be the supreme Law of the Land; and the Judges in every State shall be bound thereby, any Thing in the Constitution or Laws of any State to the Contrary notwithstanding.

The Senators and Representatives before mentioned, and the Members of the several State Legislatures, and all executive and judicial Officers, both of the United States and of the several States, shall be bound by Oath or Affirmation, to support this Constitution; but no religious Test shall ever be required as a Qualification to any Office or public Trust under the United States.

Article. VII.

The Ratification of the Conventions of nine States, shall be sufficient for the Establishment of this Constitution between the States so ratifying the Same.

DONE in Convention by the Unanimous Consent of the States present the Seventeenth Day of September in the Year of our Lord one thousand seven hundred and Eighty seven and of the Independence of the United States of America the Twelfth. In witness whereof We have hereunto subscribed our Names,

G. Washington—Presidt
and deputy from Virginia

New Hampshire { John Langdon
Nicholas Gilman

Massachusetts { Nathaniel Gorham
Rufus King

Connecticut { Wm Saml Johnson
Roger Sherman

New York { Alexander Hamilton

New Jersey { Wil: Livingston
David Brearley
Wm Paterson
Jona: Dayton

Pennsylvania	B. Franklin Thomas Mifflin Robt Morris Geo. Clymer Thos FitzSimons Jared Ingersoll James Wilson Gouv Morris
Delaware	Geo: Read Gunning Bedford jun John Dickinson Richard Bassett Jaco: Broom
Maryland	James McHenry Dan of St Thos Jennifer Danl Carroll
Virginia	John Blair— James Madison Jr.
North Carolina	Wm Blount Richd Dobbs Spaight Hu Williamson
South Carolina	J. Rutledge Charles Cotesworth Pinckney Charles Pinckney Pierce Butler
Georgia	William Few Abr Baldwin

Attest: William Jackson, Secretary

Appendix F

A Chart for Article I, Section 8, of the United States Constitution

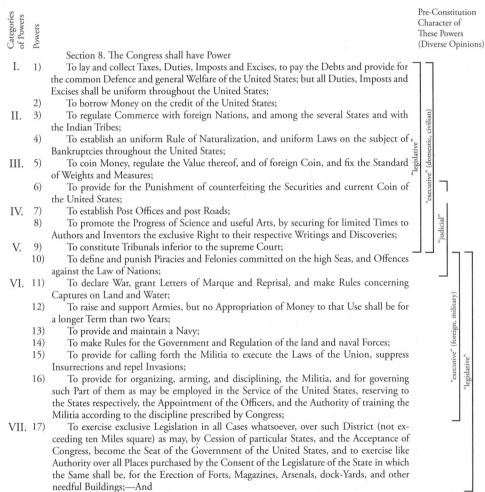

Section 8. The Congress shall have Power

I. 1)   To lay and collect Taxes, Duties, Imposts and Excises, to pay the Debts and provide for the common Defence and general Welfare of the United States; but all Duties, Imposts and Excises shall be uniform throughout the United States;

    2)   To borrow Money on the credit of the United States;

II. 3)   To regulate Commerce with foreign Nations, and among the several States and with the Indian Tribes;

    4)   To establish an uniform Rule of Naturalization, and uniform Laws on the subject of Bankruptcies throughout the United States;

III. 5)   To coin Money, regulate the Value thereof, and of foreign Coin, and fix the Standard of Weights and Measures;

    6)   To provide for the Punishment of counterfeiting the Securities and current Coin of the United States;

IV. 7)   To establish Post Offices and post Roads;

    8)   To promote the Progress of Science and useful Arts, by securing for limited Times to Authors and Inventors the exclusive Right to their respective Writings and Discoveries;

V. 9)   To constitute Tribunals inferior to the supreme Court;

    10)   To define and punish Piracies and Felonies committed on the high Seas, and Offences against the Law of Nations;

VI. 11)   To declare War, grant Letters of Marque and Reprisal, and make Rules concerning Captures on Land and Water;

    12)   To raise and support Armies, but no Appropriation of Money to that Use shall be for a longer Term than two Years;

    13)   To provide and maintain a Navy;

    14)   To make Rules for the Government and Regulation of the land and naval Forces;

    15)   To provide for calling forth the Militia to execute the Laws of the Union, suppress Insurrections and repel Invasions;

    16)   To provide for organizing, arming, and disciplining, the Militia, and for governing such Part of them as may be employed in the Service of the United States, reserving to the States respectively, the Appointment of the Officers, and the Authority of training the Militia according to the discipline prescribed by Congress;

VII. 17)   To exercise exclusive Legislation in all Cases whatsoever, over such District (not exceeding ten Miles square) as may, by Cession of particular States, and the Acceptance of Congress, become the Seat of the Government of the United States, and to exercise like Authority over all Places purchased by the Consent of the Legislature of the State in which the Same shall be, for the Erection of Forts, Magazines, Arsenals, dock-Yards, and other needful Buildings;—And

Necessary and Proper Clause   To make all Laws which shall be necessary and proper for carrying into Execution the foregoing Powers, and all other Powers vested by this Constitution in the Government of the United States, or in any Department or Officer thereof.

225

Sources: There is provided here an amended version of the chart developed in George Anastaplo, *The Constitution of 1787: A Commentary* (Baltimore: Johns Hopkins University Press, 1989), 53–57, 280. See Part One, Essays Eight and Thirteen, of these *Reflections.* See also, William W. Crosskey, *Politics and the Constitution in the History of the United States* (Chicago: University of Chicago Press, 1953).

Appendix G

The Amendments to the
United States Constitution (1791–1992)

Articles in Addition to, and Amendment of, the Constitution of the United States, Proposed by Congress and Ratified by the Several States, Pursuant to the Fifth Article of the Original Constitution

Amendment I [1791]

Congress shall make no law respecting an establishment of religion, or prohibiting the free exercise thereof; or abridging the freedom of speech, or of the press; or the right of the people peaceably to assemble, and to petition the Government for a redress of grievances.

Amendment II [1791]

A well regulated Militia, being necessary to the security of a free State, the right of the people to keep and bear Arms, shall not be infringed.

Amendment III [1791]

No Soldier shall, in time of peace be quartered in any house, without the consent of the Owner, nor in time of war, but in a manner to be prescribed by law.

Sources: See *The Declaration of Independence and the Constitution of the United States,* 96th Cong., 1st sess., House Document No. 96-143 (Washington, D.C.: Government Printing Office, 1979). See also, George Anastaplo, *The Constitution of 1787: A Commentary* (Baltimore: Johns Hopkins University Press, 1989), 237, 288–97; George Anastaplo, *The Amendments to the Constitution: A Commentary* (Baltimore: Johns Hopkins University Press, 1996), 243, 375–84. The dates of ratification of the Amendments are provided in brackets. "Sec." is written as "Section" in all Amendments.

Amendment IV [1791]

The right of the people to be secure in their persons, houses, papers, and effects, against unreasonable searches and seizures, shall not be violated, and no Warrants shall issue, but upon probable cause, supported by Oath or affirmation, and particularly describing the place to be searched, and the persons or things to be seized.

Amendment V [1791]

No person shall be held to answer for a capital, or otherwise infamous crime, unless on a presentment or indictment of a Grand Jury, except in cases arising in the land or naval forces, or in the Militia, when in actual service in time of War or public danger; nor shall any person be subject for the same offence to be twice put in jeopardy of life or limb; nor shall be compelled in any criminal case to be a witness against himself, nor be deprived of life, liberty, or property, without due process of law; nor shall private property be taken for public use, without just compensation.

Amendment VI [1791]

In all criminal prosecutions, the accused shall enjoy the right to a speedy and public trial, by an impartial jury of the State and district wherein the crime shall have been committed, which district shall have been previously ascertained by law, and to be informed of the nature and cause of the accusation; to be confronted with the witnesses against him; to have compulsory process for obtaining witnesses in his favor, and to have the Assistance of Counsel for his defence.

Amendment VII [1791]

In Suits at common law, where the value in controversy shall exceed twenty dollars, the right of trial by jury shall be preserved, and no fact tried by a jury, shall be otherwise re-examined in any Court of the United States, than according to the rules of the common law.

Amendment VIII [1791]

Excessive bail shall not be required, nor excessive fines imposed, nor cruel and unusual punishments inflicted.

Amendment IX [1791]

The enumeration in the Constitution, of certain rights, shall not be construed to deny or disparage others retained by the people.

Amendment X [1791]

The powers not delegated to the United States by the Constitution, nor prohibited by it to the States, are reserved to the States respectively, or to the people.

Amendment XI [1798]

The Judicial power of the United States shall not be construed to extend to any suit in law or equity, commenced or prosecuted against one of the United States by Citizens of another State, or by Citizens or Subjects of any Foreign State.

Amendment XII [1804]

The Electors shall meet in their respective states, and vote by ballot for President and Vice-President, one of whom, at least, shall not be an inhabitant of the same state with themselves; they shall name in their ballots the person voted for as President, and in distinct ballots the person voted for as Vice-President, and they shall make distinct lists of all persons voted for as President, and of all persons voted for as Vice-President, and of the number of votes for each, which lists they shall sign and certify, and transmit sealed to the seat of the government of the United States, directed to the President of the Senate;—The President of the Senate shall, in the presence of the Senate and House of Representatives, open all the certificates and the votes shall then be counted;—The person having the greatest number of votes for President, shall be the President, if such number be a majority of the whole number of Electors appointed; and if no person have such majority, then from the persons having the highest numbers not exceeding three on the list of those voted for as President, the House of Representatives shall choose immediately, by ballot, the President. But in choosing the President, the votes shall be taken by states, the representation from each state having one vote; a quorum for this purpose shall consist of a member or members from two-thirds of the states, and a majority of all the states shall be necessary to a choice. And if the House of Representatives shall not choose a President whenever the right of choice shall devolve upon them, before the fourth day of March next following, then the Vice-President shall act as President, as in the case of the death or other constitutional disability of the President.—The person having the greatest number of votes as Vice-President, shall be the Vice-President, if such number be a majority of the whole number of Electors appointed, and if no person have a majority, then from the two highest numbers on the list, the Senate shall choose the Vice-President; a quorum for the purpose shall consist of two-thirds of the whole number of Senators, and a majority of the whole number shall be necessary to a choice. But no person constitutionally ineligible to the office of President shall be eligible to that of Vice-President of the United States.

Amendment XIII [1865]

Section 1. Neither slavery nor involuntary servitude, except as a punishment for crime whereof the party shall have been duly convicted, shall exist within the United States, or any place subject to their jurisdiction.

Section 2. Congress shall have power to enforce this article by appropriate legislation.

Amendment XIV [1868]

Section 1. All persons born or naturalized in the United States, and subject to the jurisdiction thereof, are citizens of the United States and of the State wherein they reside. No State shall make or enforce any law which shall abridge the privileges or immunities of citizens of the United States; nor shall any State deprive any person of life, liberty, or property, without due process of law; nor deny to any person within its jurisdiction the equal protection of the laws.

Section 2. Representatives shall be apportioned among the several States according to their respective numbers, counting the whole number of persons in each State, excluding Indians not taxed. But when the right to vote at any election for the choice of electors for President and Vice President of the United States, Representatives in Congress, the Executive and Judicial officers of a State, or the members of the Legislature thereof, is denied to any of the male inhabitants of such State, being twenty-one years of age, and citizens of the United States, or in any way abridged, except for participation in rebellion, or other crime, the basis of representation therein shall be reduced in the proportion which the number of such male citizens shall bear to the whole number of male citizens twenty-one years of age in such State.

Section 3. No person shall be a Senator or Representative in Congress, or elector of President and Vice President, or hold any office, civil or military, under the United States, or under any State, who, having previously taken an oath, as a member of Congress, or as an officer of the United States, or as a member of any State legislature, or as an executive or judicial officer of any State, to support the Constitution of the United States, shall have engaged in insurrection or rebellion against the same, or given aid or comfort to the enemies thereof. But Congress may by a vote of two-thirds of each House, remove such disability.

Section 4. The validity of the public debt of the United States, authorized by law, including debts incurred for payment of pensions and bounties for services in suppressing insurrection or rebellion, shall not be questioned. But neither the United States nor any State shall assume or pay any debt or obligation incurred in aid of insurrection or rebellion against the United States, or any claim for the loss or emancipation of any slave; but all such debts, obligations and claims shall be held illegal and void.

Section 5. The Congress shall have power to enforce, by appropriate legislation, the provisions of this article.

Amendment XV [1870]

Section 1. The right of citizens of the United States to vote shall not be denied or abridged by the United States or by any State on account of race, color, or previous condition of servitude.

Section 2. The Congress shall have power to enforce this article by appropriate legislation.

Amendment XVI [1913]

The Congress shall have power to lay and collect taxes on incomes, from whatever source derived, without apportionment among the several States, and without regard to any census or enumeration.

Amendment XVII [1913]

The Senate of the United States shall be composed of two Senators from each State, elected by the people thereof, for six years; and each Senator shall have one vote. The electors in each State shall have the qualifications requisite for electors of the most numerous branch of the State legislatures.

When vacancies happen in the representation of any State in the Senate, the executive authority of such State shall issue writs of election to fill such vacancies: *Provided,* That the legislature of any State may empower the executive thereof to make temporary appointments until the people fill the vacancies by election as the legislature may direct.

This amendment shall not be so construed as to affect the election or term of any Senator chosen before it becomes valid as part of the Constitution.

Amendment XVIII [1919]

Section 1. After one year from the ratification of this article the manufacture, sale, or transportation of intoxicating liquors within, the importation thereof into, or the exportation thereof from the United States and all territory subject to the jurisdiction thereof for beverage purposes is hereby prohibited.

Section 2. The Congress and the several States shall have concurrent power to enforce this article by appropriate legislation.

Section 3. This article shall be inoperative unless it shall have been ratified as an amendment to the Constitution by the legislatures of the several States, as provided in the Constitution, within seven years from the date of the submission hereof to the States by the Congress.

Amendment XIX [1920]

The right of citizens of the United States to vote shall not be denied or abridged by the United States or by any State on account of sex.

Congress shall have power to enforce this article by appropriate legislation.

Amendment XX [1933]

Section 1. The terms of the President and Vice President shall end at noon on the 20th day of January, and the terms of Senators and Representatives at noon on the 3d day of January, of the years in which such terms would have ended if this article had not been ratified; and the terms of their successors shall then begin.

Section 2. The Congress shall assemble at least once in every year, and such meeting shall begin at noon on the 3d day of January, unless they shall by law appoint a different day.

Section 3. If, at the time fixed for the beginning of the term of the President, the President elect shall have died, the Vice President elect shall become President. If a President shall not have been chosen before the time fixed for the beginning of his term, or if the President elect shall have failed to qualify, then the Vice President elect shall act as President until a President shall have qualified; and the Congress may by law provide for the case wherein neither a President elect nor a Vice President elect shall have qualified, declaring who shall then act as President, or the manner in which one who is to act shall be selected, and such person shall act accordingly until a President or Vice President shall have qualified.

Section 4. The Congress may by law provide for the case of the death of any of the persons from whom the House of Representatives may choose a President whenever the right of choice shall have devolved upon them, and for the case of the death of any of the persons from whom the Senate may choose a Vice President whenever the right of choice shall have devolved upon them.

Section 5. Sections 1 and 2 shall take effect on the 15th day of October following the ratification of this article.

Section 6. This article shall be inoperative unless it shall have been ratified as an amendment to the Constitution by the legislatures of three-fourths of the several States within seven years from the date of its submission.

Amendment XXI [1933]

Section 1. The eighteenth article of amendment to the Constitution of the United States is hereby repealed.

Section 2. The transportation or importation into any State, Territory, or possession of the United States for delivery or use therein of intoxicating liquors, in violation of the laws thereof, is hereby prohibited.

Section 3. This article shall be inoperative unless it shall have been ratified as an amendment to the Constitution by conventions in the several States, as provided in the Constitution, within seven years from the date of the submission hereof to the States by the Congress.

Amendment XXII [1951]

Section 1. No person shall be elected to the office of the President more than twice, and no person who has held the office of President, or acted as President, for more than two years of a term to which some other person was elected President shall be elected to the office of the President more than once. But this Article shall not apply to any person holding the office of President when this Article was proposed by the Congress, and shall not prevent any person who may be holding the office of President, or acting as President, during the term within which this Article becomes operative from holding the office of President or acting as President during the remainder of such term.

Section 2. This article shall be inoperative unless it shall have been ratified as an amendment to the Constitution by the legislatures of three-fourths of the several States within seven years from the date of its submission to the States by the Congress.

Amendment XXIII [1961]

Section 1. The District constituting the seat of Government of the United States shall appoint in such manner as the Congress may direct:

A number of electors of President and Vice President equal to the whole number of Senators and Representatives in Congress to which the District would be entitled if it were a State, but in no event more than the least populous State; they shall be in addition to those appointed by the States, but they shall be considered, for the purposes of the election of President and Vice President, to be electors appointed by a State; and they shall meet in the District and perform such duties as provided by the twelfth article of amendment.

Section 2. The Congress shall have power to enforce this article by appropriate legislation.

Amendment XXIV [1964]

Section 1. The right of citizens of the United States to vote in any primary or other election for President or Vice President, for electors for President or Vice President, or for Senator or Representative in Congress, shall not be denied or abridged by the United States or any State by reason of failure to pay any poll tax or other tax.

Section 2. The Congress shall have power to enforce this article by appropriate legislation.

Amendment XXV [1967]

Section 1. In case of the removal of the President from office or of his death or resignation, the Vice President shall become President.

Section 2. Whenever there is a vacancy in the office of the Vice President, the President shall nominate a Vice President who shall take office upon confirmation by a majority vote of both Houses of Congress.

Section 3. Whenever the President transmits to the President pro tempore of the Senate and the Speaker of the House of Representatives his written declaration that he is unable to discharge the powers and duties of his office, and until he transmits to them a written declaration to the contrary, such powers and duties shall be discharged by the Vice President as Acting President.

Section 4. Whenever the Vice President and a majority of either the principal officers of the executive departments or of such other body as Congress may by law provide, transmit to the President pro tempore of the Senate and the Speaker of the House of Representatives their written declaration that the President is unable to discharge the powers and duties of his office, the Vice President shall immediately assume the powers and duties of the office as Acting President.

Thereafter, when the President transmits to the President pro tempore of the Senate and the Speaker of the House of Representatives his written declaration that no inability exists, he shall resume the powers and duties of his office unless the Vice President and a majority of either the principal officers of the executive department or of such other body as Congress may by law provide, transmit within four days to the President pro tempore of the Senate and the Speaker of the House of Representatives their written declaration that the President is unable to discharge the powers and duties of his office. Thereupon Congress shall decide the issue, assembling within forty-eight hours for that purpose if not in session. If the Congress, within twenty-one days after receipt of the latter written declaration, or, if Congress is not in session, within twenty-one days after Congress is required to assemble, determines by two-thirds vote of both Houses that the President is unable to discharge the powers and duties of his office, the Vice President shall continue to discharge the same as Acting President; otherwise, the President shall resume the powers and duties of his office.

Amendment XXVI [1971]

Section 1. The right of citizens of the United States, who are eighteen years of age or older, to vote shall not be denied or abridged by the United States or by any State on account of age.

Section 2. The Congress shall have power to enforce this article by appropriate legislation.

Amendment XXVII [1992]

No law varying the compensation for the services of the Senators and Representatives shall take effect until an election of Representatives shall have intervened.

Appendix H

Proposed Amendments to the United States Constitution Not Ratified by the States (1789–1978)

Articles in Addition to, and Amendment of, the Constitution of the United States, Proposed by Congress but Not Ratified by the States

Proposal of 1789

After the first enumeration required by the first article of the Constitution, there shall be one Representative for every thirty thousand, until the number shall amount to one hundred, after which the proportion shall be so regulated by Congress, that there shall be not less than one hundred Representatives, nor less than one Representative for every forty thousand persons, until the number of Representatives shall amount to two hundred; after which the proportion shall be so regulated by Congress, that there shall not be less than two hundred Representatives, nor more than one Representative for every fifty thousand persons.

Proposal of 1810

If any citizen of the United States shall accept, claim, receive or retain any title of nobility or honour, or shall, without the consent of Congress, accept and retain any present, pension, office or emolument of any kind whatever, from any emperor, king, prince or foreign power, such person shall cease to be a citizen of the United States, and shall be incapable of holding any office of trust or profit under them, or either of them.

Sources: See *The Declaration of Independence and the Constitution of the United States,* 96th Cong., 1st sess., House Document No. 96-143 (Washington, D.C., Government Printing Office, 1979). See also, George Anastaplo, *The Constitution of 1787: A Commentary* (Baltimore: Johns Hopkins University Press, 1989), 237, 298–99.

Proposal of 1861

No amendment shall be made to the Constitution which will authorize or give to Congress the power to abolish or interfere, within any State, with the domestic institutions thereof, including that of persons held to labor or service by the laws of said State.

Proposal of 1924

Section 1. The Congress shall have power to limit, regulate, and prohibit the labor of persons under 18 years of age.

Section 2. The power of the several States is unimpaired by this article except that the operation of State laws shall be suspended to the extent necessary to give effect to legislation enacted by the Congress.

Proposal of 1972

Section 1. Equality of rights under the law shall not be denied or abridged by the United States or by any State on account of sex.

Section 2. The Congress shall have the power to enforce, by appropriate legislation, the provisions of this article.

Section 3. This amendment shall take effect two years after the date of ratification.

Proposal of 1978

Section 1. For purposes of representation in the Congress, election of the President and Vice President, and article V of this Constitution, the District constituting the seat of government of the United States shall be treated as though it were a State.

Section 2. The exercise of the rights and powers conferred under this article shall be by the people of the District constituting the seat of government, and as shall be provided by the Congress.

Section 3. The twenty-third article of amendment to the Constitution of the United States is hereby repealed.

Section 4. This article shall be inoperative, unless it shall have been ratified as an amendment to the Constitution by the legislatures of three-fourths of the several States within seven years from the date of its submission.

Appendix I

The Confederate Constitution (1861)

The texts of the first twelve amendments to the United States Constitution of 1787 are substantially incorporated in Articles I, II, III, and VI of the Confederate Constitution, which itself works from the 1787 Constitution. The numbering and most *of the words added in 1861 to the Constitution of 1787 and to its first twelve amendments incorporated therein are underlined below. The 1861 changes in spelling, capitalization, punctuation, and italicization are* not *noted by underlining here. These changes are not uniform in all editions available to us of the Confederate Constitution of 1861.*

The Constitution of the Confederate States of America

We, the people of the <u>Confederate</u> States, <u>each State acting in its sovereign and independent character</u>, in order to form <u>a permanent federal government</u>, establish justice, insure domestic tranquility, and secure the blessings of liberty to ourselves and our posterity—<u>invoking the favor and guidance of Almighty God</u>—do ordain and establish this Constitution for the <u>Confederate</u> States of America.

Article I.

Section 1.

All legislative powers herein <u>delegated</u> shall be vested in a Congress of the <u>Confederate</u> States, which shall consist of a Senate and a House of Representatives.

Sources: See Senate Document No. 234, 58th Cong., 2nd sess. (Washington, D.C.: Government Printing Office, 1904), 909–23; Roger L. Ransom, *The Confederate States of America* (New York: W. W. Norton and Co., 2005), 265–86. See also, George Anastaplo, *The Amendments to the Constitution: A Commentary* (Baltimore: Johns Hopkins University Press, 1995), 243, 344–61. See, as well, George Anastaplo, *Abraham Lincoln: A Constitutional Biography* [preferred title, *Thoughts on Abraham Lincoln*](Lanham, Md.: Rowman & Littlefield, 1999).

Section 2.

1. The House of Representatives shall be composed of members chosen every second year by the people of the several States; and the electors in each State shall <u>be citizens of the Confederate States, and</u> have the qualifications requisite for electors of the most numerous branch of the State Legislature; <u>but no person of foreign birth, not a citizen of the Confederate States, shall be allowed to vote for any officer, civil or political, State or Federal.</u>

2. No person shall be a Representative who shall not have attained the age of twenty-five years, and <u>be</u> a citizen of the <u>Confederate</u> States, and who shall not, when elected, be an inhabitant of that State in which he shall be chosen.

3. Representatives and direct taxes shall be apportioned among the several States, which may be included within this <u>Confederacy</u>, according to their respective numbers, which shall be determined, by adding to the whole number of free persons, including those bound to service for a term of years, and excluding Indians not taxed, three-fifths of all <u>slaves</u>. The actual enumeration shall be made within three years after the first meeting of the Congress of the <u>Confederate</u> States, and within every subsequent term of ten years, in such manner as they shall by law direct. The number of Representatives shall not exceed one for every <u>fifty</u> thousand, but each State shall have at least one Representative; and until such enumeration shall be made, <u>the State of South Carolina</u> shall be entitled to choose <u>six; the State of Georgia ten; the State of Alabama nine; the State of Florida two; the State of Mississippi seven; the State of Louisiana six; and the State of Texas six.</u>

4. When vacancies happen in the representation from any State, the Executive authority thereof shall issue writs of election to fill such vacancies.

5. The House of Representatives shall choose their Speaker and other officers; and shall have the sole power of impeachment; <u>except that any judicial or other Federal officer, resident and acting solely within the limits of any State, may be impeached by a vote of two-thirds of both branches of the Legislature thereof.</u>

Section 3.

1. The Senate of the <u>Confederate</u> States shall be composed of two Senators from each State, chosen for six years by the Legislature thereof, <u>at</u>

the regular session next immediately preceding the commencement of the term of service; and each Senator shall have one vote.

2. Immediately after they shall be assembled, in consequence of the first election, they shall be divided as equally as may be into three classes. The seats of the Senators of the first class shall be vacated at the expiration of the second year; of the second class at the expiration of the fourth year; and of the third class at the expiration of the sixth year; so that one-third may be chosen every second year; and if vacancies happen by resignation, or otherwise, during the recess of the Legislature of any State, the Executive thereof may make temporary appointments until the next meeting of the Legislature, which shall then fill such vacancies.

3. No person shall be a Senator who shall not have attained the age of thirty years, and be a citizen of the Confederate States; and who shall not, when elected, be an inhabitant of the State for which he shall be chosen.

4. The Vice President of the Confederate States shall be President of the Senate, but shall have no vote unless they be equally divided.

5. The Senate shall choose their other officers; and also a President *pro tempore* in the absence of the Vice President, or when he shall exercise the office of President of the Confederate States.

6. The Senate shall have the sole power to try all impeachments. When sitting for that purpose, they shall be on oath or affirmation. When the President of the Confederate States is tried, the Chief Justice shall preside; and no person shall be convicted without the concurrence of two-thirds of the members present.

7. Judgment in cases of impeachment shall not extend further than to removal from office, and disqualification to hold and enjoy any office of honor, trust or profit under the Confederate States; but the party convicted shall, nevertheless, be liable and subject to indictment, trial, judgment and punishment according to law.

Section 4.

1. The times, places and manner of holding elections for Senators and Representatives, shall be prescribed in each State by the Legislature thereof, subject to the provisions of this Constitution; but the Congress may, at any time, by law, make or alter such regulations, except as to the times and places of choosing Senators.

2. The Congress shall assemble at least once in every year; and such

meeting shall be on the first Monday in December, unless they shall, by law, appoint a different day.

Section 5.

<u>1.</u> Each House shall be the judge of the elections, returns, and qualifications of its own members, and a majority of each shall constitute a quorum to do business; but a smaller number may adjourn from day to day, and may be authorized to compel the attendance of absent members, in such manner and under such penalties as each House may provide.

<u>2.</u> Each House may determine the rules of its proceedings, punish its members for disorderly behavior, and, with the concurrence of two-thirds <u>of the whole number,</u> expel a member.

<u>3.</u> Each House shall keep a journal of its proceedings, and from time to time publish the same, excepting such parts as may in their judgment require secrecy; and the yeas and nays of the members of either House, on any question, shall, at the desire of one-fifth of those present, be entered on the journal.

<u>4.</u> Neither House, during the session of Congress, shall without the consent of the other, adjourn for more than three days, nor to any other place than that in which the two Houses shall be sitting.

Section 6.

<u>1.</u> The Senators and Representatives shall receive a compensation for their services, to be ascertained by law, and paid out of the Treasury of the <u>Confederate</u> States. They shall, in all cases, except treason, felony, and breach of the peace, be privileged from arrest during their attendance at the session of their respective Houses, and in going to and returning from the same; and for any speech or debate in either House, they shall not be questioned in any other place.

<u>2.</u> No Senator or Representative shall, during the time for which he was elected, be appointed to any civil office under the authority of the <u>Confederate</u> States, which shall have been created, or the emoluments whereof shall have been increased during such time; and no person holding any office under the <u>Confederate</u> States shall be a member of either House during his continuance in office. <u>But Congress may, by law, grant to the principal officer in each of the Executive Departments a seat upon the floor of either House, with the privilege of discussing any measures appertaining to his department.</u>

Section 7.

<u>1.</u> All bills for raising revenue shall originate in the House of Representatives; but the Senate may propose or concur with amendments, as on other bills.

<u>2.</u> Every bill which shall have passed <u>both Houses,</u> shall, before it becomes a law, be presented to the President of the <u>Confederate</u> States; if he approve, he shall sign it; but if not, he shall return it, with his objections, to that House in which it shall have originated, who shall enter the objections at large on their journal, and proceed to reconsider it. If, after such reconsideration, two-thirds of that House shall agree to pass the bill, it shall be sent, together with the objections, to the other House, by which it shall likewise be reconsidered, and if approved by two-thirds of that House, it shall become a law. But in all such cases, the votes of both Houses shall be determined by yeas and nays, and the names of the persons voting for and against the bill shall be entered on the journal of each House respectively. If any bill shall not be returned by the President within ten days (Sundays excepted) after it shall have been presented to him, the same shall be a law, in like manner as if he had signed it, unless the Congress, by their adjournment, prevent its return; in which case it shall not be a law. <u>The President may approve any appropriation and disapprove any other appropriation in the same bill. In such case he shall, in signing the bill, designate the appropriations disapproved; and shall return a copy of such appropriations, with his objections, to the House in which the bill shall have originated; and the same proceedings shall then be had as in case of other bills disapproved by the President.</u>

<u>3.</u> Every order, resolution, or vote, to which the concurrence of both Houses may be necessary (except on a question of adjournment) shall be presented to the President of the <u>Confederate</u> States; and before the same shall take effect, shall be approved by him; or being disapproved by him, shall be repassed by two-thirds of <u>both Houses,</u> according to the rules and limitations prescribed in case of a bill.

Section 8.

The Congress shall have power—

<u>1.</u> To lay and collect taxes, duties, imposts, and excises <u>for revenue, necessary</u> to pay the debts, provide for the common defence, <u>and carry on the Government of the Confederate States; but no bounties shall be</u>

granted from the Treasury; nor shall any duties or taxes on importations from foreign nations be laid to promote or foster any branch of industry; and all duties, imposts, and excises shall be uniform throughout the Confederate States;

2. To borrow money on the credit of the Confederate States;

3. To regulate commerce with foreign nations, and among the several States, and with the Indian tribes; but neither this, nor any other clause contained in the Constitution, shall ever be construed to delegate the power to Congress to appropriate money for any internal improvement intended to facilitate commerce; except for the purpose of furnishing lights, beacons, and buoys, and other aids to navigation upon the coasts, and the improvement of harbors and the removing of obstructions in river navigation; in all which cases such duties shall be laid on the navigation facilitated thereby as may be necessary to pay the costs and expenses thereof;

4. To establish uniform laws of naturalization, and uniform laws on the subject of bankruptcies, throughout the Confederate States; but no law of Congress shall discharge any debt contracted before the passage of the same;

5. To coin money, regulate the value thereof, and of foreign coin, and fix the standard of weights and measures;

6. To provide for the punishment of counterfeiting the securities and current coin of the Confederate States;

7. To establish post offices and post routes; but the expenses of the Post Office Department, after the first day of March, in the year of our Lord eighteen hundred and sixty-three, shall be paid out of its own revenues;

8. To promote the progress of science and useful arts, by securing for limited times to authors and inventors the exclusive right to their respective writings and discoveries;

9. To constitute tribunals inferior to the Supreme Court;

10. To define and punish piracies and felonies committed on the high seas, and offences against the law of nations;

11. To declare war, grant letters of marque and reprisal, and make rules concerning captures on land and water;

12. To raise and support armies; but no appropriation of money to that use shall be for a longer term than two years;

13. To provide and maintain a navy;

14. To make rules for the government and regulation of the land and naval forces;

15. To provide for calling forth the militia to execute the laws of the Confederate States, suppress insurrections, and repel invasions;

16. To provide for organizing, arming, and disciplining the militia, and for governing such part of them as may be employed in the service of the Confederate States; reserving to the States, respectively, the appointment of the officers, and the authority of training the militia according to the discipline prescribed by Congress;

17. To exercise exclusive legislation, in all cases whatsoever, over such district (not exceeding ten miles square) as may, by cession of one or more States and the acceptance of Congress, become the seat of the government of the Confederate States; and to exercise like authority over all places purchased by the consent of the Legislature of the State in which the same shall be, for the erection of forts, magazines, arsenals, dockyards, and other needful buildings; and

18. To make all laws which shall be necessary and proper for carrying into execution the foregoing powers, and all other powers vested by this Constitution in the Government of the Confederate States, or in any department or officer thereof.

Section 9.

1. The importation of negroes of the African race, from any foreign country, other than the slaveholding States or Territories of the United States of America, is hereby forbidden; and Congress is required to pass such laws as shall effectually prevent the same.

2. Congress shall also have power to prohibit the introduction of slaves from any State not a member of, or Territory not belonging to, this Confederacy.

3. The privilege of the writ of *habeas corpus* shall not be suspended, unless when in cases of rebellion or invasion the public safety may require it.

4. No bill of attainder, *ex post facto* law, or law denying or impairing the right of property in negro slaves shall be passed.

5. No capitation or other direct tax shall be laid, unless in proportion to the census or enumeration hereinbefore directed to be taken.

6. No tax or duty shall be laid on articles exported from any State, except by a vote of two-thirds of both Houses.

7. No preference shall be given by any regulation of commerce or revenue to the ports of one State over those of another.

8. No money shall be drawn from the Treasury, but in consequence of appropriations made by law; and a regular statement and account of the receipts and expenditures of all public money shall be published from time to time.

9. Congress shall appropriate no money from the Treasury except by a vote of two-thirds of both Houses, taken by yeas and nays, unless it be asked and estimated for by some one of the heads of departments and submitted to Congress by the President; or for the purpose of paying its own expenses and contingencies; or for the payment of claims against the Confederate States, the justice of which shall have been judicially declared by a tribunal for the investigation of claims against the Government, which it is hereby made the duty of Congress to establish.

10. All bills appropriating money shall specify in Federal currency, the exact amount of each appropriation and the purposes for which it is made; and Congress shall grant no extra compensation to any public contractor, officer, agent or servant, after such contract shall have been made or such service rendered.

11. No title of nobility shall be granted by the Confederate States; and no person holding any office of profit or trust under them shall, without the consent of the Congress, accept of any present, emolument, office or title of any kind whatever, from any king, prince, or foreign state.

12. Congress shall make no law respecting an establishment of religion, or prohibiting the free exercise thereof; or abridging the freedom of speech, or of the press; or the right of the people peaceably to assemble and petition the Government for a redress of grievances.

13. A well-regulated militia, being necessary to the security of a free State, the right of the people to keep and bear arms shall not be infringed.

14. No soldier shall, in time of peace, be quartered in any house, without the consent of the owner; nor in time of war, but in a manner to be prescribed by law.

15. The right of the people to be secure in their persons, houses, papers, and effects, against unreasonable searches and seizures, shall not be violated; and no warrants shall issue but upon probable cause, supported by oath or affirmation, and particularly describing the place to be searched, and the persons or things to be seized.

16. No person shall be held to answer for a capital or otherwise infamous crime, unless on a presentment or indictment of a grand jury, except in cases arising in the land or naval forces, or in the militia, when in actual service in time of war or public danger; nor shall any person be subject for the same offence to be twice put in jeopardy of life or limb; nor be compelled, in any criminal case, to be a witness against himself; nor be deprived of life, liberty, or property, without due process of law; nor shall private property be taken for public use, without just compensation.

17. In all criminal prosecutions, the accused shall enjoy the right to a speedy and public trial, by an impartial jury of the State and district wherein the crime shall have been committed, which district shall have been previously ascertained by law, and to be informed of the nature and cause of the accusation; to be confronted with the witnesses against him; to have compulsory process for obtaining witnesses in his favor; and to have the assistance of counsel for his defence.

18. In suits at common law, where the value in controversy shall exceed twenty dollars, the right of trial by jury shall be preserved; and no fact so tried by a jury shall be otherwise re-examined in any court of the Confederacy, than according to the rules of common law.

19. Excessive bail shall not be required, nor excessive fines imposed, nor cruel and unusual punishments inflicted.

20. Every law, or resolution having the force of law, shall relate to but one subject, and that shall be expressed in the title.

Section 10.

1. No State shall enter into any treaty, alliance, or confederation; grant letters of marque and reprisal; coin money; make any thing but gold and silver coin a tender in payment of debts; pass any bill of attainder, or *ex post facto* law, or law impairing the obligation of contracts; or grant any title of nobility.

2. No State shall, without the consent of the Congress, lay any imposts or duties on imports or exports, except what may be absolutely necessary for executing its inspection laws; and the net produce of all duties and imposts, laid by any State on imports or exports, shall be for the use of the Treasury of the Confederate States; and all such laws shall be subject to the revision and control of Congress.

3. No State shall, without the consent of Congress, lay any duty on tonnage, except on sea-going vessels, for the improvement of its rivers

and harbors navigated by the said vessels; but such duties shall not con-flict with any treaties of the Confederate States with foreign nations; and any surplus revenue, thus derived, shall, after making such improvement, be paid into the common treasury. Nor shall any State keep troops or ships-of-war in time of peace, enter into any agreement or compact with another State, or with a foreign power, or engage in war, unless actually invaded, or in such imminent danger as will not admit of delay. But when any river divides or flows through two or more States, they may enter into compacts with each other to improve the navigation thereof.

Article II.

Section 1.

1. The executive power shall be vested in a President of the Confeder-ate States of America. He and the Vice President shall hold their offices for the term of six years; but the President shall not be re-eligible. The President and Vice President shall be elected as follows:

2. Each State shall appoint, in such manner as the legislature thereof may direct, a number of electors equal to the whole number of Senators and Representatives to which the States may be entitled in the Congress; but no Senator or Representative or person holding an office of trust or profit under the Confederate States, shall be appointed an elector.

3. The electors shall meet in their respective States and vote by bal-lot for President and Vice President, one of whom, at least, shall not be an inhabitant of the same State with themselves; they shall name in their ballots the person voted for as President, and in distinct ballots the person voted for as Vice President, and they shall make distinct lists of all persons voted for as President, and of all persons voted for as Vice President, and of the number of votes for each, which lists they shall sign and certify, and transmit, sealed, to the seat of the government of the Confederate States, directed to the President of the Senate; the President of the Senate shall, in the presence of the Senate and House of Representatives, open all the cer-tificates, and the votes shall then be counted; the person having the great-est number of votes for President shall be the President, if such number be a majority of the whole number of electors appointed; and if no person have such majority, then, from the persons having the highest numbers, not exceeding three, on the list of those voted for as President, the House of Representatives shall choose immediately, by ballot, the President. But

in choosing the President, the votes shall be taken by States—the representation from each State having one vote; a quorum for this purpose shall consist of a member or members from two-thirds of the States, and a majority of all the States shall be necessary to a choice. And if the House of Representatives shall not choose a President, whenever the right of choice shall devolve upon them, before the fourth day of March next following, then the Vice President shall act as President, as in case of the death, or other constitutional disability of the President.

4. The person having the greatest number of votes as Vice President, shall be the Vice President, if such number be a majority of the whole number of electors appointed; and if no person have a majority, then, from the two highest numbers on the list, the Senate shall choose the Vice President; a quorum for the purpose shall consist of two-thirds of the whole number of Senators, and a majority of the whole number shall be necessary to a choice.

5. But no person constitutionally ineligible to the office of President shall be eligible to that of Vice President of the Confederate States.

6. The Congress may determine the time of choosing the electors, and the day on which they shall give their votes; which day shall be the same throughout the Confederate States.

7. No person except a natural born citizen of the Confederate States, or a citizen thereof at the time of the adoption of this Constitution, or a citizen thereof born in the United States prior to the 20th of December, 1860, shall be eligible to the office of President; neither shall any person be eligible to that office who shall not have attained the age of thirty-five years, and been fourteen years a resident within the limits of the Confederate States, as they may exist at the time of his election.

8. In case of the removal of the President from office, or of his death, resignation, or inability to discharge the powers and duties of said office, the same shall devolve on the Vice President; and the Congress may, by law, provide for the case of removal, death, resignation, or inability, both of the President and Vice President, declaring what officer shall then act as President; and such officer shall act accordingly, until the disability be removed or a President shall be elected.

9. The President shall, at stated times, receive for his services a compensation, which shall neither be increased nor diminished during the period for which he shall have been elected; and he shall not receive within that period any other emolument from the Confederate States, or any of them.

10. Before he enters on the execution of his office, he shall take the following oath or affirmation: "I do solemnly swear (or affirm) that I will faithfully execute the office of President of the Confederate States, and will, to the best of my ability, preserve, protect, and defend the Constitution thereof."

Section 2.

1. The President shall be Commander-in-Chief of the Army and Navy of the Confederate States, and of the militia of the several States, when called into the actual service of the Confederate States; he may require the opinion, in writing, of the principal officer in each of the executive departments upon any subject relating to the duties of their respective offices; and he shall have power to grant reprieves and pardons for offences against the Confederate States, except in cases of impeachment.

2. He shall have power, by and with the advice and consent of the Senate, to make treaties; provided two-thirds of the Senators present concur; and he shall nominate, and by and with the advice and consent of the Senate, shall appoint ambassadors, other public ministers and consuls, judges of the Supreme Court, and all other officers of the Confederate States whose appointments are not herein otherwise provided for, and which shall be established by law; but the Congress may, by law, vest the appointment of such inferior officers, as they think proper, in the President alone, in the courts of law, or in the heads of departments.

3. The principal officer in each of the Executive Departments, and all persons connected with the diplomatic service, may be removed from office at the pleasure of the President. All other civil officers of the Executive Departments may be removed at any time by the President, or other appointing power, when their services are unnecessary, or for dishonesty, incapacity, inefficiency, misconduct, or neglect of duty; and when so removed, the removal shall be reported to the Senate, together with the reasons therefor.

4. The President shall have power to fill all vacancies that may happen during the recess of the Senate, by granting commissions which shall expire at the end of their next session; but no person rejected by the Senate shall be re-appointed to the same office during their ensuing recess.

Section 3.

1. The President shall, from time to time, give to the Congress information of the state of the Confederacy, and recommend to their consideration such measures as he shall judge necessary and expedient; he may, on extraordinary occasions, convene both Houses, or either of them; and in case of disagreement between them, with respect to the time of adjournment, he may adjourn them to such time as he shall think proper; he shall receive ambassadors and other public ministers; he shall take care that the laws be faithfully executed, and shall commission all the officers of the Confederate States.

Section 4.

1. The President, Vice President, and all civil officers of the Confederate States, shall be removed from office on impeachment for, and conviction of, treason, bribery, or other high crimes and misdemeanors.

Article III.

Section 1.

1. The judicial power of the Confederate States shall be vested in one Supreme Court, and in such inferior courts as the Congress may, from time to time, ordain and establish. The judges, both of the Supreme and inferior courts, shall hold their offices during good behavior, and shall, at stated times, receive for their services a compensation which shall not be diminished during their continuance in office.

Section 2.

1. The judicial power shall extend to all cases arising under this Constitution, the laws of the Confederate States; and treaties made, or which shall be made, under their authority; to all cases affecting ambassadors, other public ministers and consuls; to all cases of admiralty and maritime jurisdiction; to controversies to which the Confederate States shall be a party; to controversies between two or more States; between a State and citizens of another State, where the State is plaintiff; between citizens claiming lands under grants of different States; and between a State or the citizens thereof, and foreign states, citizens or subjects; but no State shall be sued by a citizen or subject of any foreign state.

<u>2.</u> In all cases affecting ambassadors, other public ministers and consuls, and those in which a State shall be a party, the Supreme Court shall have original jurisdiction. In all the other cases before mentioned, the Supreme Court shall have appellate jurisdiction both as to law and fact, with such exceptions and under such regulations as the Congress shall make.

<u>3.</u> The trial of all crimes, except in cases of impeachment, shall be by jury, and such trial shall be held in the State where the said crimes shall have been committed; but when not committed within any State, the trial shall be at such place or places as the Congress may by law have directed.

Section 3.

<u>1.</u> Treason against the <u>Confederate</u> States shall consist only in levying war against them, or in adhering to their enemies, giving them aid and comfort. No person shall be convicted of treason unless on the testimony of two witnesses to the same overt act, or on confession in open court.

<u>2.</u> The Congress shall have power to declare the punishment of treason; but no attainder of treason shall work corruption of blood, or forfeiture, except during the life of the person attainted.

Article IV.

Section 1.

<u>1.</u> Full faith and credit shall be given in each State to the public acts, records, and judicial proceedings of every other State. And the Congress may, by general laws, prescribe the manner in which such acts, records, and proceedings shall be proved, and the effect thereof.

Section 2.

<u>1.</u> The citizens of each State shall be entitled to all the privileges and immunities of citizens in the several States; <u>and shall have the right of transit and sojourn in any State of this Confederacy, with their slaves and other property; and the right of property in said slaves shall not be thereby impaired.</u>

<u>2.</u> A person charged in any State with treason, felony, or other crime <u>against the laws of such State</u>, who shall flee from justice, and be found in another State, shall, on demand of the Executive authority of the State from which he fled, be delivered up, to be removed to the State having jurisdiction of the crime.

3. No slave or other person held to service or labor in any State or Territory of the Confederate States, under the laws thereof, escaping or lawfully carried into another, shall, in consequence of any law or regulation therein, be discharged from such service or labor: but shall be delivered up on claim of the party to whom such slave belongs, or to whom such service or labor may be due.

Section 3.

1. Other States may be admitted into this Confederacy by a vote of two-thirds of the whole House of Representatives and two-thirds of the Senate, the Senate voting by States; but no new States shall be formed or erected within the jurisdiction of any other State; nor any State be formed by the junction of two or more States, or parts of States, without the consent of the legislatures of the States concerned, as well as of the Congress.

2. The Congress shall have power to dispose of and make all needful rules and regulations concerning the property of the Confederate States, including the lands thereof.

3. The Confederate States may acquire new territory; and Congress shall have power to legislate and provide governments for the inhabitants of all territory belonging to the Confederate States, lying without the limits of the several States; and may permit them, at such times, and in such manner as it may by law provide, to form States to be admitted into the Confederacy. In all such territory, the institution of negro slavery, as it now exists in the Confederate States, shall be recognized and protected by Congress and by the territorial government: and the inhabitants of the several Confederate States and Territories shall have the right to take to such territory any slaves lawfully held by them in any of the States or Territories of the Confederate States.

4. The Confederate States shall guarantee to every State that now is, or hereafter may become, a member of this Confederacy, a republican form of government; and shall protect each of them against invasion; and on application of the Legislature (or of the Executive, when the Legislature is not in session), against domestic violence.

Article V.

Section 1.

1. Upon the demands of any three States, legally assembled in their

several conventions, the Congress shall summon a convention of all the States, to take into consideration such amendments to the Constitution as the said States shall concur in suggesting at the time when the said demand is made; and should any of the proposed amendments to the Constitution be agreed on by the said convention—voting by States—and the same be ratified by the Legislatures of two-thirds of the several States, or by conventions in two-thirds thereof—as the one or the other mode of ratification may be proposed by the general convention—they shall thenceforward form a part of this Constitution. But no State shall, without its consent, be deprived of its equal representation in the Senate.

Article VI.

1. The Government established by this Constitution is the successor of the Provisional Government of the Confederate States of America, and all the laws passed by the latter shall continue in force until the same shall be repealed or modified; and all the officers appointed by the same shall remain in office until their successors are appointed and qualified, or the offices abolished.

2. All debts contracted and engagements entered into before the adoption of this Constitution shall be as valid against the Confederate States under this Constitution, as under the Provisional Government.

3. This Constitution, and the laws of the Confederate States, made in pursuance thereof, and all treaties made, or which shall be made, under the authority of the Confederate States, shall be the supreme law of the land; and the judges in every State shall be bound thereby, anything in the Constitution or laws of any State to the contrary notwithstanding.

4. The Senators and Representatives before mentioned, and the members of the several State Legislatures, and all executive and judicial officers, both of the Confederate States and of the several States, shall be bound by oath or affirmation to support this Constitution; but no religious test shall ever be required as a qualification to any office or public trust under the Confederate States.

5. The enumeration, in the Constitution, of certain rights shall not be construed to deny or disparage others retained by the people of the several States.

6. The powers not delegated to the Confederate States by the Constitution, nor prohibited by it to the States, are reserved to the States, respectively, or to the people thereof.

Article VII.

1. The ratification of the conventions of <u>five</u> States shall be sufficient for the establishment of this Constitution between the States so ratifying the same.

2. When five States shall have ratified this Constitution, in the manner before specified, the Congress under the Provisional Constitution shall prescribe the time for holding the election of President and Vice President; and for the meeting of the Electoral College; and for counting the votes, and inaugurating the President. They shall, also, prescribe the time for holding the first election of members of Congress under this Constitution, and the time for assembling the same. Until the assembling of such Congress, the Congress under the Provisional Constitution shall continue to exercise the legislative powers granted them; not extending beyond the time limited by the Constitution of the Provisional Government.

Adopted unanimously by the Congress of the Confederate States of South Carolina, Georgia, Florida, Alabama, Mississippi, Louisiana and Texas, sitting in Convention at the capitol, in the city of Montgomery, Alabama, on the Eleventh day of March, in the Year Eighteen Hundred and Sixty-One. . . .

Appendix J

Roster of Cases and Other Materials Drawn On

Cases

Baker v. *Carr,* 369 U.S. 186 (1962).

Bakke, Regents of the University of California v., 438 U.S. 265 (1978).

Barron v. *Mayor and City of Baltimore,* 32 U.S. 243 (1833).

Black and White Taxicab and Transfer Company v. *Brown and Yellow Taxicab and Transfer Company,* 276 U.S. 518 (1928).

Bolling v. *Sharpe,* 347 U.S. 497 (1954).

Brown v. *Board of Education I,* 347 U.S. 483 (1954).

Brown v. *Board of Education II,* 349 U.S. 294 (1955).

Bush v. *Gore,* 531 U.S. 98 (2000).

Calder v. *Bull,* 3 U.S. 386 (1798).

Child Labor Tax Case, 259 U.S. 20 (1922).

Civil Rights Cases, 109 U.S. 3 (1883).

Cohen v. *California,* 403 U.S. 15 (1971).

Colgrove v. *Green,* 328 U.S. 549 (1946).

Corfield v. *Coryell,* 4 Wash. C. C. 371, 6 Fed. Case 546 (1823).

Dean Milk Company v. *City of Madison,* 340 U.S. 349 (1951).

Dred Scott v. *Sandford,* 60 U.S. 393 (1857).

Erie Railroad Company v. *Tompkins,* 304 U.S. 64 (1938).

Gibbons v. *Ogden,* 22 U.S. 1 (1824).

Gratz v. *Bollinger,* 539 U.S. 244 (2003).

Grutter v. *Bollinger,* 539 U.S. 306 (2003).

Hammer v. *Dagenhart,* 247 U.S. 251 (1918).

Hirabayashi v. *United States,* 320 U.S. 81 (1943).

H. P. Hood & Sons v. *Du Mond,* 336 U.S. 525 (1949).

Kassel v. *Consolidated Freightways Corporation,* 450 U.S. 862 (1981).

Korematsu v. *United States,* 323 U.S. 214 (1944).

Kuhn v. *Fairmont Coal Company,* 315 U.S. 349 (1910).

Langbridge's Case (Common Bench, 1345; reported Year Book, 19 Edw. III, 375).

Lochner v. *New York,* 148 U.S. 45 (1905).

Lucas v. *Forty-Fourth General Assembly,* 377 U.S. 713 (1964).

Marbury v. *Madison,* 5 U.S. 137 (1803).

Martin v. *Hunter's Lessee,* 14 U.S. 304 (1816).

M'Culloch v. *Maryland,* 17 U.S. 316 (1819).

Missouri v. *Holland,* 252 U.S. 416 (1920).

Plessy v. *Ferguson,* 163 U.S. 537 (1896).

Regents of the University of California v. *Bakke,* 438 U.S. 265 (1978).

Roe v. *Wade,* 410 U.S. 113 (1973).

San Antonio Independent School District v. *Rodriguez,* 411 U.S. 719 (1973).

Shelley v. *Kraemer,* 334 U.S. 1 (1948).

Slaughter-House Cases, 83 U.S. 36 (1872).

Somerset v. *Stewart,* 98 Eng. Rep. 499 (1772).

Southern Pacific Company v. *Arizona,* 325 U.S. 761 (1945).

Steel Seizure Case, 343 U.S. 579 (1952).

Swift v. *Tyson,* 41 U.S. 1 (1842).

United States v. *Lopez,* 514 U.S. 549 (1995).

Wickard v. *Filburn,* 317 U.S. 111 (1942).

Youngstown Sheet & Tube Company v. *Sawyer,* 343 U.S. 579 (1952).

Other Materials

Anastaplo, George. Bibliography. In *Leo Strauss and His Legacy: A Bibliography,* ed. John A. Murley. Lanham, Md.: Lexington Books, 2005, 29, 733–855, 871.

————. "Did Anyone 'In Charge' Know What He Was Doing? The Thirty Years War of the Twentieth Century." In *Campus Hate-Speech Codes, Natural Right, and Twentieth Century Atrocities.* Lewiston: Edwin Mellen Press, 1999, 49–70.

————. "September Eleventh, The ABC's of a Citizen's Responses: Explorations." 29 *Oklahoma City University Law Review,* 165–382 (2004).

Articles of Confederation and Perpetual Union (1776–1789).

Constitution of the United States and Amendments.

Crosskey, William W. *Politics and the Constitution in the History of the United States.* Chicago: University of Chicago Press, 1953.

Declaration of Independence (1776).

Dictionary of American Biography. New York: Charles Scribner's Sons, 1937.

Du Bois, W. E. Burghardt. *The Souls of Black Folk.* Chicago: A. G. Mc-Clurg and Co., 1903.

Encyclopedia of the American Constitution. New York: Macmillan, 1986.

Fisher, Louis. "The Curious Belief in Judicial Supremacy." 25 *Suffolk University Law Review* 85, 113–14 (1991).

The Guide to American Law: Everyone's Legal Encyclopedia. St. Paul: West Publishing Company, 1984.

Magna Carta.

Murley, John A., ed. *Leo Strauss and His Legacy: A Bibliography.* Lanham, Md.: Lexington Books, 2005.

Northwest Ordinance (1787).

Strauss, Leo. *Natural Right and History.* Chicago: University of Chicago Press, 1953.

University of Chicago Weekly, October 21, 2004, 8 (on diversification of the student body).

Weaver, Richard M. *Ideas Have Consequences.* Chicago: University of Chicago Press, 1948.

Index

About the Author

George Anastaplo was born in St. Louis, Missouri, in 1925, and grew up in Southern Illinois. After serving three years as an aviation cadet and flying officer during and just after World War II, he earned A.B., J.D., and Ph.D. degrees from the University of Chicago. He is currently lecturer in the liberal arts at the University of Chicago (in the Basic Program of Liberal Education for Adults), professor of law at Loyola University of Chicago, and professor emeritus of political science and of philosophy at Dominican University. See http://hydeparkhistory. org. See also http://cygneis.com/Anastaplo.

His publications include a dozen books and two-dozen book-length collections in law reviews. His scholarship was reviewed in seven articles in the 1997 volume of the *Political Science Reviewer*. A two-volume Festschrift, *Law and Philosophy*, was issued in his honor in 1992 by the Ohio University Press. Between 1980 and 1992 he was nominated annually for a Nobel Peace Prize by a Chicago-based committee that had as its initial spokesman Malcolm P. Sharp (1897–1980), professor emeritus of the University of Chicago Law School.

Professor Anastaplo's career is assessed in a chapter in *Leo Strauss, the Straussians, and the American Regime* (Rowman & Littlefield, 1999). A bibliography of his work is included in *Law and Philosophy* (v. II, pp. 1073–1145). See also "George Anastaplo: An Autobiographical Bibliography (1947–2001)," 20 *Northern Illinois University Law Review* 581–710 (2000); "George Anastaplo: Tables of Contents for His Books and Published Collections (1950–2001)," 39 *Brandeis Law Journal* 219–87 (2000–2001). See as well the massive bibliography in political philosophy compiled by John A. Murley, Rochester Institute of Technology, *Leo Strauss: A Bibliographical Legacy* (Lexington Books, 2005), pp. 733–855.